The French Communist Party
and the Crisis of
International Communism

CENTER FOR INTERNATIONAL STUDIES
MASSACHUSETTS INSTITUTE OF TECHNOLOGY

Studies in International Communism

The French Communist Party
and the Crisis of
International Communism

François Fejtö

THE M.I.T. PRESS

Massachusetts Institute of Technology
Cambridge, Massachusetts, and London, England

PREFACE

François Fejtö had originally planned to write a chapter on French communism for the second volume of *Communism in Europe,* but, happily, he wrote a book instead.

He is, I think, uniquely qualified to write about the *Parti communiste français* (PCF). Of Hungarian origin, he was, in the mid-thirties, in Budapest, where along with the great Hungarian poet Attila Jószef and the essayist Pál Ignotus, he was one of the editors of the left-wing journal *Szep Szó.* Thereafter he left Horthy's Hungary and has lived in France for nearly thirty years. His historical works on Central Europe include a biography of the Austrian Emperor Joseph II and the standard *Histoire des démocraties populaires.* More recently he has published the only serious work in French on the Sino-Soviet dispute, *Chine-U.R.S.S., la fin d'une hégémonie: Les origines du grand schisme communiste, 1950–1957* (Paris: Plon, Vol. 1, 1964; Vol. 2, 1966). Also a publicist, he contributes regularly to French literary and political journals and for some years has been in charge of Communist affairs for Agence France Presse in Paris.

Fejtö's treatment of the PCF has, I think, several particular advantages. First, it is firmly embedded in the history and politics of France. Second, it places the PCF in the complex currents of world politics and French foreign affairs, notably the Algerian war. Third, it also places the PCF in the world of international communism, especially with respect to the Soviet, Chinese, and Italian Communist parties. Fourth, it summarizes and interprets the domestic and external factors which have led the PCF to change somewhat its domestic and international line since the fall of Khrushchev.

I was greatly assisted in editing this book by my research assistant, Dr. Robin Remington, and in the final preparation of the book for publication by Miss Mary Patricia Grady. The manuscript was typed by Mrs. Lila T. Fernandez and Mrs. Micheline Khachadourian and indexed by Mrs. Edward E. Colt. I am grateful to the Center for International Studies and to its director, Max F.

Millikan, for their support in publishing this volume in the Studies in International Communism series. Its publication was made possible by a generous grant to M.I.T. by the Ford Foundation for research and teaching in international affairs.

WILLIAM E. GRIFFITH

Munich, Germany
August 23, 1966

ACKNOWLEDGMENTS

For his invaluable assistance in editing, as well as in compiling the documentation for this study I am particularly grateful to my friend, G. S., who, through excessive modesty, wishes to remain anonymous. Nevertheless, I should like to call attention to the important part he has played in our joint effort to analyze the behavior of the PCF in the crisis of authority and doctrine that has shaken the international Communist movement since Stalin's death.

I am grateful also to Professor William E. Griffith, who suggested that I expand my essay on this subject in *Arguments,* Nos. 25 and 26 (Paris, 1962), as a contribution to this series.

FRANÇOIS FEJTÖ

CONTENTS

ix

*The French Communist Party
and the Crisis of
International Communism*

CHAPTER ONE

INTRODUCTION

The death of Maurice Thorez on July 11, 1964 marked the end of an epoch in the history of both the French Communist Party (Parti communiste français—PCF) and the international Communist movement.[1] Why, then, has the French Communist Party continued to remain an important ally of the Soviets? Shortly before burying the man who had led the party for thirty-four years, the PCF had created for him the position of party president. On this occasion and at the French Communist Party's Seventeenth Congress, Mikhail Suslov, Secretary of the Soviet Communist Party and one of the most important personalities in the Soviet hierarchy, was present, thus emphasizing Moscow's specific interest in French communism. The question of why this Soviet interest should have continued is even more pertinent because in recent years certain weaknesses of the PCF have become all too evident: decline in active membership, newspaper circulation, and militant activity; heavy losses at the polls with only small subsequent gains; the lack of any real alliance with other important political groups in France; and finally, on another level, the party's hesitation and reserve with regard to implementing de-Stalinization.

However, these weaknesses have been balanced by other factors that have increased the importance of the French Communist Party

---

1 For the history of the French Communist Party, see the following sources: André Ferrat, *Histoire du Parti Communiste Français* (Paris: Bureau d'Éditions, 1931); Jacques Fauvet, *Histoire du Parti Communiste Français: De la guerre à la guerre, 1917–1939*, Vol. I (Paris: Fayard, 1964); PCF Central Committee, *Histoire du Parti Communiste Français—Manuel* (Paris: Éditions Sociales, 1964), edited by Jacques Duclos and François Billoux; Maurice Thorez, *Oeuvres de Maurice Thorez* (Paris: Éditions Sociales); *Histoire du Parti Communiste Français*, Vol. I, *Des origines à 1940* (Paris: Édition Veridad, 1960), Vol. II, *De 1940 à la Libération* (Paris: Éditions Unir, undated); Gérard Walter, *Histoire du Parti Communiste Français* (Paris: Somogy, 1948); and the romanticized biography of Maurice Thorez, *Fils du peuples*, the successive editions of which contain important changes. For a more detailed bibliography see Gérard Walter, *op. cit.*

1

from the Soviet viewpoint. First, there has been the situation created by the intensifying Sino-Soviet dispute. Among the capitalist and uncommitted countries (that is, non-Communist countries) of any importance at all, it was possible to see that in two of them, Japan and Indonesia, the official Communist party belonged to the Chinese camp; in two others, India and Brazil, the party was split by the Sino-Soviet schism. The small Communist parties in the United States, Great Britain, and West Germany carried no weight. The Finnish, Greek, Spanish, and Portuguese parties were more significant, but the modest size of their respective countries and, in the case of the last three, their semilegal and clandestine status greatly limited the importance of their policy positions. In the face of the opposition of the Italian Communist Party (Partito comunista italiano—PCI), which systematically obstructed preparations for an international Communist conference designed to excommunicate the Chinese, Khrushchev had no choice but to lean heavily on the support of the French Communist Party, then as secure an ally as the Czechoslovak Communist Party.[2] He needed this support in order to overcome the reservations felt by the membership, as well as the leadership, of every Communist party in power. After a great West European party such as the PCF had called for a conference,[3] Soviet insistence no longer appeared simply as pressure by the Soviet Communist Party, behind which stood the interests of the Soviet state.

Moreover, the idea of a conference somehow acquired greater ideological substance and international sanction from the fact that the French Communist Party did not seem directly interested in the excommunication of the Chinese. Nor should it be underestimated that Soviet leaders must have been extremely conscious of their vulnerable ideological position and sensitive to the criticism of those who, echoing the Chinese attacks, accused the Soviets of having demolished Stalin, to whom they owed their training and rise to power. It was not enough for the Soviets to preach a return

2 We shall return to the affinities between these two parties, an element as important as the rivalry and divergence of opinion between the PCF and the PCI. For a parallel between the French and Czech Communist parties, see François Fejtö, *Chine-URSS, la fin d'une hégémonie—Les origines du grand schisme communiste, 1950–1957*, Vol. I (Paris: Plon, 1964), pp. 188–190. By 1966 the Japanese Communist Party again became neutral between Moscow and Peking.

3 The PCF was the first major party to call for an international conference on October 6, 1963. It took up the call again on March 26, 1964, a few days before the publication of Mikhail Suslov's report in which the CPSU declared itself officially in favor of such a conference.

to Lenin and allegiance to Leninism, in order to justify a policy whose essential traits gave evidence of a very eclectic empiricism; they needed support and approval. For some time, particularly between 1953 and 1957, they had seemed ready to pay a high price to Mao Tse-tung for such support. Later, when Sino-Soviet hostilities became overt, with Mao claiming himself heir to Leninism and accusing Khrushchev of having fallen into "modern revisionism" and "great-power chauvinism," Khrushchev began to attach great value to everything that could prove he had remained faithful to doctrinaire orthodoxy and to proletarian internationalism. This accounts for his efforts to obtain the support of Fidel Castro, and even of Ben Bella, both of whom were held to symbolize the revolutionary movements in the uncommitted world.[4] It also accounts for the Soviet quest for support of the major Communist parties of Western Europe, which stood for the working class in developed industrial countries. And to the extent that Italian Communist support seemed to give way, as evidenced by the publication of Togliatti's testament,[5] the support of the French Communist Party assumed still greater weight.

Yet the deepening crisis in the international Communist movement was only one factor involved in the PCF's status with the Soviet leaders. A second factor, the pivotal position of France in international politics, was and is perhaps even more fundamental. It is not necessary to argue at length that of all the West European countries France has been the most important to the Soviet Union, and, incidentally, to China as well. This will be so as long as Anglo-American solidarity remains more or less intact and as long as the Federal Republic of Germany remains an obstacle to Soviet policy and the mere existence of East Germany prevents a rapprochement between Moscow and Bonn. Undoubtedly, Gaulist policies exacerbated the differences already existing between France and its NATO allies, and these differences led to a serious crisis within the alliance as early as the French rejection of the European Defense Community in 1954. However, the presence in France of a Communist party ready to echo various initiatives of Soviet diplomacy and possessing at the same time a strong tendency—transcending the political left and extending into business circles—toward de-emphasizing the American (and German) alliance offered,

---

4 The Soviet press gave considerable prominence to the statements made by Fidel Castro and Ben Bella at the time of their visits to Moscow (Apr. 27–June 3, 1963, and Apr. 26, 1964, respectively).

5 *Rinascita*, Sept. 5, 1964.

and still offers, considerable possibilities for maneuver. Such possibilities never existed in Italy. Also, since France occupies a key position strategically in the communications system between the United States and all of Western Europe and retains much influence within her former colonies, despite their political independence today, it is not surprising that a Communist party operating on such a terrain is of particular interest to Moscow.

Third, in contrast to what developed during the most intense period of the Cold War (1947–1953), current political developments within France tend to increase at least the potential importance of the French Communist Party. Most hypotheses about French politics after de Gaulle rest ultimately on the support (that is, at least the benevolent neutrality and possibly the participation) of the French Communist Party. Moreover, Gaullists themselves may well need French Communist support in order to resist the inroads of the advocates of European and Atlantic integration. The possibility of trading upon this support, on the part of de Gaulle or his opponents, gives the French Communist Party an interesting strategic position in the French political game.

In sum, changes in international relations resulting from internal splits in each of the two great blocs have increased the weight of the French Communist Party both in France and within the international Communist movement. Paradoxically, this is happening at the same time that the fighting spirit and ardor of the PCF, the rhythm of its daily activities, and the effects of its slogans—in short, its ability to create a real mass movement and assume the role of a revolutionary party in line with Leninist conceptions—appear weaker than they have ever been.

Although this is primarily a study of the PCF, the role of French communism within the international Communist movement is closely intertwined with that of Italian communism and has been considered from that standpoint. Scarcely more than a month after the death of Thorez, the leader of the Italian Communist Party, Palmiro Togliatti, died on August 21, 1964. Except for Mao Tse-tung, Thorez and Togliatti were the last of the top-ranking leaders of what could be called the heroic period of the Third International. Such East European leaders as Tito, Gomułka, Kádár, and Gheorghiu-Dej made their appearance on center stage only after Stalinism had triumphed over various opposition groups in the struggle that began immediately after Lenin's death. Dolores Ibarruri of Spain, Luis Carlos Prestes of Brazil, and the Vietnamese Ho Chi Minh, veterans themselves, played no particularly important role in the international Communist machine before the mid-thirties. Thorez and Togliatti had won their spurs in the international Communist movement in Lenin's time, actively participated in the ideological battles of the second half of the twenties, and from 1930 on exercised unchallenged leadership of the Communist parties in their respective countries. Although Togliatti may have played a more important role than Thorez in the apparatus of the Comintern before the Second World War, the French Communist Party had by that time become a powerful mass party, while the Italian Communist Party in Fascist Italy was still nothing but a small, clandestine sect, most of whose members were actually dispersed in various groups of *émigrés* abroad.

Between Thorez and Togliatti there were as many differences as similarities. What they had in common, after Hitler crushed German communism, was their leadership of the only two major Communist parties in large, fully developed industrial countries; and both leaders adopted a political orientation that led to the integration of their revolutionary parties into the political institutions of their bourgeois states and, in the postwar period, Communist participation in coalition governments. In the area of foreign policy, if not of ideology (this reservation refers to Togliatti), that orientation was reflected in a regular alignment with the positions adopted by the Soviet Union.

On this common basis, differences later developed, whose origins are to be found in the personalities of the leaders, in national traditions, and social and internal political conditions—differences that were to become greater after Stalin's death and particularly after the Twentieth CPSU Congress. Differences between the "intellectual" Togliatti and the "mine-worker" Thorez were paralleled by differences between the "revisionist" Italian Communist Party and the seemingly "orthodox" French Communist Party and between the "de-Stalinizing" temerity of the Italians and the nostalgia for Stalin on the part of the French. The significant episodes of rivalry between the French and Italian Communist parties in which the respective personalities of their leaders played an important part will be discussed later.

CHAPTER TWO

THE APPEALS OF COMMUNISM IN FRANCE

As the importance of French communism to Moscow rests in part upon the widespread appeal of the PCF within France, it is important to understand that appeal. To do so we must return to the PCF's origins. For if the Communist Party of France in 1966 seemed to have lost much in common with the party born in December 1920 at the Congress of Tours, it nevertheless retained the marks of its ancestry.

In her extensive study, *Les origines du communisme français (1914–1920)*,[1] the historian Annie Kriegel, an old Communist militant notable for her "activity among the intellectuals," has described in great detail the period between the Congress of Tours and the beginning of the First World War. She concluded that the adherence of the overwhelming majority of the Socialist Party to the Third International in 1920 can be explained only by the concurrence of certain specific circumstances in the French labor movement—that is, the Socialist defeat in the election of November 1919, followed by the failure of the Syndicalist attempt at "total revolution" (the rail workers' strike), which was harshly suppressed in May 1920. Seeing their hopes shattered, the French Socialists could not but "discover" bolshevism, which had just overcome civil war and foreign intervention in Russia. Adherence to the Third International, and thus the establishment of a link with the victorious Russian Revolution, made it possible

to capture the dynamism and revolutionary energy of victorious bolshevism and inject it into French and European socialism, without absorbing everything which made bolshevism a specifically Russian product.[2]

In sum, for the French Socialists, adherence to the twenty-one conditions of the Communist International was to remain a formality.

[1] Annie Kriegel, *Les origines du communisme français* (2 vols.; Paris and The Hague: Mouton, 1964).

[2] Introduction to Annie Kriegel, *Le Congrès de Tours* (Collection "Archives"; Paris: Julliard, 1964), p. 23.

Jaurèsism had inherited from radicalism the art of making divergent and often much more empirical practices coexist with the sacred texts, whereas for the Russian Bolsheviks the essential point was to capture the masses of the party and leave their bolshevization until later.

Moreover, the Russians, in turn, had no illusions; they knew that their new French recruits were not authentic bolsheviks. But in 1920 the leaders of the Soviet Union were uncertain about their global perspective:

> If . . . the European revolution has a chance to win in short order, the entire bolshevik effort should concentrate on German socialism, which occupies a key position; . . . but if a long-term strategy is required, France will increase in importance. Since the distinction between victors and vanquished will gradually disappear, Germany might eventually crumble under a revolutionary push from the West just as well as from the East.[3]

This observation is all the more interesting because it throws some light on why the Soviet Communist Party and the Communist International came to consider the French Communist Party so important. While the German Communist Party was, in a certain sense, born under the banner of imminent revolution, engendered by the revolution and for the revolution, the French Communist Party seemed destined from the beginning to play its role in the form of a "longer-term" strategy. From its inception it was, so to speak, the party of revolution for the day after tomorrow.

The reasons are historical. The period during which Thorez consolidated his power in the Communist Party of France coincided with the first Five-Year Plan, the liquidation of the German Communist Party, and the triumph of Stalinism in the Soviet Union. (The year 1934 ended with Kirov's assassination, which ushered in the era of the great trials.) From 1934 on, the proletarian revolution and the conquest of political power disappeared as aims from the programs of Western European Communist parties. In France the leading group around Maurice Thorez, the survivors of which are Jacques Duclos, Benoît Frachon, and two defectors from the "Barbé-Célor" group, Raymond Guyot and François Billoux (as well as Étienne Fajon and Waldeck Rochet, who joined later), had been trained in the practice of revolutionary gesturing. The PCF grew and attained its greatest power as well as its national and international prestige, however, through the practice of a united front strategy that included a large part of the bourgeoisie, a line

3 *Ibid.*, p. 30.

carried out so well that by 1936 the Communist Party had managed to outflank the Socialists on the latter's right. For this strategy it had the blessings of the Comintern, at whose Seventh Congress in August 1935 the French section had been held up as a shining example to all other members—this time without the slightest hint of criticism in the eulogy—and Thorez was given a long ovation.[4]

The profoundly significant triumph of the French Communist Party at the Seventh Comintern Congress was soon followed by popular front victories at the polls in France; for a very long period the Communist movement renounced all revolutionary perspective in the highly developed industrial countries. The parties born in the wake and under the influence of the Russian Revolution of October 1917 first organized to prepare for the world revolution and entered the political game in the bourgeois countries under the label of antifascism. Even though this new strategy was inspired primarily by concern about the defense of that fortress of socialism, the Soviet state, it could not fail to have deep repercussions within these parties. From 1935 on, with regard to one entire sector of its activities, the French Communist Party no longer differed from a reformist party.

It can therefore be said that the PCF entered its period of maturity, and Thorez entered fully into Stalin's good graces, during a period of retreat on the part of the world revolutionary forces—a retreat epitomized by the disintegration of the German Communist Party. Like Stalin's triumph in the Soviet Union, Thorez' rise in France was closely tied to the receding of the revolutionary wave. When in 1936 France was again hit with a wave of sit-down strikes, Thorez did not hesitate to place his full authority in the service of "appeasement": "One should know how to end a strike," "not everything is possible," "communism will not arrive in France tonight or even tomorrow morning"—these were the answers Thorez gave to workers who were not content with the Matignon agreements.[5]

[4] Leon Trotsky, in his *Journal d'exil—1935* (Paris: Gallimard, 1960), p. 49, wrote on February 14, 1935:
What goes by the name of "popular front"—that is, the radical bloc in favor of parliamentary struggle—is the most bastardly betrayal of the people ever to be sanctioned by the workers' parties since the war. [Editor's translation.]
See also Trotsky, *Écrits 1928–1940* (Paris: Publications de la Quatrième Internationale), Vol. II, *Où va la France?*, and Vol. III, *La Tragédie de la classe ouvrière allemande—La révolution espagnole.*

[5] The Matignon agreements, signed on the night of June 7–8, 1936 by the delegations of the reunited CGT (Confédération Générale du Travail) and the Conseil National du Patronat Français, covered in particular a general increase in wages and the establishment of joint methods of procedure.

Thus in 1936 the Communist Party of France attained its quasi-definitive form. After a flirtation with Trotsky,[6] Maurice Thorez, formerly a sectarian, had shown great astuteness in adapting himself to the Stalinist line by turning around and declaring himself (with the blessing of the Soviets) a pillar of bourgeois democratic society.

However, it is the fact that communism took root in French political reality which is of interest to us. How did this happen? The success of French communism has been largely due to the ability with which it has been able profitably to assimilate certain traditions of the French labor movement: the revolutionary tradition of anarchosyndicalism, the parliamentary tradition of Jaurèsian socialism, the internationalist tradition, and the Jacobin tradition—that is, the patriotism, in both its chauvinist and centralizing aspects, passed on by the petite bourgeoisie to the labor movement.

Thus every year the party commemorates not only the massacre of the Communards at the Mur des Fédérés in 1871 but also the assassination of that great Socialist Jean Jaurès in 1914. It commemorates July 14, 1789 and November 11, 1918—and even the feast day of Joan of Arc, which before the Second World War was traditionally a holiday of the extreme right. Tied organically by its origins to the multiple traditions that nourished the French labor movement itself, the Communist Party rooted itself in French national consciousness. Without ceasing to declare itself the champion of proletarian internationalism, it has played upon traditional French chauvinist emotions after 1941 with its "anti-Boche" policy and, after 1947, its anti-American propaganda.

These various traditions, extremely contradictory in themselves, existed side by side during the first years of the Communist Party's existence, though not always peaceably. Thorez' accomplishment was to fuse them by sterilizing them. The resulting amalgam has existed long enough to be considered by now a Thorezian or Stalinist tradition.

6 In his La révolution prolétarienne, written before the war, Boris Souvarine published letters written by Maurice Thorez in 1924, during a period when, as a Trotskyite sympathizer, he had distributed copies of Trotsky's pamphlet Cours Nouveau (see Le Figaro, Dec. 8, 1961). (After Liberation Thorez' letters were reprinted in Est & Ouest.) But as soon as Thorez realized that Trotsky had lost the game, he decided to adhere to the most rigid Stalinist obedience. Togliatti, on the other hand, compromised himself seriously with Bukharin. (See the correspondence between Togliatti, alias Ercoli, and Jules Humbert-Droz, then secretary of the Communist International, in J. Humbert-Droz, "L'Oeil de Moscou" à Paris, [Collection "Archives"; Paris: Julliard; 1964], especially pp. 242–250, and Giulio Seniga, Togliatti e Stalin [Milan: Sugar, 1961], pp. 8 and 25).

In analyzing this process one must keep in mind how great the weight of tradition is and how particularly heavy it is in France, where, to use Marxist language, the ideological and political super-structures reflect the comparative slowness of social evolution dur-ing the last century, the strong resistance to change with regard to certain methods of production, economic organization, and the persistence of anachronistic institutions such as dispersed small in-dustry, disorganized distribution machinery, and a fragmented agri-culture that permits a near marginal farmer to live or, rather, to vegetate. In fact, the superstructures inherited from the past some-times persist with great vigor, even though the economic and social context that gave rise to them has undergone a profound transfor-mation.

For these reasons, "pure" sociology is incapable of explaining the geographical distribution of political currents in France. Why did the Nord and the Pas-de-Calais remain strongholds of the Socialist Party when that party was very weak in industrialized Lorraine, Paris, or Lyon? Why is the Communist Party so powerful in the rural areas where small proprietors dominate (some departments in the Center, Southeast, and Midi), while other rural regions, some-times poorer and more open to economic evolution and ready to question their archaic and paralyzing social structures, still incline toward the right? (This is the case, typically, in western Brittany.) The weight of the past—the republican and anticlerical tradition in one area, the battles of the Maquis elsewhere, or, in contrast, the hold of the Catholic Church—is often decisive.[7]

We are not dealing here with a specifically rural phenomenon. The same seeming lack of pattern can be found in the cities. Com-munist influence, very considerable in Marseilles, Nice, Le Havre, Nîmes, and Béziers, all cities very unequally industrialized, is small in Bordeaux or Rennes, and insignificant in Metz, Mulhouse, and Strasbourg.

Many sociologists, economists, and political observers tend to be-lieve that the changes in French society after World War II—a better living standard for the working class; full and almost perma-nent employment; higher wages for still insufficient numbers of skilled workers; disappearance of hunger, unemployment, very low

[7] From the extensive literature on the geography and sociology of elections, see Jacques Fauvet, *Les forces politiques en France* (Paris: Éditions "Le Monde," 1951), and *La politique et les paysans* (Paris: Armand Colin, 1958). See also François Goguel, *La politique des partis sous la IIIème République* (2 vols.; Paris, 1946); André Siegfried, *Tableau des partis en France* (Paris, 1930).

salaries, and flagrant injustices; the development of employment guarantees and a system of social security; a massive increase in the consumption of durable goods, financed by consumer credit; growth of the number of cadres, technicians, and altogether of the "third" sector; the emergence of a certain planning of the national economy, contrasting with the liberalism associated with the memory of crises and depressions—should have had the effect of reducing the role of the French Communist Party, with its "Stalinist" profile sculptured by Thorez.[8] But even if such reasoning might apply in the long run, the error frequently committed has been to underestimate the capacity of the French Communist Party to adapt itself to a changing situation.

For example, immediately after the very serious 1958 electoral defeat suffered by the French Communist Party many commentators pointed out that Communist losses had been even greater in urban and working-class centers than in certain of its rural strongholds in the center and south of France. To move from such evidence to the conclusion that the French Communist Party was condemned to decline quickly in advanced industrialized zones and expanding regions, and would maintain itself well only in backward and marginal regions, was only one step.

It became clear later that this way of looking at things was too simple. In the course of subsequent elections the French Communist Party made a very good recovery, and even new gains, in industrial centers.[9] In 1958 the Communist electorate had complained bitterly about the defeat suffered several months before, when their party had not been able to prevent de Gaulle from coming to power. The urban electorate had supported de Gaulle. Yet in 1962, by adjusting its propaganda and its actions to the new situation and by concentrating on strategic points where it seemed in danger of losing power, the French Communist Party regained most of its traditional bastions.

The real point is that the French Communist Party as an electoral movement is very complex. Some vote for it from a "Leninist"

8 This was primarily the viewpoint defended by Serge Mallet in *France-Observateur*, 1958–1959. (For a more subtly argued opposition to this position, see Alain Touraine, "Une classe ouvrière en devenir," *Arguments*, No. 12–13 [Jan.–Feb.–Mar. 1959], pp. 15–21.) Analyses of this sort played a considerable part in encouraging the formation of the Parti Socialiste Unifié, which for a long time had hopes of winning over what it called the "new classes" created by the evolution of modern capitalist society.

9 See the Appendix for a comparative table of the PCF's election returns.

position, with the intention of sending deputies to Parliament who will use it as a platform to reflect mass movements; others vote for it simply to demonstrate that they belong to the working class, in contrast to the bourgeoisie; others vote for the largest opposition party to express their dissatisfaction; still others vote for it out of solidarity with the poor, even though they themselves are financially secure. Finally, some vote for the PCF under the influence of the party's daily propaganda; that is, they vote for those who defend the claims of one or another category of citizens, for the defense of national independence, "against revanchist Germany," or "against the Americans."

In the majority of cases, however, what determines why people vote Communist is that a vote for the PCF is a vote for the party furthest to the left; whether it is an act of faith, subversion, or simply protest, those who vote Communist have the feeling that it is simply impossible to vote otherwise.

Thus the Communist Party, the "inheriting" party par excellence, has succeeded largely through the efforts of Maurice Thorez in absorbing the most diverse and even the most contradictory legacies.[10] For example, exploiting the old adage of "the struggle of the little fellows against the big fellows," the PCF has been able to pose as the relentless defender of the small agricultural, commercial, or even industrial proprietor, ready to support demands for prices and profit margins contrary to the interests of the wage earners. With the help of the parliamentary system, the PCF has thus been able to make itself the representative of all those who hold to these diverse traditions.

As a result of the representative nature it acquired, the French

[10] A striking manifestation of how tradition will survive, underground as it were, may be seen in reading over the principal speeches delivered at the Congress of Tours (in Annie Kriegel, *op. cit.*). Each speaker (including the minority who were opposed to joining the Third International, as well as those who represented various majority opinions) continued not only to pursue the objectives appropriate to his position but also to refer to his particular standards and heroes. Jules Guesde and Jean Jaurès were, in turn, invoked by the "rightists," Marcel Sembat and Léon Blum, and the majority supporters, Marcel Cachin and Ludovic-Oscar Frossard. Each, however, brandished *his* Guesde and *his* Jaurès. Marcel Cachin's Guesde was the Marxist theoretician who advocated the revolutionary conquest of political power by the proletariat, while Marcel Sembat's Guesde pledged the socialists to "rally 'round the flag"; this Guesde would have participated in the government in August 1914 under the slogan of national defense. The confusion was all the greater since Cachin and Frossard, who advocated joining the Third International, did not lessen their efforts to justify the patriotic positions they had adopted during World War I.

Communist Party became a genuine political institution[11] even in the eyes of its opponents. In a way, its role has become similar to that of the second party in two-party regimes. Its leadership is the "shadow cabinet," its machinery the possible replacement and reserve in case of accident. But, on the other hand, the PCF has differed from parties that play a comparable role in two-party systems because, at least until the beginning of the sixties, it was based on a centralized structure not only on the national level but, more important, on the international level as well. This structure is, in turn, supported by two myths, very strong in France, that give it a much greater force than that of any other party machine: the myth of the Soviet Union, based in part upon the cult of Stalin, and the myth of organization.

Although the myth of the Soviet Union was based on the tradition of internationalism, the myth distorted and transformed that tradition, for internationalism had become entirely confused with attachment to the Soviet Union; that is, internationalism had been reduced to support for Moscow. For the French Communists, internationalism, crystallized and limited in this attachment to the Soviet Union, became a matter of faith rather than a principle inspiring concrete actions. For example, despite the power of its Communist party, France was one of the few European countries where protests against the Anglo-French-Israeli expedition against the Suez Canal remained purely verbal, without ever being expressed in the streets. But on November 7, 1956, that is, at the same time, the Communist party succeeded in the course of a few hours in mobilizing the majority of its Paris militants to answer the attack of extreme rightists who, in the wake of a demonstration of solidarity with the Hungarians crushed by the Red Army, had set fire to the offices of the Communist Party and its paper, L'Humanité. To be sure, the reflex of self-defense had played its part, but the remarkable fact remains that despite the general unpopularity of the Soviet intervention in Hungary (doubts assailed even the ranks of Communist workers, at least during the few days that followed the event, when Soviet tanks fired on the workers of Budapest) the French Communist Party selected this occasion for its "reassessment," after a period of vacillation. As a result of the circumstances in which it took place, this demonstration became a manifestation of support for the Soviet Union in the very domain where the

11 Serge Mallet has often used the expression *poujadisme* to describe the PCF's systematic defense of its demands.

latter's action had profoundly trouble many of its most faithful defenders.[12]

Seen from a certain angle, an analogy comes to mind between the fanaticism with which the French Communists have always defended the Soviet Union against all "calumnies" and the attitude of integralist Catholics, who represented a minority sect in France (but always a very dynamic and powerful one) and who confound the catholicity of the Church with an absolute cult of the Papacy. In France as in Italy, the Communist Party has been the only one to offer those dechristianized elements of the working classes who were still unconsciously religious an ersatz for the Church that they had left in the form of Communist myths and organization.

The Communist church has its popularized Marxist dogmas, within easy reach of all in the form of a work such as *Fils du peuple,* the autobiography of Maurice Thorez. This is more readily available than the sacred texts of Marx, Engels, and Lenin, of which most people knew only a few sentences they had learned by heart. It has its saints, its martyrs, its ceremonies, its rites, its priests who belonged to a rigid hierarchy, its vocabulary of initiation, its more or less practicing members,[13]—all of which have been inextricably tied to the cult of Stalin, which appeared very early in France. In his message to the Sixteenth Congress of the CPSU (Bolshevik) in June 1930, Maurice Thorez was already expressing himself in these terms in the name of the Central Committee of the French Communist Party:

[12] The attack on party headquarters, in which a number of recently emigrated Hungarians participated, was a veritable godsend for the leaders of the PCF (most of whom were at the Soviet embassy when the raid occurred, attending a reception in honor of the thirty-ninth anniversary of the October Revolution). The "oppositionists" went so far as to suspect the Politburo of having arranged the demonstrations through the infiltration of *agents provocateurs* but were never able—for good reason—to find proof of or make public their accusations. The fact remains that party propaganda, starting with the allegation that Hungarians in France were protected by the fascists who set fire to the party's organizational headquarters, found the going easier when it asserted that the Hungarian uprising was inspired by fascists and reactionaries.

As an example of how the PCF's propaganda makes use of arguments totally extraneous to communism, the reader is referred to Léo Figuères, who wrote, in *L'Humanité-Dimanche,* that the Hungarian attitude was not surprising in view of the fact that Hungary had been an ally of Germany—in 1914–1918 and 1939–1940. Likewise, in order to present in an acceptable fashion to party militants the suppression of the workers in East Berlin in June 1953, the PCF counted on an "anti-Boche" chauvinism; the riots were held to be the work of Nazi revanchists.

[13] For the "religious" aspect of the Communist Party, see Fauvet, *Les forces politiques en France, op. cit.,* pp. 11–16.

We greet Comrade Stalin, the foremost fighter of the Communist Party of the Soviet Union, and assure him of our deepest sympathy, arising from our gratitude for his merits as the chief of all Bolsheviks. . . . Long live the Central Committee of the Communist Party of the Soviet Union and its respected leader Comrade Stalin![14]

It is possible to trace through the years the evolution of the tone used in the documents of the French Communist Party. On the eve of the Second World War, in a speech on January 21, 1939 at the National Conference of the French Communist Party at Gennevilliers, Maurice Thorez spoke of Stalin as "the friend and continuator of Lenin," referred on several occasions to the "Leninist-Stalinist method" and to "the purity of the principles of the doctrine of Marx, Engels, Lenin, and Stalin," and proclaimed "unshakable loyalty to our party, our International, and its leaders, Dimitrov and Stalin," celebrating the latter as "the heir of the Russian revolutionary workers' movement and also of the international workers' movement."[15] The respected chief of 1930 had taken on the rank of theoretician, the equal of the greatest; and "profound sympathy" had become "unshakable loyalty."

This cult reached its culmination during the years of the Cold War (1947–1952). Without exaggeration, it would take a whole book to reproduce the eulogies to Stalin found in the texts of the French Communist Party during that period.

How profoundly this cult influenced the PCF may be seen in the fact that more than a year after Stalin's death, when the French Communist leaders could no longer ignore the trend in the Soviet Union toward de-Stalinization, Jacques Duclos opened the Eighth Congress of the French Communist Party (at Ivry, June 3–7, 1954) by

evoking, at the threshold of our labors, the exceptional life and work of this prestigious architect of communism, this master of socialism, whose lessons inspire and guide us in our struggles."

Next Duclos asked for a "minute of silence in memory of our great Comrade Stalin."[16]

14 *La Correspondence Internationale*, No. 66 (Aug. 6, 1930), reprinted from *Oeuvres de Maurice Thorez* (Paris: Éditions Sociales, 1950), Book II, Vol. I, pp. 40, 43. See the report on the Central Committee meeting of December 5–7, 1952, at Gennevilliers in *Cahiers du Communisme*, Jan. 1953.

15 "Discours de Maurice Thorez à la Conférence nationale du P.C.F. 21–22–23 janvier 1939 à Gennevilliers," *La brochure populaire*, No. 94, pp. 3, 25–26.

16 "Pour le changement de la politique française, pour l'indépendance nationale et la paix," report on the activity of the Central Committee of the PCF, presented by Jacques Duclos, PCF pamphlet, p. 2.

Yet French communism has another face, complementary to and inseparable from its transcendental aspect. Communism remains close to the people, as did the Church in the early period of Christianity. It listens to the murmurs of the dissatisfied masses. For the French sympathizer communism is represented not only by the faraway and marvelous Kremlin, the Red Vatican, or the majestic and somber Paris headquarters of the Central Committee, which resemble an austere bishop's seat installed in the building of an insurance company. Communism is at the same time embodied in the person of the activist, who within the working-class milieu plays something akin to the role of the country priest in old Catholic rural society. He may be the trade union delegate of the Régie Renault or Electricité de France, attentive to the daily preoccupations of the workers, devoted to the defense of the small demands of his comrades, whether they concern salaries, working hours, the distribution of clothes, vacations, or some professional injustice.

For many workers who are not party members, this militant Communist is a strange person, a little irritating, a man who sometimes speaks an incomprehensible language and who devotes his spare time to inexplicable rites, but also the man who devotes himself to others, who defends them, who speaks in their name. Projected to the national level, this image of Communists at the factory level becomes the image of the party.

The myth of organization, without which the edifice constructed by the Communist Party would remain quite shaky, was, undoubtedly, the most difficult to introduce into the French labor movement. Under the pretext of safeguarding the unity of the workers' ranks in the class struggle, it demands respect for strict discipline and an organizational structure within which political decisions are taken at the summit and passed on to the lower levels. Leaders at all levels are infallible, at least as long as the higher echelon has not authorized criticism of them.[17]

This military-type organization was only reluctantly accepted because revolutionary syndicalism, which had provided bolshevism with its first converts in France, was steeped in libertarian tenden-

---

[17] Thus no party member dared raise any objection to the often brutal methods employed by André Marty in his capacity as secretary of the PCF. But when Marty was arraigned by the Politburo in 1952, the party militants who had been the butts of his humorous sallies brought up their grievances, in some cases retained for years, at cell meetings, sectional meetings, etc. Marty's collaborators, Léon Feix, Jacques Kahn, André Voguet, *et al.*, found themselves free at last to discharge the animosity accumulated against their former patron during long months of working together.

cies. In order to impose its myth of organization, the French Communist Party had to rely on contrasting tendencies of petit bourgeois origin: the French taste for militarism, a remnant of the great epoch of the French Army; and a leaning toward Bonapartism, which found expression on several occasions in modern France —in particular during the time of Napoleon III and General Boulanger—and which even today prevents the PCF from openly attacking General de Gaulle.

Despite the difficulties of the task, the PCF's leadership under the command of Maurice Thorez has fully succeeded in this respect. The current still called "anarchosyndicalist" persists in the form of an inclination or leaning, but it has been emptied of all substance. It is no longer represented in the leadership of the movement. The term *"anar"* has become synonymous with lack of discipline, hotheadedness, lack of conscience and political education, and it is customary to make fun of it indulgently. On great occasions these *anars* reappear; they are invited to attend meetings and demonstrations of the party, to vote, to go out into the streets. Some representatives of this species may still be found among the party activists at the lowest level; their dynamism and their combativeness are exhausted there in skirmishes. When there is a strike or demonstration, accompanied by clashes with the police, they are in the forefront.

These "anarchosyndicalist" types still represent considerable numerical force, but only potentially; their aversion to any form of organization prevents them from playing an active role in party life. Thus, many workers who will vote Communist and follow the directives of the CGT manifest their disagreement with the Communist myth of organization by refusing to join the party (and the trade unions as well). However, they are de facto supporters of party and union organization, for they vigorously oppose any effort that might lead to weakening the organization of the working class.

At the same time as it imposes in practice its authority on the workers, even though they are repelled by its authoritarian methods, the PCF commands the respect of its bourgeois enemies. In periods when the regime is shaky, this organization alone is capable of disciplining the movement of the masses and making them return to law and order. We have mentioned Maurice Thorez' role in the strikes of 1936. In his memoirs,[18] de Gaulle has explained why he asked five Communists, among them Thorez, to participate in his government of November 21, 1945:

[18] Charles de Gaulle, *Le Salut* (Paris: Plon, 1959), Vol. III, p. 276.

I did it on the basis of my judgment that at least for some time their rallying under my control could serve social peace, of which the country was in such great need.

An anecdote told by a Communist militant admirably illustrates the image of the French Communist Party held by circles far removed from Communist sympathies. This activist had been asked, along with some of his comrades, to represent the Communist list in a voting place in Paris on election day. After the closing of the polls, he had been discussing in a café the events of the day with some policemen in civilian clothes who, like the Communist delegates, had watched the election operations from morning until evening. Not hiding his admiration, the policeman said: "After all, there are only two administrations in France that work: yours and ours." The police and the Communist Party!

Let us add that a very long period of legality has made their task easier for the leaders of the French Communist Party. Even during times when the party was effectively isolated, it was not really ostracized by French society. Whether it was from 1920 to 1934 or from 1947 to 1952, its isolation was only relative; the channels of communication with the external world and the ties between certain militant Communists and the rest of society were never really completely cut. The PCF's one period of complete isolation and clandestine existence was very short: it lasted from September 1939 to June 1941, from the declaration of war to the invasion of the Soviet Union by Hitler. This was actually the most difficult period in the party's history. In fact, the Nazi-Soviet pact had been badly received even in the ranks of the party itself, though the dismay was much greater at the base than at the summit. But this crisis left few lasting traces, except for a bad conscience on the part of the leaders which still existed twenty-five years later, for the massive participation of the French Communist Party in the Resistance during the following three years allowed it to recover and surpass what it had lost during the first eighteen months of the war.

To sum up, of those five years of illegal existence the PCF was really completely outside the law for only less than two years. The contrast with the Italian Communist Party, which was forced by fascism to exist as a clandestine organization from 1926 to 1943, must be emphasized.

CHAPTER THREE

POLITICAL AND ORGANIZATIONAL MANIFESTATIONS OF THE CULT OF STALIN WITHIN THE PCF

The period of dithyrambs for and deification of Stalin coincided with the furious campaign unleashed on an international scale against Yugoslavia and Tito, and prolonged in the people's democracies by the great trials (Rajk in Hungary, Kostov in Bulgaria, Slánský in Czechoslovakia). In this campaign the French Communist Party distinguished itself by especial fury.

For example, in his "Homage to Stalin," Maurice Thorez said:

The trials of the traitors Rajk and Kostov have revealed the monstrous crimes committed by these spies and the chief of their gang, Tito. The trials revealed that all these scoundrels were employed for a long time by the Anglo-American intelligence service. . . . Some people still call that traitor Tito a "Communist," a "revolutionary" who built socialism in his country! With American dollars! As though Mussolini had not been a "socialist," and as though the precursors of Tito, too, had not pretended to fight capitalism and build socialism![1]

To be sure, Maurice Thorez jumped at the chance offered him to take revenge for the criticism that the Yugoslavs had dared level at the first meeting of the Cominform in September 1947 against the timid attitude of the French (and Italian) Communists on the occasion of the liberation of Europe.[2] On July 8 and 9, 1948, on the day after the second meeting of the Cominform at which Yugoslavia had been condemned, the Central Committee of the French party had made haste to adopt a resolution inviting "the entire

---

[1] *Cahiers du Communisme,* Vol. 27, No. 1 (Jan. 1950), p. 32.

[2] On this subject see François Fejtö, *Histoire des démocraties populaires* (Paris: Éditions du Seuil, 1952), and Eugenio Reale, *Avec Jacques Duclos au banc des accusés à la Réunion constitutive du Kominform à Szklarska Poręba* (Paris: Plon, 1958).

party to derive inspiration from this rich document to improve its own activity."[3] From then on, the PCF's anti-Yugoslav campaign became more and more violent. The capital crime of "petit bourgeois nationalism" had led Tito to "anti-Sovietism," while "the cornerstone for all parties and political militants, today, as well as thirty years ago, is their attitude toward the Soviet Union." This formula, taken from an article by Étienne Fajon in *Cahiers du Communisme* of September 1948,[4] was for years repeated in all the propaganda of the French Communist Party. Following the Stalinist pattern, "Tito and his clique" could not help but degenerate into a "band of spies and assassins in the pay of imperialism."[5] Speaking of Catholic and Socialist workers, Léon Mauvais wrote in *Cahiers du Communisme* of May 1950: "We can and must loyally stretch out our hand to them. But does this also go for the Titoists? Is Titoism a deviation, a trend?" He answered: "There is no Titoist deviation, any more than there is a Titoist trend; any more than there is a Hitlerite or Trotskyite deviation or trend."[6]

This was a major excommunication. The French Communist Party would have liked to continue holding out its hand to the right and to the left. But all contact with Tito was forbidden, all travel to Yugoslavia brought automatic exclusion of the "culprit" from the ranks of the party; all reservations with regard to the fantastic accusations that Soviet propaganda, relayed by the French Communist Party, showered on the Yugoslav leaders, or any doubt regarding the veracity of the "confessions" on which the trials in Budapest, Sofia, and Prague rested, entailed an immediate and brutal break with a person thus suspect of "Titoist" sympathies.

One could fill pages with all the literature published in the years 1949 to 1952 by the French Communist Party denouncing and insulting Tito, or condemning Rajk, even after his death. Just a small sample, from among hundreds: "Tito screamed very loudly after Rajk's confessions. Dogs act the same: when someone steps on their tail, they bark. . . ."[7] Thus, the publicist André Wurmser was made

---

[3] Victor Joannes, "Dans le secteur français du camp anti-impérialiste et démocratique," *Cahiers du Communisme*, Vol. 25, No. 9 (Sept. 1948), p. 957.

[4] *Ibid.*, pp. 914–915.

[5] Maurice Thorez, *Rapport au 12ème Congrès National du P.C.F.* (Apr. 6–7 1950 at Gennevilliers), published by the PCF under the title *La lutte pour l'indépendance nationale et pour la paix*, p. 19.

[6] Léon Mauvais, "La vigilance révolutionnaire et la lutte pour la paix," *Cahiers du Communisme*, Vol. 27, No. 5 (May 1950), p. 62.

[7] André Wurmser, *Réponse à Jean Cassou* (Éditions *La Nouvelle Critique*), p. 3.

to answer his brother-in-law, the writer Jean Cassou, a fellow traveler who had fought for many years on the side of the Communists.

There had been some unrest at the base among intellectuals and youth who had traveled in Yugoslavia before the Cominform meeting and returned full of enthusiasm, believing, incidentally, that they were completely "in line." Some militants withdrew; others were expelled. The language with which the leaders of the French Communist Party castigated the Titoist heresy and criticized the "lack of vigilance" of the PCF cadres testified to the witch-hunt atmosphere that reigned in the party at that time. According to the article by Léon Mauvais cited earlier,[8] a report of the Communist federation of Haute-Marne contained this passage: "In our federation we have not yet discovered any Titoist deviation." Such naïveté was not unique: "In certain departments," continued Léon Mauvais, "the leaders fail to denounce the machinations of Tito and his clique under the pretext that so far no apparent Titoist activity has been revealed."[9] But "one must never forget that the Titoists, like the Trotskyites, do their dirty work cunningly, infiltrate wherever they are, and do everything not to reveal their true aims."[10] In a word, if no Titoist had so far been discovered, this was an additional proof that there were some. Léon Mauvais admonished "certain comrades," particularly of the Rhône federation, that there were still some who felt that "to tell the party about machinations, declarations, and acts contrary to the general line was to be an informer."[11] He demanded that this petit bourgeois prejudice be abandoned.

Eventually the difficulties produced by the anti-Yugoslav campaign, namely its excesses and its absurdities, undoubtedly led to a loss of party members. This loss had begun in 1948, that is, the year after the Communists had been excluded from the French government. But at the level of the cadres, in the *apparat,* the French Communist Party registered hardly any losses: when certain leaders on the local or regional level were relieved of their functions or blamed for insufficient anti-Titoist "vigilance," this was often a mere pretext to settle old accounts. As in the people's democracies, one began to suspect the veterans of the International Brigades in Spain of "Titoism," and also the old leaders of the Resistance in France. But not until 1952 did the French Communist Party orga-

8 Mauvais, *op. cit.,* p. 62.
9 *Ibid.,* p. 63.
10 *Ibid.*
11 *Ibid.,* p. 66.

nize its "great trial" against two of its leaders, André Marty and Charles Tillon.

With regard to the "Marty-Tillon Affair," which had simmered for several months (the actual indictment by Léon Mauvais made the beginning of the inquiry go back to before May 26, 1952),[12] it was made public after the Central Committee meeting of September 3–4, 1952. The first indiscretions found their way into the bourgeois press even before the cadres had been officially informed. Even today, it remains rather difficult to untangle the exact motives of those who launched the affair at that moment and the method chosen to conduct it.

The interpretation of this affair seems all the more complex for none of the sources to which one might refer can be considered an objective, impartial document: neither the indictment drawn up by the French Communist Party; nor the book devoted to his defense by André Marty himself, under the title *The Marty Affair*, as he was already under the influence of alienated, particularly Trotskyite, elements of the French Communist Party; nor the passages devoted to the event by witnesses such as Auguste Lecoeur ("Expected Self-Criticism") or Pierre Hervé ("Letter to Sartre").

One thing seems certain: to combine the Marty Affair and the Tillon Affair was artificial. It was the application, in France, of the well-known technique that had been used before in Moscow in conducting the trials of the "block of Trotskyites and Bukharinites"; in Budapest against Rajk and Jusztusz; or to make it appear, in Prague, as though Slánský and Clementis had been acting together. André Marty and Charles Tillon were associated only through memories: in 1919 both had participated in the Black Sea Revolt—mutiny of the French fleet against the intervention in Russia—and then again in the years 1936 to 1939, at the organization of International Brigades in Spain. In fact, with regard to these two events, Charles Tillon had played a much more effective role than had André Marty, of whom party propaganda had made a sort of living symbol of solidarity with the Soviet Union and then with Republican Spain—a real storybook legend. But while André Marty, French delegate to the Secretariat of the Communist International, found himself in Moscow in 1939, at the moment of the declaration of war, and left the Soviet Union only to lead the delegation of the Central Committee in *liberated* Algiers in 1943, Charles Tillon led, on national soil, the military organization of

12 Léon Mauvais's report in *Cahiers du Communisme*, Vol. 29, No. 10 (Oct. 1952), p. 1034.

the Resistance created by the French Communist Party, the Franc-Tireurs, and the French Partisans.

Thus, one trait the two men might have shared was a certain disdain for the "bureaucrat" Maurice Thorez, who during his career as an activist had taken only a minimum of physical risks. This disdain was probably aggravated when, in the absence of Thorez, whose experience and flexibility had been able to limit friction, his wife, Jeannette Vermeersch, tried to exercise a delegated authority to which she was not entitled. Actually, in his report, Léon Mauvais accused André Marty of "having talked tirelessly of the leaders of the party, in terms that were violent and unfriendly, discrediting them with those to whom he talked."[13] And Marty accused Charles Tillon of having

displayed responses and attitudes of an unfriendly, not to say insulting, nature with regard to our Comrade Jeannette Vermeersch, and indirectly with regard to our Comrade Maurice Thorez.[14]

However, the link established between the two men by their common past and their common aversion against the leader and his wife was not enough to create a political group. On that plane, Marty and Tillon found themselves instead at opposite poles. From the libertarian ideals of his youth, Marty had undoubtedly retained his leftist tendencies; in any event, militant workers and sympathizers recognized him instinctively, by his gestures, his language, and the memory of his long years in prison (1919–1923) as a "revolutionary" leader, in contrast to the "parliamentarian" Duclos, or an *apparatchik* like Thorez. Tillon, on the other hand, could be suspected of "nationalism": the leading role he had played in the Resistance in France had led him to show some irritation with the "resisters from Moscow" (that is, men who had resisted Hitler from the safety of their Moscow refuge).

Thus it is quite probable that André Marty had really stated in private to the cadres that the Communist Party had "missed the boat" in 1944. The accusation leveled by the Politburo in its document of October 3, 1952 ("André Marty has declared to his comrades that the dissolution of the patriotic militias was a mistake"),[15] was effectively corroborated by the analysis that Marty made of this period in his book, after his expulsion. Yet, all in all, it does not seem that Marty's protestations during the entire time when

13 *Ibid.*, p. 1038.
14 *Ibid.*, p. 1044.
15 Document of the Politburo of Oct. 3, 1952, *Cahiers du Communisme*, Vol. 29, No. 10 (Oct. 1952), p. 942.

he was secretary of the party, together with Maurice Thorez and Jacques Duclos, went beyond mere verbal outbursts, or manifestations of bad temper in the course of private conversations.

Finally, the precise charges that the party could level against Marty were so thin that the Politburo accused him of "duplicity" consisting in "publicly approving the Party's decision" when he had had "the possibility of defending his opinions in the Secretariat." Of course, if he did not submit his divergent opinions to this organ, it was because his "conceptions, contrary to those of the party, would have been contested." The principal points of the accusation consisted in the declarations by Beyer, an old member of the Central Committee, removed in 1950, who stated that Marty had asked him in February–March 1949 to publish a factional bulletin and that in the spring of 1951 a conversation between Marty and Tillon had taken place in his apartment.

But it so happens that in 1951 Charles Tillon, as representative of the French Communist Party to the National Movement of Peace, had opposed the leadership of the French Communist Party and the World Council of Peace on grounds regarded as "nationalist." At the bottom of this disagreement was Tillon's desire to conserve for the French peace movement a certain autonomy against the World Council (in other words, Moscow) but also against the leadership of the French Communist Party. In Tillon's opinion, such autonomy would have made it possible to make of the movement a true mass organization, leading its own life independently of that of the party; and this evidently constituted a danger for the leadership of the latter.

It actually seems that the proposal for a factional bulletin in 1949 was an invention on the part of Beyer; as far as the conversation between Marty and Tillon is concerned, even if it had taken place without the knowledge of the other members of the Politburo, it apparently had no sequel in the course of the following eighteen months. It is therefore difficult to believe that the leadership of the party, at the moment the affair was launched, could have felt itself threatened by some pressing danger of "conspiracy."

One may therefore hypothesize that the launching of the affair, the objective foundations of which were so fragile, was due to circumstances prevailing in the second half of 1952. A leadership crisis in the French Communist Party had resulted from the absence of Maurice Thorez, who had been under treatment in Moscow since his stroke in Paris in October 1950. The members of the PCF Politburo seemed to tolerate only with impatience the tendency by Jeanette Vermeersch, the wife of Maurice Thorez, to give instructions in the name of her husband. There was the failure of the insurrectional exercise at the end of May and beginning of June,[16] on the one hand; and on the other, particularly, there was the frenetic campaign of "vigilance" on the international level. It was also in 1952 that Slánský and his codefendants in Czechoslovakia were liquidated, that Ana Pauker was eliminated in Romania, and that a new purge was in preparation in the Soviet Union. It was therefore necessary, in France as well, to hit at the left and the right; to find "infiltrated enemies" in the leadership of the party; and to find them among the militants who had links with the international machinery, and against whom it was possible to level, no matter how implausibly, the accusation of "anti-Sovietism."

Thus Marty and Tillon were selected as sacrificial lambs essentially because they stood out as personalities with a certain prestige. The fact that they had been fighters in the Spanish Civil War contributed, in the crazed atmosphere of Stalin's final months, to increasing the presumption of guilt, as in the case of Rajk in Hungary. Moreover, popular among the masses, André Marty had often made himself unpopular with the militants of the apparatus by his verbal outbursts, his brutality, his fits of temper, so much in contrast with the demagogic good-fellowship of Maurice Thorez or Jacques Duclos. Marty had never really been integrated into

16 The failure of the strike of February 2, organized as a protest against the prohibition of a commemorative demonstration of the days of February 1934, was acknowledged by the Central Committee (see Étienne Fajon in *Cahiers du Communisme*, Vol. 29, No. 3 [Mar. 1952], pp. 235–237), but far from learning its lesson, the committee decided to repeat the experiment on an even larger scale. This political strike launched with slogans concerning internal politics was followed by a campaign entirely directed toward foreign policy. This was the campaign to mobilize violent demonstrations, of an insurrectional character, against the arrival in France of General Ridgway, who was regarded as responsible for "bacteriological warfare" in Korea and had been called by Communist propaganda "Ridgway-the-Plague," "Microbe Killer," "Great War Criminal," and so forth. (See editorial by Victor Michaut in *ibid.*, Vol. 29, No. 6 [June 1962], pp. 565 and 568.) On May 28, 1952, the PCF militants received bludgeons, clubs, bricks, and bottles to face the police, and the riots were at times bloody. Under somewhat obscure circumstances Jacques Duclos was arrested on the evening of that day of riots, not far from the place of the demonstrations, while carrying a notebook of notes taken during the Politburo meetings. On June 4 an effort by militant Communists to push the workers into a general strike against the arrest of Duclos met with disaster. Where they succeeded in causing work stoppages, as in the Renault works, the militant Communists were met by violent opposition from their fellow workers the next day. There were several scuffles, and several hundred of the Communist cadres, union delegates, and others lost their jobs.

the inner circle of the French Communist Party. They had collaborated with him because the legend created around him when he paid in jail for his actions during the Black Sea mutiny had rendered his presence indispensable; but he always remained to some extent a foreign body, a residue of the old French anarcho-syndicalism, not fully assimilated by the bureaucratic millieu. With regard to Tillon, he was much less known, and the fear that his past as a partisan leader aroused in Thorez and his wife was due more to guilt on their part than to any real danger.

Besides, shortly thereafter, the difference between the two men became clear: while Marty refused to extend the "self-criticism" demanded of him to the humiliating point of confessing imaginary actions, Tillon succeeded in obtaining clemency. He was simply sent back to the base—which did not stop constant insinuations in the whole party, on the basis of a charge by Léon Mauvais that he had misappropriated certain Resistance funds.[17]

Marty, on the other hand, was quickly expelled from the party, after his successive self-criticisms were rejected as "insufficient"; and after December 7, 1952, the Central Committee spoke of the problem of "his connection with police elements."[18]

On January 21, 1953, in a speech at the Mutualité, Auguste Lecoeur, secretary of the party, went even further:

As far as Marty is concerned, we have had confirmation, after sanctions taken against him by the Central Committee, that he was connected with the police services. . . . It is up to the police of the Socialist leaders to defend their colleague Marty.[19]

From then on, as in the "message to Maurice Thorez" approved by the delegates of the National Conference of the French Communist Party on March 5, 1953 at Gennevilliers (". . . under your direction we have been able to unmask and stop the criminal attempts of the police agent, Marty"),[20] the epithet of "police agent" was linked to Marty's name in Communist propaganda in France.

[17] "Deux dépôts d'argent étaient conservés par le camarade Charles Tillon à l'insu de la direction du Parti" (report by Léon Mauvais), Cahiers du Communisme, Vol. 29, No. 10. (Oct. 1952), p. 1034.

[18] Resolution by the Central Committee at Gennevilliers (Dec. 7, 1952) in Cahiers du Communisme, Vol. 30, No. 1 (Jan. 1953), p. 92.

[19] Auguste Lecoeur, "Sous la conduite de Staline, les idées du léninisme éclairent le chemin du communisme et guident le parti de Maurice Thorez" (speech on the 29th anniversary of the death of Lenin), Cahiers du Communisme, Vol. 30, No. 2 (Feb. 1953), pp. 159–160.

[20] Cahiers du Communisme, special issue, Mar. 1953, p. 398.

Strictly on the political plane, François Billoux, in his report to the Central Committee of December 5, 6, and 7, 1952 at Gennevilliers, well expressed the absence of principle that had been notable in the entire affair:

Marty and Tillon, by abandoning the principles of Marxism-Leninism, are the living incarnation of what a mixture of opportunism and sectarianism can produce on the basis of a hard core of opportunism under the cover of leftist phrases and gestures.[21]

It was absolutely necessary to charge the accused with all crimes at the same time, particularly with all the crimes committed by the party leaders.

Reading the Communist press in the fall of 1952 and the winter of 1952–1953 confirms what many militants actually felt in the cells at the base of the party: that the "Marty-Tillon Affair" brought on a rather serious malaise; the accusations of collaboration with the police were particularly poorly received; and the overzealous propagandists who had made this connection between Marty and the police go back for more than thirty years were forced to reverse themselves. However, those militants who asked questions, left the party, or were expelled on this occasion did not belong to the higher echelons.

In sum, in the French party, as in the international Communist movement, the year 1952 marked, without doubt, the death throes of Stalinism. It was a Stalinism gone mad, infected by persecution mania, and incapable of adopting any but very short-term tactics.

In the same way, the party "swallowed," without any important ripples at the level of the cadres, the Doctors' Plot, which was part of the "anti-Zionist" offensive in Moscow and of which a previous episode, the Slánský trial, had taken place in Prague. In the same speech at the Mutualité quoted earlier, Auguste Lecoeur declared:

... Honest doctors will not forget that at present one does not merely try to camouflage the monstrous crimes of Nazi doctors with the white coat of their profession, but also the crimes of their murderous colleagues who have just been arrested in the Soviet Union. ... The attempts on the part of the warmongers to camouflage their crimes with the rabbinical vestment, the doctor's coat, or the priest's cassock are classic maneuvers that may still fool some timid bourgeois, but are much too worn-out to be able to move the working class.[22]

21 François Billoux, *La politique du Parti et l'action pour les libertés* (report delivered at the Central Committee meeting of December 5–7, 1952 at Gennevilliers) (PCF pamphlet), p. 29.

22 *Cahiers du Communisme*, Vol. 30, No. 2 (Feb. 1953), p. 158. The "Doctors' Plot" had been launched by a communiqué published in *Pravda*, Jan. 13, 1953.

As a result of delays in printing, the March 1953 issue of *La Nouvelle Critique* (periodical of the French Communist Party for the intellectuals) appeared after Stalin's death, with four fifths of its contents devoted to the struggle against "Zionism" and the affair of the "criminal doctors."

The main article of this issue, called "Criminal Physicians or Perverted Science," appeared over the signature of Dr. Louis Le Guillant, chief physician of a psychiatric hospital and one of the most gifted French specialists. Dr. Le Guillant, after quoting the Pravda communiqué announcing the arrest of the doctors and giving their "crimes" in less than ten lines, wrote:

As far as we know, there is as yet no technical indication supporting this information. Therefore on the basis of fact, there is no reason to question it at all.[23]

Thus, in connection with such a monstrous accusation leveled against eminent doctors, some of world-wide reputations and, moreover, almost all of them Jews, the absence of all precise data—far from justifying doubts or reservations—reinforced the conviction of their Communist French colleague. And the latter calmly finished his article with the following lines: "Also, as far as I am concerned, I simply congratulate myself that the Soviets have caught some doctors who perverted and dishonored my profession."[24] The twenty-six bewildering pages ending with this conclusion were built entirely on the following "argumentation": "The participation of German doctors in Nazi atrocities during the Second World War is proof that doctors can be assassins."[25]

Ten years later, Maurice Thorez raised the question again at Ivry at the Central Committee meeting of October 5, 1963, but this time in a completely different context. It was then in connection with an attack on the Chinese Communist Party, which was accused by the Secretary-General of the French Communist Party of defending Stalin among other things, that Maurice Thorez evoked the transgressions of the "cult of personality."

This evil could be felt not only in the Soviet Union but in all other Socialist countries and in the entire international Communist movement. I will take a single example from our own party; the affair of the "white coats" that concerned those doctors most of whom I knew personally be-

23 *La Nouvelle Critique*, Vol. 5, No. 44 (Mar. 1953), p. 32.
24 *Ibid.*, p. 58.
25 Dr. Le Guillant allegedly had a nervous breakdown after he heard that the Soviet doctors, whom he had believed guilty, had been rehabilitated. He has not renewed his party membership card for the last several years.

cause they had spent whole weeks, day and night, at my bedside. They were arrested, thrown into prison, beaten, and they barely escaped death. They were liberated the very day that I left Moscow.

Ah well! At the time *pressure was exerted* on our Communist doctors in France to sign without delay a text approving such arbitrary violence against their own Soviet colleagues for acts of which they knew nothing.[26]

With this convenient expression Thorez, at the time still in the Soviet Union, deflected the responsibility on others whom he did not name. His allusion might have been aimed at any of the other members of the Politburo of the time: Jacques Duclos or Étienne Fajon—or those who were eliminated later, such as Auguste Lecoeur and still more probably Laurent Casanova, who at the time was responsible for Communist Party work among the intellectuals.[27]

Yet the explanation given *a posteriori* by Maurice Thorez seemed quite thin to those who were interested. The generation of French Communist doctors who had personally experienced the events had suffered too deeply as a result of this affair and its consequences to be satisfied with such a version. First of all, they had had to convince themselves of the guilt of their Soviet colleagues and over-come their first reaction of incredulity. They had had to place over every moral and scientific consideration their confidence in their party and in its discipline, sacrifice their reputations, and see them-selves ostracized in their profession. They remembered the terribly charged atmosphere of those first months in 1953: all around them inside the party every doctor was suspect of being at least able to commit murder, just as all militant Jews became suspect of "Zion-ism." For the most compelling reasons the Jewish doctors—and most of the French Communist doctors were Jewish—became the allegedly legitimate objects of "vigilance." At times they felt obliged to go the others "one better," to show that for them the

---

26 *L'Humanité*, Oct. 10, 1963 [My italics—F.F.].

27 It may have seemed opportune to insinuate that Casanova was to blame; for, beginning in 1957, the latter had begun to intrigue against Thorez, particularly in intellectual and student circles, aided undoubtedly by some powerful Soviet supporters. Though it is often difficult to be sure of accurate information on this subject, it seems that Casanova's "line" consisted in advocating a more vigorous de-Stalinization in the PCF and a more realistic domestic policy, and that he made efforts to persuade Moscow that the French leadership was in league with the Chinese Communist Party. Apparently, Casanova wanted the post of Secretary-General of the PCF for himself. Elim-inated in 1961, but still a PCF member and close to Italian and Soviet mili-tants on the highest level, Casanova could still have appeared sufficiently dan-gerous for Thorez to try to discredit him (all the more as the Communist intellectuals still remembered Casanova's extreme sectarianism in the fifties, through 1956). We shall return to the role played by this important personality.

party spirit was stronger than professional or "racial" solidarity. Outside the party, they met with consternation, reproaches, and sarcasm, which became particularly unbearable after Moscow had announced the rehabilitation of those accused.

Six of the ten doctors who had signed the declaration demanding "exemplary punishment" for their Soviet colleagues—a declaration published in the January 27, 1953 issue of *L'Humanité*—have since then either left the Communist Party or taken up notoriously "oppositional" positions. One of them, Dr. Jean Dalsace, has revealed[28] that the text which appeared in *L'Humanité* with his signature "had no relationship to the text which had been submitted to me for my approval in principle."

The anti-Yugoslav campaign, the "trial" of André Marty, and the Doctors' Plot illustrate the phenomenon of the *quasi-mystical participation* of the French Communists, particularly the intellectuals, in a world from which they were excluded in every way. They lived in a world where the French Communist Party was like a province or republic of the Soviet Federation, and they vibrated in complete unison with it. To be sure, the same "sacrifices of intellect" had been observed in Hungary, for example, where a thinker as brilliant and original as György Lukács had humiliated himself before the mediocre leaders who ruled "cultural life" with the same methods of discipline and expediency that they applied in other domains. But in that country the Communist Party at least held power and controlled the state apparatus. *In France, through the pressure of its machine alone, the Communist Party succeeded in the tour de force of obtaining the participation of all its faithful, intellectuals above all, in this furious pursuit of heresy.* When reading the works of old Communists, such as *Autocritique* by Edgar Morin,[29] or *La somme et le reste* by Henri Lefebvre,[30] one begins to realize that this pressure was as strong and effective as if the party had also had full control of all secular power. For the "Marty Affair" is typical in this respect: it was really a trial where only the means to make the sentence physically effective were lacking. The French Communist Party went to the ultimate limits set by objective conditions in France: Marty was deprived of his dwelling; his wife was forced to leave him; his correspondence was stolen; his name was effaced from the history of the party; and even his

28 In the organ of the "Association for the Defense of the Interests of Old Members of the French Communist Party," *Le Débat Communiste*, Feb. 1964.
29 Collection "Lettres Nouvelles"; Paris: Julliard, 1959.
30 Éditions La Nef de Paris, 1959.

likeness was removed from old photographs where he appeared next to other militants. He could not be locked up; so he was rejected. Unable to make use of the police, the party itself became the police; and its victim, Marty, was charged with the crime of being a "police agent." It was a great accomplishment to have brought the Inquisition to a country where the party was not in power.

We have found it necessary to evoke this period rather lengthily in order to make more comprehensible the worried stupefaction, the near panic, that gripped the French Communist leaders and many of the militants at the news of the death of Stalin. Just at that time a National Conference of the French Communist Party had met at Gennevilliers on the morning of March 5, 1953. The next day, on March 6, several hours after the official announcement of Stalin's death, the President of the meeting, Victor Michaut, declared:

In the terrible sorrow which wrings our hearts, the Central Committee that has met here has decided to adjourn the National Conference of the French Communist Party as a sign of mourning. . . . The Central Committee asks all delegates to return to their federations in order to take there all decisions demanded by the situation created by the terrible and brutal blow that has hit all peoples, all workers, all defenders of the peace. . . . We have lost Comrade Stalin; Stalinism lives and will live eternally in the hearts of men.[31]

Clearly, this last statement was primarily meant by the leaders of the French Communist Party to reassure themselves. They were too well informed and too experienced not to grasp reality: with Stalin dead, Stalinism as a whole was in danger of disintegrating. For those who knew how to read between the lines, the text published in Moscow on the night of March 5–6 by the leaders of the Soviet party and state, with its insistence on "the iron unity and monolithic cohesion of the party ranks," clearly signified that this unity was in peril. The decision to adjourn the National Conference in Gennevilliers, in haste and without having passed any resolution, betrayed the prevailing profound confusion of the French leaders, brutally deprived of the man whom Jacques Duclos, in a brief speech, had called "our beloved master."[32]

31 *Cahiers du Communisme*, Mar. 1953, special number, p. 395.
32 *Ibid.*, p. 267.

CHAPTER FOUR

FROM THE DEATH OF STALIN TO FEBRUARY 1956

The following three years—from March 1953 to February 1956—were marked by a sort of long interregnum in the international Communist movement. Factions (or potential factions) existing at the time of Stalin's death had no choice but to settle their accounts and turn their attention to the struggle for power. It was difficult for other Communist parties to ascertain who would be the victor. In France the party reacted in conformity with its prudent nature: it attempted to maintain the purity of the Stalinist cult while modifying some of its more exaggerated manifestations and its inquisitorial aspect. Plans were cautiously drawn up for a "benevolent offensive" to follow Moscow's "liberal" policy, which emphasized peaceful coexistence and production of consumer goods. On the other hand, Soviet declarations that had begun to emphasize, in very general terms, the necessity of "collective leadership" and to criticize the "personality cult" were, if not censored outright by the French Communist press, certainly not distributed to the general public. In other words, instead of publishing such Soviet texts conspicuously in *L'Humanité*, the PCF relegated them after considerable delay to its more esoteric publications with a limited circulation. For example, an important article by F. Yakovlev entitled "Collective Leadership, Major Principle of Party Leadership," appeared in the July 1953 issue of *Kommunist* but was not published in France until October—and then only in a collection of pamphlets entitled "Études et documents théoretiques," which had a very limited circulation.

Indeed, the summer of 1953 proved sorely trying for the leadership of the PCF, including Maurice Thorez, who had returned to his post. On June 7, 1953, the PCI's success at the polls sounded an alert: the party on the other side of the Alps had succeeded in braving the years of the Cold War without losing its effectiveness;

it had maintained its alliance with the Socialist Party and was still gaining in influence. In the competition already existing between the two great Communist parties of Western Europe, the Italians had scored an important point for the leadership of the movement in that part of the world.[1] In the same month a genuine workers' insurrection had been crushed by the Red Army in East Berlin and all of East Germany, while the Central Committee of the Hungarian Workers' Party had disavowed the disastrous policies of Rákosi and named his old enemy, Imre Nagy, Prime Minister. The government program read to the Assembly on July 4, 1953 by the new Premier of Hungary was entirely contrary to Stalinist policy.

In July 1953 the French Communist leaders learned that Beria was nothing but an agent of "international imperialism." They announced the news to their activists in the most traditional style, more or less in the same way as they had announced the discovery of the Doctors' Plot:

Repeated provocations against the international workers' movement and against the countries of the democratic camp, considerable sums of money devoted to finance espionage operations, sabotage, and terrorist diversion in countries liberated from the imperialist yoke show the intention of the American imperialists and their accomplices not to shrink from any means of re-establishing capitalism in those countries that have freed themselves from it. Under these conditions they try to introduce agents into the Communist and workers' parties in order to pursue their criminal activities, not unlike those to which the traitor Beria lent himself. Fortunately, he was unmasked and prevented from doing further damage by the disciples and followers of Lenin and Stalin.

Such was the comment devoted to Beria's fall in a PCF Politburo declaration of July 23, 1953.[2] However, it is now known that in a secret meeting held by the leaders of Communist parties with membership in the Cominform, convened from July 12–14, 1953 in

---

1 This rivalry had been publicly expressed when, right after the war, the PCF had declared itself in favor of the return of Trieste and its environs to Yugoslavia. However, the Yugoslav attacks against the PCF and PCI blended into a joint charge of opportunism at the first Cominform session, and the subsequent common approval by the two great Western parties of Tito's excommunication could not but entail a rapprochement. It was possible only for insiders to understand that Togliatti, when he stressed the value of maintaining his party effectives and his alliance with Italy's Socialist Party, meant "as distinguished from the PCF." Similarly, Thorez, when he boasted about the ideological and organizational cohesiveness of the PCF and his refusal to collaborate with social-democratic ideology, was indirectly attacking the Italian "fraternal" party.

2 *Cahiers du Communisme,* Vol. 30, No. 8–9 (Aug.–Sept. 1953), p. 925.

Moscow[3] under the chairmanship of Malenkov, Molotov, and Khrushchev, the representative of the French Communist Party, Jacques Duclos, had been informed of most of the accusations that were to appear in Khrushchev's secret report at the Twentieth Congress in 1956. Thus the French Communist leaders who three years later were to feign "surprise" at the "painful revelations made by Khrushchev" knew in 1953 that the "criminal activity" of which Beria was accused had been desired, ordered, and covered up by Stalin. Told in the course of this same session that they would have to change their methods of directing the party, they did nothing about it. This was the first time that the PCF leaders permitted themselves to disregard completely a compelling suggestion by the "great Soviet brethren."[4]

On July 28, 1953, the signature of the armistice at Panmunjong marked the end of the war in Korea. Would it now also become necessary for the PCF to drop its anti-American line, for six years one of the constants in French Communist propaganda? The confusion in the French Communist leadership was very profound; in fact, it was so deep that when in August 1953 a vast movement of spontaneous strikes broke out in France in the public sector affecting several hundred thousand workers, the Communist political and trade union leaders were the first to be surprised by the scope, duration, and intensity of the strikes. These strikes had broken out for strictly professional reasons. (They began as protests against decrees of Laniel's rightist government jeopardizing certain guarantees of workers in state and nationalized enterprises.) However, the movement was quick to spread and ended by making much larger demands, concerning general salary increases, an end to the war in Vietnam, and so on. But the leaders of the Communist Party were paralyzed by their *attentisme*. To begin with, they were handicapped by the fact that the first strikes had been sparked by the *Force Ouvrière* (SFIO), while the majority of the CGT leaders, not expecting anything in the summer months, traditionally unfavorable in France for any such movements, were on vacation. The CGT, which had hastily joined the movement, restricted itself

[3] For an account of that meeting, with a photocopy of the transcribed text of the speech by the PCI delegate Pietro Secchia, see Giulio Seniga, *Togliatti e Stalin* (Milan: Sugar, 1961).

[4] The report of the information meeting made to the PCF and PCI in the course of the Cominform session ended with these words: "You, too, must change your methods of leadership, because, as the personality cult, personal leadership and disregard of party rules did considerable harm to us in the Soviet Union, such harm would be even greater in your case since you have not yet taken power." (*Ibid.*, p. 13.)

to celebrating the refound unity with the SFIO; but the Communist leaders, in the absence of any clear directions emanating from their party, lagged behind the union members at the base. The joint leadership of the *Force Ouvrière* and the CFTC (the Catholic trade unions) offered the CGT an almost providential escape hatch by negotiating a resumption of work with the government. The CGT jumped at the chance. While it denounced the "treason of the splittist leaders," it gave orders at the same time to resume work "in order to consolidate the unity" broken by the other leaders. Thus the French Communist Party resigned itself to the inglorious miscarriage of the most powerful strike wave France had known since 1947–1948. The French working class drew its lesson from this: During the two years that followed there was not again in France any large-scale, long-term labor unrest staged by many different trade union organizations.

While in 1936 the French Communist Party had wanted to accommodate Stalin by putting the brake on the strikes, its incapacity in 1953 to direct them toward any objective was a direct consequence of Stalin's death; in the absence of the leader the compass needle was off its track. However, it should be noted that in the confusion the natural reflexes of the Communist chiefs had enabled them to accept defeat and reject "adventurism."

After drifting for several months, the French Communist Party at the end of 1953 again found a prime objective: to bring about the failure of the treaties guaranteeing the European Defense Community. This choice was of great importance, for it led the French Communist Party to seek an alliance with the Gaullists and the entire nationalist right. Both sides were equally opposed, for different reasons, to a European army. Jacques Duclos defined this policy at the Central Committee plenum at Drancy (October 22–23, 1953):

Conscious of the need to act quickly throughout the country to prevent the adoption of the treaties that would create a European army, we Communists declare that we are ready, together with all Frenchmen, whoever they may be—we say deliberately, whoever they may be—and, who, like us, do not want a new Wehrmacht, to participate in any political action that can and must be organized in a powerful campaign throughout France.

To this solemn declaration the Communists added that

we for our part are ready to contribute by all parliamentary means to the defeat of the promoters and defenders of the European army.[5]

5 *Cahiers du Communisme,* Vol. 30, No. 11–12 (Dec. 1953), p. 1108.

And before the same Central Committee plenum, Maurice Thorez added:

Nothing is more important, nothing more urgent than the rallying of all good Frenchmen for the purpose of making the agreements between Bonn and Paris fail.[6]

As there was "nothing more important, nothing more urgent," one could for the moment make certain concessions to the "good Frenchmen" of the right with whom one wanted to "rally." This led to the necessity of avoiding labor demands that might frighten such allies or reduce the vigor of the campaign against the war in Vietnam, and served to keep protests against France's colonial policies in North Africa within limits. The political choice made by the Central Committee at Drancy was to have very long-term repercussions. The entire history of the relations of the French Communist Party with the Algerian insurrection was to be influenced by it. It is not even impossible that the French Communist Party might really have believed, in its exacerbated egocentrism, that the launching of the Algerian insurrection in November 1954 was an effort by rabid *provocateurs* to ruin its policy of "rallying of all good Frenchmen."

The Thirteenth Congress of the French Communist Party, meeting at Ivry from June 3–7, 1954, confirmed the line of the Central Committee of Drancy. The watchwords of struggle against the war in Vietnam and of solidarity with the African peoples were an important part of the "thesis on the political situation and the tasks of the French Communist Party" adopted by the Congress, while its principal emphasis was on the affirmation of the party's "national character" and on unity against the EDC. In the course of the preparatory discussion prior to the Congress, this orientation had been criticized, albeit in very cautious terms, in various section conferences and even in the "discussion column" in *L'Humanité*, where the most noteworthy position was taken by Victor Leduc, a former collaborator with François Billoux in the ideological section of the Central Committee and an influential personality among Communist intellectuals. Despite the careful language of these "leftist" criticisms, which proposed only simple amendments to the draft theses, Louis Aragon and Georges Cogniot devoted long passages to refuting them.[7] Another amendment, which

---

6 *Ibid.*, p. 1101.

7 Speech by Louis Aragon, published in *Cahiers du Communisme*, Vol. 30, No. 6–7 (June–July 1954), special number, p. 842, and Georges Cogniot, "Rapport de la Commission politique," *ibid.*, pp. 896–903.

went so far as to demand the institution of a permanent discussion forum in the columns of *L'Humanité,* was also violently attacked by Georges Cogniot.[8]

It is interesting to note that since 1954 the two principal themes around which the oppositionists of 1956 were to regroup themselves were expressed—timidly, to be sure—in the preparation of the congress: namely, criticism of opportunism and "nationalism," and aspiration toward more internal democracy. Furthermore, the Thirteenth Congress ratified the condemnation of the former organizational secretary, Auguste Lecoeur:

> The ultimate expression of the liquidating current has appeared in the formulation of an opportunistic line that would have led the party to renounce its independent policy and its vanguard role, to become a mere supporting force, and, on the level of organizing work, in the surrender, combined with the institution of cell instructors, of the essential principles appropriate for a workers' party of the new type.[9]

Contrary to those leveled against Marty in 1952, the charges against Lecoeur were confined to the political area. Another sign of the times: Lecoeur's expulsion was not announced until January 1955, and then it was only temporary, for one year. Despite this change in form, the methods remained fundamentally identical: Lecoeur served mainly as a convenient scapegoat, responsible for the recent failures of party policies and organization. It would appear that Auguste Lecoeur, who had risen very rapidly in the Communist hierarchy thanks to the protection of Maurice Thorez, in this affair was made to pay for the arguments he had had with Jeannette Vermeersch during Thorez' illness. Like Tillon, Lecoeur had committed the imprudence, in the course of relatively secondary incidents, of alluding to his past as a fighter in Spain and in the French Resistance. But outside of these insinuations, considered rather unfriendly by Thorez and his wife, hardly any trace of those personal policy positions imputed to him in order to justify this new purge can be found in Auguste Lecoeur's activity up until 1954. (The organizational measures for which the Congress made him responsible had been formulated by the entire Politburo.)

Incidentally, the Lecoeur affair had only very minor repercussions among PCF activists. Much less known than Marty, the former organizational secretary had made himself unpopular among party intellectuals by his clumsy interference in artistic and literary questions. Moreover, it had been easy to blame Lecoeur for the system

8 *Ibid.,* pp. 887–888.
9 *Ibid.,* p. 926.

of cell instructors. Actually, the activists were very hostile to this system, which forced them to carry cards and stamps to the homes of "phantom" adherents, that is, those who did not participate in meetings or other activities of the party.

The summer of 1954, which saw the fall of the Laniel government, gave the French Communist Party an occasion to apply the policies defined at Drancy and the Congress of Ivry. On June 17 the Communist members of Parliament voted for Pierre Mendès-France's investiture as Premier. Within a few weeks Mendès-France succeeded in liquidating the war in Vietnam through the Geneva accords, in gaining acceptance for the internal autonomy of Tunisia, and in obtaining the rejection of the EDC. However, the new and very unusual style adopted by the new chief of government (who had, moreover, decided not to count the Communist votes in his majority) made him appear personally responsible for these results. In turn, the French Communist Party, by simply offering Mendès-France its agreement with no concessions in return, had effectively limited itself to playing a supporting role. From the PCF ranks criticism arose against the abstention of Communist deputies on the occasion of the vote on government economic and financial projects. In Doubs and Belfort the federal bureau protested against this attitude of the PCF parliamentary group. Alarmed, the party secretariat published a long reply justifying its attitude.[10]

In the meantime, the signature of the London and Paris agreements replacing the EDC treaty put an end to the PCF's support of Mendès-France's government. It was under these circumstances that the Algerian insurrection broke out on November 1, 1954, after Maurice Thorez, in an article in *L'Humanité* of October 28, 1954, had declared that the struggle against German rearmament and therefore for the moment, against the ratification of new agreements was the PCF's central task.

Once more the French Communist Party was caught off guard by the course of events. There was of course an Algerian Communist Party, but it had been kept constantly in tutelage by the "overseas" section of the French Communist Party (previously called the "colonial" section), which actually directed from Paris all Communist activities in French possessions around the world. The paternalistic methods of the "colonial specialists" of the French Communist

10 "Réponse aux camarades du Bureau fédéral du Doubs et du Territoire de Belfort," *Cahiers du Communisme*, Vol. 30, No. 8–9 (Aug.–Sept. 1954), pp. 1113–1115.

Party were strangely reminiscent of those of both the French colonizers and the Russians in their foreign territories (including the people's democracies). Forced to subordinate its policies to the demands of the French Communist Party, the Algerian Communist Party had lost all influence among the Moslem masses and was composed mainly of activists of European or Jewish origin. Transplanted to Algeria, the slogans of the priority of the struggle against American imperialism, and then against the EDC and German rearmament, could hardly find much response. Isolated in their own country, the Algerian Communists remained completely ignorant of the preparations for the rebellion and of the state of mind of the masses, who were ready for armed struggle against France. The split in the principal nationalist movement, the MTLD (Mouvement pour le triomphe des libertés démocratiques), between the old leader Messali and his Central Committee confirmed the Algerian and French Communists in their conviction that no serious explosion could be expected in Algeria in the near future. The action of a group of second-level militants, who had formed the CRUA (Comité révolutionnaire pour l'unité et l'action) before establishing the FLN, had passed completely unnoticed.

Because of its campaign against German rearmament, which appealed particularly to nationalist arguments, the French Communist Party could not afford to support the Algerian "separatists," or to compromise the alliance which it sought to establish with those sectors of public opinion hostile to Germany by tradition but also attached to a "French Algeria." This explains the considerable embarrassment reflected in the declaration of the Politburo of the French Communist Party of November 8, 1954. While declaring itself entirely against repression in Algeria and recognizing the existence of "political problems of a national character," the declaration in essence took a position against the insurrection:

Under such circumstances, true to the teachings of Lenin, the French Communist Party cannot approve any recourse to individual acts that play into the hands of the worst types of colonists, even if such acts are not fomented by them. The French Communist Party assures the Algerian people of the solidarity of the French working class in its mass struggle against repression and for the defense of its rights.[11]

From all indications this was a restrictive solidarity: it was "mass struggle" as opposed to armed struggle. This declaration, which made the initiators of the national rebellion in Algeria look like

11 "Déclaration du P.C.F. sur la situation en Algérie," *Cahiers du Communisme*, Vol. 30, No. 11–12 (Nov.–Dec. 1954).

provocateurs, was to ruin whatever credit the French Communist Party still had in Algeria after the default of its local branch.

In the Algerian affair, which was to dominate all French political life for the next eight years, the French Communist Party thus restated its choice, in conformity with Soviet policy: solidarity with the colonial peoples or the underdeveloped world was relegated to second place, behind the European policy objective of the systematic exploitation of all possibilities of splitting the Atlantic Alliance. Within this choice was already contained the germ of the PCF's future opposition to the theses of the Chinese Communist Party which, on the contrary, considered the unaligned world as the primary theater of operations in the "struggle against imperialism."

On February 5, 1955, the French Communist Party joined the votes of its deputies to those of the Right to overthrow the government of Mendès-France. A few days later, Bulganin replaced Malenkov as the head of the Soviet Government. In France as well as in East European countries this new change of Soviet leadership was apparently considered the signal for a hard line. *Cahiers du Communisme* of March 1955 published a lead article by Maurice Thorez devoted to the thesis of the "absolute pauperization" of the working class. This article tried to "demonstrate" that the purchasing power of the workers in capitalist countries, particularly in France, was constantly declining.[12] In the April issue of the same magazine there appeared a letter by Thorez to one Bordage, editor of the Communist journal *Les Nouvelles de Bordeaux et du Sud-Ouest,* who had published a special issue "against the agreements of London and Paris and against the menace of atomic war." With respect to the last point, Maurice Thorez charged the *Nouvelles de Bordeaux* with having indulged in "exaggerations" when speaking of the possibility "of destruction in a few hours of all forms of life even in the most remote regions of France." According to Thorez:

Such exaggerations are only water on the mills of the American imperialists, who would like to prepare atomic war with impunity by spreading ideas among the masses such as: "There's nothing one can do. Why fight? It's the end of the world!"

In conclusion, Maurice Thorez invoked a notion still unassailable at the time:

12 Maurice Thorez, "La situation économique de la France—mystifications et réalités," *Cahiers du Communisme,* Vol. 31, No. 3 (Mar. 1955), pp. 259–279.

Comrade Molotov, in his last speech (highly recommended to our activists), has given the precise answer to those who speak of the "annihilation of civilization"; it is not world civilization which will perish, no matter how great may be the damage done by a new aggression, but it is the system which is already rotten, its imperialist base drenched in blood, the system which has seen its day, which is doomed by reason of its aggressiveness and hated because it exploits the workers and the oppressed peoples.[13]

The particularly warm reference to Molotov doubtless indicated the direction of Maurice Thorez' secret preferences with regard to the Soviet leaders. But it should be noted above all that Molotov's thesis, taken up in turn by the leaders of the French Communist Party, was to be denounced several years later as a dangerous manifestation of irresponsibility, a cold-blooded acceptance of the idea of nuclear war in order to install socialism on the ruins of humanity. In between times, it is true, the Soviet and French Communist parties had rejected this thesis, which Mao Tse-tung had defended in his turn in very similar terms at the 1957 Moscow Conference. In April 1955, however, the positions in the Communist movement were almost opposite: at the moment when Thorez, following in Molotov's steps, asked his colleague Bordage "not to exaggerate" the dangers of atomic war, Chou En-lai developed at Bandung the five principles of peaceful coexistence!

At the end of May 1955 the arrival of Bulganin and Khrushchev in Belgrade, followed by the reconciliation with Tito, plunged the majority of PCF activists into great confusion. Although they had been alerted about Soviet intentions a whole year earlier, on the occasion of a secret meeting of the Cominform in Prague,[14] the French Communist leaders had done nothing to prepare their party for the end of the anti-Yugoslav campaign. The very next day the Yugoslav "gang of assassins and Fascist spies" again became the leaders of a Communist party and of a state engaged in building socialism. However, in an article in *L'Humanité* of June 8, 1955, Étienne Fajon still showed some reservations: "The resolution on the Yugoslav situation issued by the Cominform in 1948 contained some perfectly normal criticisms." Only the 1949 resolution, "based on documents forged by Beria," was "in error and

---

[13] *Ibid.*, Vol. 31, No. 4 (Apr. 1955), pp. 525–526.

[14] According to Giulio Seniga in *Togliatti e Stalin, op. cit.*, p. 49, this meeting took place at the same time as the Congress of the KSČ (June 10–15, 1954). As a security measure, and to avoid the use of interpreters who were a possible source of leaks, Khrushchev first informed the PCI delegate d'Onofrio (who knew Russian well) and instructed him to transmit the information directly to Jacques Duclos.

inadmissible." But this explanation did not seem to satisfy many militants: with the Marxist-Lenininst compass as a guide, how could anyone, even on the basis of trust in forged documents, have made such gross errors about the nature of the Yugoslav state, which the PCF had called fascist for six years?

Despite the difficulties of the PCF leadership, the legislative elections of January 2, 1956, were relatively successful for the Communists. This success seemed quite spectacular because the Communist Party managed to regain a great number of parliamentary seats, lost in 1951 as a result of a simple electoral technicality permitting some parties to "ally" among themselves. But even though this law had remained in force, the disintegration of the center coalition, which had been victorious in 1951, thanks to the electoral alliances among coalition groups, worked out in such a way in 1956 that the representation of the various parties in the new Assembly was more or less in proportion to the votes received in the country. With respect to its total vote, the Communist party regained a little of the terrain it had lost in 1951 but did not reach the record percentage that it had attained in 1946. In their turn, the vote of the parties grouped together under the label of *Front Républicain* —Socialists, Radicals, the UDSR (Union Démocratique et Socialiste de la Résistance), a center-left group—and those few *Républicains Sociaux* who had escaped the shipwreck of the Gaullist RPF increased considerably. The increase in votes was not, however, reflected in a corresponding gain of seats, again because of the same electoral laws, which had favored them in 1951.

The *Front Républicain* had carried on its campaign under the slogan of "Peace in Algeria." This had led the French Communist Party in turn to develop this theme to its profit in the last weeks of 1955, with less restraint than during the preceding months. (Yet when the demonstrations against the recall of draftees for North Africa took a violent and even dangerous form, the Communist party had preferred to stay behind the leftist Catholic or nonorganized groups, to counsel moderation to the young soldiers, and to denounce the demonstrations as "provocations" in some cases. The Communist leaders systematically avoided anything which could bring against them charges of "provoking the disobedience of military personnel." At the same time, they deceived those young soldiers who counted on the Communist party to coordinate their spontaneous movements with those of the civilian population.)

In large measure the *Front Républicain* owed its success to the popularity that peace in Vietnam had given to Mendès-France.

Though it had gone into the elections without any kind of partnership with the Communist party, the great new fact in the Assembly of January 2 was the virtual existence of a leftist majority—if the votes of the Communist deputies were added to those of the *Front Républicain* together.

In its session of January 18, 1956, the Central Committee of the French Communist Party cavalierly abandoned the line of the "Rally of all good Frenchmen" in favor of the "new Popular Front" and renewed its offer of unity of action to the leadership of the Socialist and Radical parties. It demanded "a government of the left resting firmly on the leftist majority in the National Assembly" which would open "negotiations with qualified representatives of the Algerian people."[15] (The FLN was not referred to by name in French Communist documents of that period.) Among the factors favoring unity of action with the Socialists, Jacques Duclos did not forget to place high on the list the announcement of an early visit to Moscow by a delegation of the directorate of the SFIO.

The moderation of Algerian policy proposed by the French Communist Party to its eventual partners in the "new Popular Front" was expressed by Léon Feix, who handled all North African questions for the Politburo, in an article in *Cahiers du Communisme* of January-February 1956, entitled "For a Genuine French Union" —a revealing title. Without contesting Algeria's right to independence, Léon Feix dwelt mainly on the following themes:
"The right to divorce, Lenin said, does not imply the obligation of divorce. . . . Moreover, one should not confuse independence and separation." In his conclusion Feix evoked "the fruits that are yet to be expected" of "a true French union."[16]

Thus the broad lines of policy which the French Communist Party had to follow after the CPSU Twentieth Congress were sketched out.

---

15 Jacques Duclos, "Développer l'action des masses pour un nouveau front populaire," *Cahiers du Communisme*, Vol. 32, No. 1-2 (Jan.–Feb. 1956), p. 21.
16 Léon Feix, "Pour une véritable Union Française," *ibid.*, pp. 35 and 46.

CHAPTER FIVE

THE TWENTIETH CPSU CONGRESS

The news of the Twentieth CPSU Congress in Moscow did not hit France like a bolt out of the blue. On January 20, 1956, less than a month before the opening of the congress, a book by Pierre Hervé, *La révolution et les fétiches,* was published by Éditions de la Table Ronde. The personality of Pierre Hervé, long the best-known and most talented journalist of the French Communist press, a leader in the Resistance, a former deputy, and finally the private secretary of Jacques Duclos, guaranteed major repercussions. Written rapidly, sometimes brilliant, sometimes confused, the book was confined to the theoretical plane and omitted personal attacks; but it violently castigated intellectual dogmatism, theoretical arteriosclerosis, and in particular the theory of "absolute pauperization," which had been recently exhumed by Maurice Thorez. Above all, Pierre Hervé committed the crime of clearly formulating the revisionist implications of the policy of "peaceful coexistence" as it was to be defined at the Twentieth Congress. Applying Lenin's reasoning in a 1916 article to the new situation, he wrote:

Let us suppose that the assumption of power by the Communists in our country could actually lead to war between the Soviet Union and the United States. What should we do in such a case if not to declare ourselves against taking power? And even more so, if a world war were to unleash an atomic fury and produce a great decline in human civilization, if not the extermination of the human race, what should we do but adjourn the revolution, even if on the national level all objective and subjective conditions for it existed? Obviously one cannot draw the same conclusions for all countries in the world. We are in the domain of probabilities here. This does not make it less certain, however, that the question is posed in Western Europe.[1]

Following the logical course of his argumentation, Pierre Hervé

1 Pierre Hervé, *La révolution et les fétiches* (Paris: Éditions de la Table Ronde 1956), p. 17.

44

went on to suggest that the classic schema of taking power might be replaced by the struggle for a program of reforms

that would be provisionally inapplicable in the political situation, but could, in view of their attraction for the masses, push the struggle forward and create conditions in which they might be put into practice.[2]

It was not hard to see here the influence of the Italian Communist Party, one of whose principal leaders, Giuseppe Di Vittorio, Secretary-General of the Communist-led trade union, the CGIL had already formulated similar theories in October 1953 before the Congress of the World Federation of Trade Unions, of which he was president. Defending his confederation's "work-plan" (*Piano di Lavoro*) that foresaw "an organic development of industry, sources of energy, transport, agriculture, housing, schools, and hospitals, and as a result the gradual abolition of unemployment, aimed at full employment," Di Vittorio declared:

Through the work-plan the Italian working class has shown the rest of the world that it does not take a negative position on basic problems of national life; that it does not limit itself to protests or to denouncing the evil doings of the monopolies; that it does not relegate all possible constructive solutions to a time after the radical overturn of social relations; that it is capable of proposing immediate positive solutions to vital problems of the people, suitable for the betterment of their lot and their living conditions.[3]

But if *L'Humanité* could only censor Di Vittorio and the "reformist" practices of the Italian Communists, the entire press of the French Communist Party fell upon Hervé's book in order to tear it apart. Six party leaders and responsible intellectuals were mobilized to "demolish" it in various publications of the French Communist Party: Guy Besse, Jean Kanapa, Jacques Arnault, Suret-Canale, André Voguet, and Victor Michaut. The PCF leaders were all the more in a hurry because they knew that the CPSU Twentieth Congress would adopt positions on certain essential points very similar to those of Hervé. On February 14, 1956, the rebel was expelled from the party, against the recommendation of the cell to which he belonged. That February 14 was the very day on which the Twentieth Congress opened in Moscow.

Aside from articles in *L'Humanité* giving a daily account of the

2 *Ibid.,* p. 119.
3 Giuseppe Di Vittorio, *Les tâches des syndicats pour le développement économique et social, la lutte pour l'indépendance nationale et les libertés démocratiques dans les pays capitalistes et coloniaux* (Éditions SFEPSI), Supplement to *Mouvement Syndical Mondial*, No. 9 (Paris: 32 Rue Montholon, 1953).

discussions at the congress, the PCF activists had to wait until March 8, 1956 for Jacques Duclos to make the party's first public comment on it, at the Salle Wagram before several thousand Parisian Communists. In the course of his speech Duclos laid particular stress on Khrushchev's theses on unity with social democracy (not without attributing importance to the declaration of the new Socialist Minister of Foreign Affairs, Christian Pineau, in favor of an improvement of Franco-Soviet relations and critical of the United States), as well as on peaceful coexistence, the noninevitability of war, and the diversity of the various possible forms of transition to socialism. Only in the last part of his speech did Duclos' talk touch on the question of the personality cult. However, on that subject he remained far behind even the public sessions of the Twentieth Congress:

Naturally, the enemies of communism and of the Soviet Union want to make it understood that from here on in Stalin's name will be erased from the history of the Soviet Union and the international workers' movement, and that the role which he played will be completely forgotten. Nothing could be more wrong. It is true that during a certain period of Stalin's activity the principle of collective leadership was not always applied. It is also true that under these conditions some mistakes were made.

But after attacking as "enemies of communism and the Soviet Union" those who "demanded the rehabilitation of traitors such as Trotsky and Co., who were beaten and had to be beaten to keep the country of socialism from being delivered to the enemy," Duclos indulged in a veritable apologia of Stalin:

Nobody can forget that among the leaders of the party and the Soviet state Stalin played a role of the very first order in the necessary defense of the gains of the October Revolution. Nor can anybody forget the role played by Stalin in the construction of socialism in the Soviet Union or in the conduct of the war against the Hitlerites. Nobody can forget the role played by Stalin in the training and development of Communist parties. Comrade Stalin's merits are inscribed in history; they are part of the heritage of the international workers' movement.[4]

And Duclos saw to it that there were several minutes of acclamation after this sentence, with everybody standing, just as during the heyday of the "cult."[5]

In this month of March 1956 the leadership of the French Communist Party found itself in a particularly delicate situation. At

---

4 *L'Humanité*, Mar. 10, 1965.

5 However, a very small minority did not rise, leaving the rest of the audience shocked at this display of sacrilege.

the very moment when it had to try to absorb the shock of the revelations made at the Twentieth Congress, the application of its line of the "new popular front" was seriously compromised by the direction that Guy Mollet, the Socialist chief of government, took in his Algerian policy. A single day of uprisings by French Algerians on February 6 in Algiers had been enough to obtain Mollet's capitulation before the demands of demonstrators armed with tomatoes and other improvised missiles. The Premier sacrificed General Catroux, who had just been appointed in Algiers with a view toward initiating negotiations, and replaced him with Robert Lacoste, a Socialist known to be a convinced partisan of "French Algeria." After that it was clear that the government, while continuing to talk about peace, applied itself to the intensification of the war.

But the French Communist Party, which had staked everything on its new campaign of unity with the Socialists, obstinately refused to recognize the evidence. Instead of taking advantage of the reservations expressed by men like Mendès-France, traditionally situated to the right of the SFIO (and of a strong minority in that same party) in order to regain its liberty of action, the Communist Party increased its concessions, apparently without demanding anything in return. On March 2, 1956, the Politburo declared: "We are in favor of the existence of permanent, special political, economic, and cultural ties between France and Algeria." Independence was nowhere mentioned in this declaration, which limited itself to invoking "the necessary recognition of the fact of a national Algeria." The authors of this text went so far as to conclude that

The last word will be spoken by France if Communists and Socialists unite to impose negotiations and peace in Algeria, in alliance with all democrats and patriots.[6]

In this way the Politburo, despite the strong discontent of many of its activists, pretended to believe in the peaceful intentions proclaimed by Guy Mollet and his ministers. Ten days later, on March 12, the Communist deputies voted for the "special powers" demanded by the government, which continued to affirm its desire to make peace rapidly, but did not hide its intention to have recourse to military measures for the time being, which included sending young draftees to Algeria.

While declaring that Communists "could not approve" these

6 *Cahiers du Communisme*, Vol. 32, No. 4 (Apr. 1956), pp. 493–494.

measures, Jacques Duclos, in the ensuing debate, explained the vote of the Communist group by the necessity of checking

the plans of the reactionaries . . . aimed at preventing the development of the first manifestations of a foreign policy different from that of preceding governments. . . . Our vote will express our very clear desire to set up obstacles to all maneuvers of the reactionaries, by developing unity of action between the working class and the popular masses. . . . Our vote will also express our firm resolution to neglect nothing in our advance along the road that must end with a cease-fire in Algeria and lead to negotiations that will transform the Algerian people into friends and allies of the French people.[7]

This "also" implicitly signified that the Communist Party was ready to let the Algerian question play second fiddle to the all-important unity theme.

According to indiscretions by former Communist parliamentarians who had participated in the meeting at which the decision to vote in favor of special powers for Guy Mollet had been taken, the majority of deputies had favored a "no" vote or abstention, and it had been Jacques Duclos who, with his authority as the PCF delegate just back from the CPSU Congress, had imposed the "yes" vote.[8]

The PCF leaders themselves could not hide the fact that on the whole this vote was badly received by the activists. This time not just the intellectuals but also workers and young people at the age to serve in the army in Algeria protested. In the workers' suburbs of Paris there were quite a few stormy PCF section conferences, and even representatives of the central party headquarters were in the minority (as in Gentilly, where the conference was resumed after more careful "preparation"). In an article in the May 1956 *Cahiers du Communisme,* Waldeck Rochet himself had to admit that "for some time the vote of March 12 was very much discussed in the party organizations."[9]

In the meantime, Maurice Thorez, silent since his speech at the Twentieth Congress, had been forced in his turn to descend into the arena in order to take the shaken party in hand again. In his March 27, 1956 *L'Humanité* article the PCF Secretary-General tried at length to justify the vote of March 12, which, according to him,

was not inspired just by preoccupation with parliamentary tactics. . . . It was the result of larger and higher considerations. The Communist

7 *Ibid.,* p. 496.
8 Private information.
9 *Cahiers du Communisme,* Vol. 32, No. 5 (May 1956), p. 517.

party did not want to sacrifice the whole for the part. It merely subordinated its attitude in a very important, yet limited, matter to the essential aim that inspires it: to preserve the possibilites of a great development of a united front with the Socialist workers, including a cease-fire and a peaceful solution of the Algerian problem. The Communist deputies were right not to compromise this general perspective by permitting a rupture over this special issue, concerning which they are not in accord with the policies of the government.[10]

Maurice Thorez made unequivocally clear what this "general perspective" was, of which the "whole" was well worth the sacrifice of a part"—that is, the support of the struggle of the Algerians:

The French Communist Party congratulates itself on the imminent journey of a Socialist Party delegation to Moscow. . . . This contact with the country of the builders of communism and its leaders can only help in the elimination of prejudices, contribute to the development of common action in France, and facilitate the international union of the forces of the working class.

In this same article, although it was entitled "Some Important Questions Posed at the CPSU Twentieth Congress," Thorez discreetly passed over the entire Stalin problem. To be sure, he said a little more about it than Duclos had two weeks earlier: he particularly mentioned "Stalin's mistaken opinion according to which the class struggle had to increase in the Soviet Union in the same measure as the construction of socialism succeeded," and he acknowledged that "this erroneous thesis led to grave shortcomings with regard to party democracy and Soviet legality itself."

However, Thorez immediately limited the scope of this statement by adding that the Soviet Union and the people's democracies

are exposed to blows from the outside and to the pressure of class enemies who try to recruit even on their soil degenerate elements in order to make them instruments of their criminal plans.

Thorez then summed up all of the severe criticism of Stalinist methods voiced in Moscow in the following very narrow formula:

The fault of Comrade Stalin was to misunderstand, in the last period of his activity, certain rules of life and of the party leadership which he himself had taught to Communists throughout the entire world, particularly in his work, *Problems of Leninism.*

In short, Stalin's principal fault was not to have been a good enough Stalinist—and only toward the end of his life! For the

10 *Ibid.,* No. 4 (Apr. 1956), p. 390.

rest, Thorez, like Duclos, pretended to be indignant about "speculations" by "reactionaries":

As though the necessary criticism of certain errors could in any way de-
tract from the historical merits of Stalin.

These merits he thereafter complacently enumerated.

Several days later it was the turn of the Chinese Communist
Party's Politburo to take a position on the CPSU Twentieth Congress in a *Jen-min Jih-pao* article of April 5 entitled "On the
Historical Experience Concerning the Dictatorship of the Proletariat," written after an enlarged meeting of the Politburo. Most
specialists attribute this article to Mao Tse-tung himself.[11]

As subsequent Chinese documents, after the beginning of the
polemics with Moscow, trace the origins of the differences to the
Twentieth Congress,[12] it is interesting to compare the first official
reactions of the two parties, the French and the Chinese, before
the event. The comparison appears all the more valid because the
two articles followed one another at an interval of less than ten
days.

In fact the *Jen-min Jih-pao* article of April 5, 1956[13] contained
a certain number of implicit reservations with respect to the Twentieth Congress and in particular the secret speech by Khrushchev,
the content of which had not yet become public. Mao Tse-tung,
like Thorez and Duclos, developed at length the thesis of Stalin's
historical merits, insisted on the necessity to "go on studying atten-
tively Stalin's works," though in "nondogmatic" fashion, and maintained that "Stalin was a great Marxist-Leninist." But the Chinese
article dwelt at much greater length than did Thorez on the nature of the errors with which Stalin was charged. It even carefully

11 See Stuart R. Schram, *The Political Thought of Mao Tse-tung* (New York:
Praeger, 1963), p. 49.
12 Particularly "The Origin and Development of the Differences Between
the Leadership of the CPSU and Ourselves—Comment on the Open Letter of
the Central Committee of the CPSU by the Editorial Departments of *People's
Daily* and *Red Flag*," *Jen-min Jih-pao* and *Hung Ch'i*, Sept. 6, 1963, quotation
from *Peking Review*, Vol. VI, No. 37 (Sept. 13, 1963), pp. 7–23. On p. 7, the
following statement occurs: "The truth is that the differences of principle within
the international Communist movement began more than seven years ago. To
be specific, they began with the Twentieth Congress of the CPSU in 1956. The
Twentieth Congress of the CPSU was the first step along the road of revisionism
on the part of the CPSU leadership."
13 "On the Historical Experience Concerning the Dictatorship of the Proletariat," *Jen-min Jih-pao*, Apr. 5, 1956; Peking, New China News Agency
(NCNA) in English, Apr. 5, 1956 (quotations from *Current Background*, No.
383 [Apr. 9, 1956]).

sketched out a protest against the partial and insufficient character of the criticisms aimed at Stalin alone: "Both his rights and wrongs were features of the international Communist movement and bear the imprint of the times." This apparently cryptic passage made sense only in that it followed a long passage, reminding the reader in detail of all the deviations the present Chinese leaders had had to fight in their own party between 1924 and 1953, from Ch'en Tsu-hsu's "rightist opportunism" before 1927 to Kao Kang's "anti-party bloc," liquidated the previous year. For the initiated, however, the allusion was clear: of the different "deviations" mentioned the first corresponded to "certain erroneous viewpoints expressed by Stalin," as was confirmed seven years later by the article "On the Question of Stalin," which appeared in *Jen-min Jih-pao* and *Hung Ch'i* on September 13, 1963. The Kao Kang affair was most likely an attempt by the Soviet Union to grab Manchuria, China's principal industrial province.[14] A careful reading of the April 5, 1956 Chinese article also revealed that its author was systematically trying to show how a proper political orientation, meaning of course that of the Chinese, could even redress the errors of others:

But because our party had drawn the lessons from the previous two revolutionary periods, we did not allow this wrong line[15] to develop and it was set right by the Party's Central Committee within a comparatively short period.

And further:

From this it will be seen that our Party's historical experience is also that of being tempered in the course of its own struggle against various erroneous lines and because of [it] this achieved great victories in the revolution and construction. Local and particular mistakes often occur in work. It is solely due to reliance on the collective wisdom of the Party and the wisdom of the mass of the people, and the prompt exposing and overcoming of these mistakes, that they have no chance to grow and become nationwide, protracted mistakes and do not become major errors endangering the people.

In the same fashion the article in *Jen-min Jih-pao* cited the Chinese Communist Party as an example of the way in which the "cult of the personality" could be avoided. Without doubt, there was a "trace of irony"[16] in Mao's compliment to the "courageous self-

14 See François Fejtö, *Chine–U.R.S.S., la fin d'une hégémonie: Les origines du grand schisme communiste, 1950–1957* Vol. I (Paris: Plon, 1964), pp. 95–97.

15 That is, "opportunism of the right," represented by Wang Ming during the Sino-Japanese War.

16 As I have shown; Fejtö, *Chine–U.R.S.S.,* Vol. I, *op. cit.,* p. 154.

criticism by the Communist Party of the Soviet Union of its past errors." It was enough to see how the homage rendered to the fraternal party was immediately followed by the glorification of the Chinese party's practice:

The Chinese Communist Party congratulates the Communist Party of the Soviet Union on its important achievements in the historic struggle against the cult of the individual. The experience of the Chinese revolution, too, testifies to the fact that only by relying on the wisdom of the masses of the people on democratic centralism and on the system of combining collective leadership with individual responsibility can our Party obtain great victory and achievements in times of revolution and in times of national construction. The Chinese Communist Party has waged continuous struggle in the revolutionary ranks against elevating the individual above the masses, and against individual heroism.

In short, it was with some condescension that the Chinese Communist Party judged the Soviet party, which had allowed its errors to reach disturbing proportions, while the Chinese Communist Party had always succeeded in checking them in time.

Of these "grave errors" by Stalin, the article in *Jen-min Jih-pao* gave a much more detailed list than Thorez had given in *L'Humanité*:

[He] carried the problem of eliminating counterrevolutionaries to excess, showed lack of necessary vigilance on the eve of the anti-Fascist war, failed to pay proper attention to the further development of agriculture and to the material welfare of the peasantry, advocated certain erroneous lines in the international Communist movement especially on the question of Yugoslavia.

Thus while keeping their distance, the Chinese, softening their tone and employing euphemism, reiterated extensively and independently most of the concrete charges leveled against Stalin at the Twentieth Congress.

Moreover, the *Jen-min Jih-pao* article had the advantage of setting forth a theoretical explanation of these "errors." Though certainly timid, it nevertheless was less simplistic than the explanations at the Twentieth Congress, which had attributed everything to the caprices of an aging despot:

The cult of the individual is a putrid carryover from the long history of mankind. The cult of the individual has its roots not only in the exploiting class but also in the small producers. . . . The cult of the individual is also a force of habit of millions and tens of millions. Since this force of habit still exists in society, it can influence many government functionaries, and even such a leader as Stalin was no exception. The cult of the individual is a reflection in the minds of a people of a social phenomenon. . . .

Behind the clumsy and sometimes confusing formula may be detected an argumentation reminiscent of the Trotskyite position. In the development of Stalinism in the Soviet Union the Trotskyites had seen a reflection of the petit bourgeois and peasant structure of Russian society in the Soviet party and state apparatus. For them, Stalin was only the foremost representative of this type of bureaucracy.

In passing, the *Jen-min Jih-pao* article underlined somewhat complacently that "it is naive to assume that contradictions can no longer exist in a Socialist society," thus summarily reiterating a theme dear to Mao Tse-tung, who had already treated it in 1937 in his famous article "On Contradiction" and was to develop it further in his famous report of February 1957.[17]

From the preceding excerpts it may be concluded that, without recourse to provocative tones and in the guise of approving the CPSU Twentieth Congress, the Chinese Communists implied that the CPSU had played its role of leader of the international Communist movement badly, and that, therefore, Chinese political experience, both theoretical and practical, justified the candidacy of the Chinese Communist Party to the leadership of the international Communist movement. Though the article still spoke at the end of the "Camp of peace and socialism . . . with the Soviet Union at its head," Mao Tse-tung had thus already made his bid to become the brain that this head lacked.

---

[17] "On the Correct Handling of Contradictions Among the People," speech by Mao Tse-tung to the Eleventh Session (enlarged) of the Supreme State Conference, February 27, 1957. Only one edited version of this speech exists, in *Jen-min Jih-pao*, June 18, 1957; the original has never been published. For English translations, see Peking NCNA English, June 18, 1957 in *Current Background*, No. 458, June 20, 1957; and *The New York Times*, June 19, 1957. See also Fejtö, *Chine–U.R.S.S., la fin d'une hégémonie, op. cit.*, Document XIV, pp. 314–329 (excerpts).

CHAPTER SIX

ADJUSTING TO DE-STALINIZATION

Developments within the PCF

Under the circumstances analyzed earlier, it was not surprising that opposition elements in the PCF, who began to organize support particularly among intellectuals in the spring of 1956, should have regarded and used the *Jen-min Jih-pao* article as a weapon in their struggle against the leadership of their party. In section conferences and at cell meetings held in preparation for the PCF's Fourteenth Congress, numerous activists contrasted the Chinese efforts at explanation with the theoretical poverty of the texts put forward by the French leaders.[1]

At the same time, Palmiro Togliatti, in his report of March 13, 1956 to the Central Committee of the Italian Communist Party, stressed strongly the merits that his own party had acquired in its search for an "Italian road of development toward socialism" and "the utilization of Parliament to make progress toward socialism." In short, he let it be understood that the PCI had already under Stalin succeeded in launching itself successfully on the line defined by Khrushchev at the Twentieth Congress.[2] However, Togliatti still proceeded with great caution when the question arose of giving a theoretical formulation of his revisionism in practice:

I pass over other objections that have been raised against us, for example, the claim that we have become reformists. The reformists are precisely those who have never extracted from Parliament any real, radical and profound socialist transformation of society.[3]

This type of gyration made PCI statements hard to handle in the internal struggle of the PCF at that time, except in certain initiated circles close to the *apparat*.

The backwash of this struggle, though limited, nevertheless dis-

1 From private sources.
2 *L'Unità*, Mar. 15, 1956.
3 *Ibid.*

turbed the PCF leaders. At the end of a course of study for Communist deputies on April 14, 1956, Maurice Thorez admitted that

some intellectual comrades are troubled by the noise made by the enemy. They are ready to question everything including the principles and organization of the party. Their "independence of spirit" consists in repeating the enemy's calumnies instead of answering them as Communists.[4]

Thorez argued helter-skelter against all criticism of the theory of "absolute impoverishment," against "the criticism from the left by many irresponsible petit bourgeois voices" in connection with the March 12 vote on Algeria, and against the position in favor of birth control expressed by certain PCF activists, particularly physicians. On this last point Maurice Thorez and his wife organized a regular diversionary campaign. Fearing in particular that Communist physicians might demand a discussion on the responsibilities of the leaders who had encouraged them to take a position against the Doctors' Plot, Thorez took advantage of a book favorable to birth control written by the Communist journalist Jacques Derogy[5] in order to launch an artificial debate on the problem of "neo-Malthusianism."[6]

Meanwhile, at the Central Committee plenum at Arcueil (May 9–10, 1956), Thorez had been forced to deal with certain problems created by the Twentieth Congress that had until then been avoided. He now took a defensive position. Thus with respect to the vote of March 12 he said:

Naturally there was some excitement in the party as a result of that vote. I think it is not necessary to get too upset when activists demand explanations: on the contrary, it would have been disturbing if there had been no questions. . . . Of course, one must also take into account the fact that our vote permitted the Socialist leaders to cover themselves to a certain extent.[7]

These formal concessions to the activists treated only the month before as "irresponsible petit bourgeois" were probably the result

[4] *Cahiers du Communisme,* Vol. 32, No. 5 (May 1956), p. 638.

[5] Jacques Derogy, *Des enfants malgré nous* (Paris: Éditions de Minuit, 1956). Here Derogy takes up the issues examined earlier in an article he published in the progressive daily *Libération*—an article that elicited strong reaction on the part of the editors.

[6] See Maurice Thorez' letter of April 30, 1956, "Au camarade Derogy— Contre le néo-malthusianisme réactionnaire, nous luttons pour le droit à la maternité et pour l'avenir de la France," *Cahiers du Communisme,* Vol. 32, No. 5 (May 1956), pp. 640–642.

[7] "Intervention de Maurice Thorez au Comité Central d'Arcueil," *ibid.,* No. 6 (June 1956), pp. 764–765.

of fear on Thorez' part of a possible conspiracy within the PCF leadership, conceivably supported by Khrushchev, to bring about changes at its highest level. In any event, there was a rumor to that effect in Communist circles at the time, and the names most frequently mentioned as heading the "conspiracy" were those of Benoît Frachon and Waldeck Rochet. The latter, having been confined for a long time to his role of specialist on agricultural questions, now began to appear in the very first rank of political affairs in general. In actual fact, this project of a "palace revolution" does not seem to have gone beyond the state of conversations among several Central Committee members, and it disintegrated without ever having been put to the test.

In his speech at Arcueil, Maurice Thorez launched a strong counterattack against everything concerning "internal party democracy," "criticism and self-criticism," and in particular the charges, directed against himself, of a "cult of personality." He defended himself by insinuation:

The formula "Maurice Thorez' party" must be condemned, and I will not even examine here how it could have arisen in the first place. I must say that I have protested against this formula many times to the Politburo and *L'Humanité*. I regret that this was not brought more quickly to the attention of the Central Committee.[8]

In other words, his Politburo colleagues were now responsible for the cult of the personality of Maurice Thorez, organized by them against his wishes! In the same fashion, recognizing that "certain anniversaries had been celebrated a little too much," Thorez illustrated this curious "self-criticism" with the case of a federal secretary who had celebrated his twenty-fifth birthday![9] Thorez was quite ready to admit that there had also been "an excess of public mentions of individuals." But when he came to this point, Thorez indignantly rejected

what the enemies of the party are now claiming. One must not confuse manifestations of affection and confidence with the cult of personality.

Moreover,

democracy was not violated in our party. Congresses were held regularly. We have collective leadership. If we look at the theses and closing speech of the Eighth Congress, we do not find many errors.[10]

With regard to all essential points Thorez rated himself satisfactory.

8 *Ibid.*, pp. 776–777.
9 *Ibid.*, p. 777.
10 *Ibid.*, pp. 777 and 778.

But while he practically refused to admit that he himself was responsible for any errors, he used harsher words about "Stalin's errors":

. . . He [Stalin] went as far as to avoid true criticism and self-criticism. He permitted himself to become complacent and presumptuous. . . . The cult of personality led him to forget the creative role of the masses and to minimize the role of the party, and thus of all the people, particularly in the war against Nazi Germany. From this arose theoretical errors, which were not corrected but propagated and aggravated, because dogmatism spread, and people were content to echo Stalin. No more living thought or profound analysis remained, but only the fear of offending.[11]

With regard to police repression, as well, Thorez used harsher language:

. . . with the violation of the principle of collective leadership and the impeding and strangling of internal democracy there ensued, little by little, blows against Soviet legality, party legality, and unjustified repression against party activists.[12]

With less success than the Chinese, Thorez tried to find an explanation that could serve at the same time as a justification for his own behavior:

It would be childish to say that errors of judgment, for example, were simply the will of one man, or of a few men. The situation is much more complicated. One must not forget the manner in which a whole atmosphere was created including intervention and external pressures; there existed at the time an objective situation that cannot be completely disregarded when one thinks of these questions now, in 1956.[13]

All this led to a surprising conclusion, which had already figured in declarations made at the Twentieth CPSU Congress but had not been so crassly juxtaposed there with the mention of the errors: "Whatever faults and errors there may have been, the general line was right. It has been confirmed by the facts. . . ." And a little further on: "The errors, which accumulated bit by bit, could, had they persisted, have led to great catastrophes."[14] Under the pretext of "understanding how the comrades could have become involved in this" Maurice Thorez criticized the Soviet leaders in very veiled terms:

It is also true that Stalin's presence weighed on certain comrades. This must be taken into account. When speaking of the personality cult, one

11 *Ibid.,* p. 774.
12 *Ibid.,* p. 775.
13 *Ibid.,* p. 775.
14 *Ibid.*

must think the matter through to the very end, to the actual psychological realities: those men are also men of flesh and blood.

This came down to saying, indirectly, that Stalin's companions had lacked foresight and courage. Further developing this Jesuitical criticism where the essential is restriction of thought, Thorez continued:

The essential thing is that the correction of errors has taken place in the most profound political spirit, vis-à-vis the Soviet Union and the entire world. We are not dealing here with words but actions: it is in actions that the correction of errors is demonstrated.[15]

For those who could understand this language, these words meant clearly that it had been wrong to publish "phrases" about the correction of errors instead of limiting oneself to "actions." It also followed that the formula of "unconditional attachment to the Soviet Union" was not the happiest formula.

In fact, our profound attachment to the Soviet Union is conditioned exactly by the fact that we are dealing here with the first Socialist country, with the base of the international workers' movement. . . . The cause of the Soviet Union is the cause of the international workers' movement.[16]

These were important words because they constituted the beginning of a disassociation of the cause of the Soviet Union, which was to remain a sacred symbol of the unity and centralization of the movement, from that of the Soviet leaders, who were only fallible men. Thus Thorez' reaction on this point came close to that of the Chinese Communist Party, which for several years continued to demand that the Soviet Union go on playing the role of the center, of the "head" of the socialist camp and of the world Communist movement, while at the same time more and more violently contesting the capacity of the Soviet leaders to exercise this leadership.

In reality, Maurice Thorez was even more precise in his May 9 speech in expressing his reservations with regard to Khrushchev:

Our adversaries accuse us of not "aligning" ourselves quickly enough. This is a strange contradiction coming from those who accuse us also of "servility." They find that we go too fast and too slow at the same time, but we proceed at our pace and will continue to do so. What is the real question? It is not our task to correct errors that are not our errors. . . .[17]

All these reservations, expressed in rather subtle fashion, did not assume their full significance until, shorn of their artificial style,

15 *Ibid.*
16 *Ibid.,* pp. 775–776.
17 *Ibid.,* p. 776.

they became the responses of the delegates of the Central Committee and the federal bureaus on the occasion of the lower-level meetings preceding the PCF Fourteenth Congress. When oppositionists, or simply bewildered activists, asked why, in connection with certain points (such as criticism of the personality cult in the PCF, or the cultural terrorism that during the Zhdanov period had extended even into the sciences, or the proposal to institute secret voting in the party organization) inspiration was not sought from the Soviet Communist Party, the delegates of the leadership answered, with an edge of nationalism in their voices:

What the Russians do is their business. Moreover, part of the difficulties we encounter comes precisely from the mistakes they have made. Who can tell us that they are not still making others, and why should it be necessary for us to follow them?[18]

On the subject of Yugoslavia, for example, Thorez stuck to his reservations:

When we discussed the matter in the Cominform, the criticisms that were formulated on several points with regard to the Yugoslav Communist Party were completely normal between Communist parties. We believe that they were justified. . . . The proof? The man who expressed the most extreme point of view within the erroneous line then followed, in our opinion, in Yugoslavia, had to be eliminated. It was Djilas. . . . Where were we wrong? Only when passing from such criticism to an inadmissible intervention in the life of the Yugoslav Communist Party. We exceeded the rights of the Cominform. The erroneous decision with regard to Yugoslavia opened a breach in the socialist camp. Further opportunities of this kind should not be provided to the imperialists. The Soviet comrades have done well . . . to sweep away the obstacles to the resumption of normal relations with the Yugoslav people and to try to normalize the relations with the Yugoslav Communists.[19]

From all the evidence "normalization" was seen here from a purely diplomatic angle, as an attempt to close the open breach in the socialist camp, and with a certain skepticism as to the results. "One must hope," added Thorez, apparently with even less conviction, "that we will succeed in renewing good relationships with our Yugoslav comrades, particularly under present conditions."[20]

This is reminiscent of the state of mind in which the Chinese Communist Party accepted Tito's "rehabilitation." Their attitude was expressed in a letter of the Central Committee of the CCP to

18 Information from a private source.
19 "Intervention de Maurice Thorez au Comité Central d'Arcueil," *Cahiers du Communisme*, Vol. 32, No. 6 (June 1956), p. 776.
20 *Ibid.*

the Central Committee of the CPSU, dated June 10, 1954 and made public in a *Jen-min Jih-pao* article of September 26, 1963, entitled "Is Yugoslavia a Socialist Country?" The Chinese said:

In its letter of June 10, 1954, to the Central Committee of the CPSU, the Central Committee of the CCP pointed out that the fact should be taken into account that as the leaders of Yugoslavia had already gone quite far in their dealings with imperialism, they might reject our effort to win it over and refuse to return to the path of socialism.[21]

In that case, in any event "it would further expose the hypocrisy of the Yugoslav leaders before the people of Yugoslavia and the world." For Thorez, as for Mao, all this was more in the nature of a tactical maneuver to make Tito "unmask himself" than a true effort at rapprochement.

To be sure, the Yugoslavs did not fail to take up Thorez' reservations, which were repeated in the draft theses presented at the PCF Fourteenth Congress. In a *Borba* article of May 20, with excerpts reprinted by *L'Humanité* on June 4, 1956, the organ of the League of Communists of Yugoslavia complained of the

non-Marxist manner in which the PCF leadership judges the activity of the Cominform and the events of the year 1948. . . . Thorez reduces the "error" of the Cominform and the PCF to a procedural error. . . . But today, at least, it is more than evident that the error was not purely procedural. . . . This manner of reasoning could still have been tolerated in 1952 or in 1953. Today it is inadmissible. It shows that there are people who absolutely do not understand the character of actual events. It is hard to believe that Thorez, if he is incapable of understanding the events of 1948, can understand the problems that the working class and the French Communist Party face today.[22]

This was purely and simply a declaration of no confidence with respect to Maurice Thorez, who was considered basically incapable of a sincere change of heart and definitely unqualified for leadership. It should also be remembered that several days later, on May 28, 1956, Palmiro Togliatti arrived in Belgrade, where his conversations with Tito and other Yugoslav leaders took place in a friendly atmosphere and marked the resumption of a collaboration that was to become ever closer.

[21] "Is Yugoslavia a Socialist Country?—Comment on the Open Letter of the Central Committee of the CPSU (3), by the Editorial Departments of *Jen-min Jih-pao* and *Hung Ch'i*," *Peking Review*, Vol. VI, No. 39 (Sept. 27, 1963), pp. 14–27, at p. 25; excerpts in William E. Griffith, *The Sino-Soviet Rift* (Cambridge, Mass.: The M.I.T. Press, 1964), pp. 462–465.
[22] *Borba*, May 20, 1956; *L'Humanité*, June 4, 1956 (excerpts).

At the same time, a Bulgarian delegation designated to go to Yugoslavia had to cancel its trip because, according to *L'Humanité* of June 2, 1956, "the Yugoslav government tried to establish a discriminatory policy by itself selecting the interlocutors with whom to conduct discussions." Only the evening before (June 1, 1956) a short item in *L'Humanité*, entitled *"Borba* Attacks Enver Hoxha," alluded to the refusal of the Secretary-General of the Albanian Workers' Party to rehabilitate Koci Xoxe and to *Borba*'s reaction to this, concluding with the question: "Can *Borba*'s attacks facilitate an understanding? [between the two neighboring countries]." If one adds to this that on June 2 Tito arrived in Moscow, where he was received very warmly, it will be understood that Thorez, placed in the same camp as Hoxha and the Bulgarians vis-à-vis Tito, Khrushchev, and Togliatti, found himself in an uncomfortable situation.

The anonymous article published in *L'Humanité* on June 4, 1956 in reply to *Borba* also betrayed considerable embarrassment. Its author pointed out that *Borba*'s attack was aimed at the "theses of the Central Committee and not at the theses of Maurice Thorez" and that those, moreover, only repeated the evaluation contained in the documents of April 17, 1956 which constituted the dissolution of the Cominform, signed by its eight member parties. In other words, why not address oneself to the Soviets or to the Italians? The article in *L'Humanité* justified the criticisms made of the Yugoslav party in 1948 by the criticisms the Yugoslavs had made in 1947 of the policies of the French Communist Party, which they termed "opportunistic." Still on the level of procedure, the point was to show that neither party had exceeded its rights in criticizing the other, even when the criticisms themselves were without foundation. In reality, the argumentation of *L'Humanité* was addressed to the Italian Communist Party, to remind it that in 1947 it had been on the same side as the fraternal French party and had been accused of opportunism by the Yugoslavs. It was also addressed to the Soviets, reminding them that on the same occasion the Yugoslavs had described the policy of collaboration with the Socialist Party and the search for "new ways toward socialism," that is, Khrushchev's 1956 policies, as opportunism.

Nevertheless, *L'Humanité* made a new concession by admitting that already "in a passage of the 1948 resolution" the parties of the Cominform had in fact "exceeded their rights" and that

this error has led our party to accept, without verification, grave accusations with regard to the Yugoslav party which were unjustified and unfounded and which are now being cleared up and which have been the object of necessary corrections.

Once this small step forward with regard to the declarations by Maurice Thorez at Arcueil was made, the French Communist Party refused to go further; rather, in its turn, it played the role of the persecuted:

. . . We consider it inadmissible for *Borba* to mix in the internal affairs of the French Communist Party and particularly to make open attacks against its policies, leadership, and Secretary-General.

It appeared as though it was not only the "interference by *Borba*" that was being aimed at in this sentence, but also that of Khrushchev, who was suspected of acting through Belgrade to provoke the fall of the PCF leadership. In short, the point of the statement was to make Khrushchev aware that the PCF was quite ready to fall into line on condition that he would refrain from attempts to destroy its leadership. This also explains the ambiguous conclusion of the article:

We reaffirm that we attach great value to the re-establishment of contacts and relationships with the Yugoslav Communists [as well as to the strengthening of] our relations with the Communist and workers' parties of different countries.

In *Cahiers du Communisme* of June 1956, Waldeck Rochet, suspected of being the crown prince chosen by Khrushchev, was given the task of paraphrasing the argumentation against *Borba* employed in the very *L'Humanité* article whose measured and firm language he praised. On one point, however, Rochet expressed himself still more clearly than had the anonymous writer in *L'Humanité*:

Having recognized that it committed the error of mixing in the internal affairs of the Yugoslav party, our party considers that in the future the principle of noninterference must be respected by all parties, including those who in the past have had most to suffer from the violation of this principle.[23]

In the meantime, while continuing to demand a certain amount of autonomy, the PCF did not yield in its basic attitude of determining its policies in accordance with Soviet diplomatic needs. For this reason the PCF press gave much space to the visit of the SFIO

23 Waldeck Rochet, "Le projet de thèses pour le XIVème Congrès et quelques problèmes du parti," *Cahiers du Communisme*, Vol. 32, No. 6 (June 1956), p. 673.

delegation to Moscow, which was followed by negotiations between representatives of the Soviet and French governments (April 28–May 14 and May 15–19, 1956). However, the results of these discussions were quite meager, with the exception of a decision to increase commercial and cultural exchanges substantially between the two countries. The Franco-Soviet declaration, signed on May 19 by Guy Mollet, Christian Pineau, Bulganin, Khrushchev, and Molotov, was otherwise limited to generalities on peaceful coexistence, disarmament, and assistance to underdeveloped countries. Perhaps the most important passage was a little sentence at the end concerning Algeria:

The Soviet ministers have expressed the hope that, in the liberal spirit that animates it, the French government will find it possible to solve this important problem in a manner appropriate to the spirit of our times and the interest of the peoples.

This statement at one and the same time accorded to the Mollet government the label of "liberalism," expressed in extremely vague terms confidence in his ability to find a definite solution, and encouraged moderation on the part of the PCF.

The PCF followed Moscow's advice: In the June 5 vote of confidence for the government, despite the latter's increasingly obvious orientation toward large-scale military operations in Algeria, the Communist group limited itself to abstaining. Nevertheless, at the joint meeting of the PCF Central Committee and parliamentary group before the vote, several Communist deputies favored a negative vote. The official communiqué of the Central Committee session mentioned that "54 comrades" participated in the discussion and, contrary to custom, did not state that the decision was unanimous. Waldeck Rochet was designated (in order to compromise him) as the speaker charged with explaining the vote of the Communist group to the Assembly.[24]

In the meantime, Le Monde[25] became the first paper in France to publish Khrushchev's secret report to the Twentieth Congress, made public by the Department of State! The excitement among PCF activists on reading the text in Le Monde, in the face of the silence of the Communist press, was such that the carefully prepared tactic to make of the PCF Fourteenth Congress a demonstration of unity in support of the leadership threatened to break down. As we have seen, the PCF Central Committee had, up to this point,

[24] Ibid., p. 784.
[25] Between June 6 and 19, 1956.

entirely endorsed the CPSU Twentieth Congress and had increasingly expressed its agreement, after some hesitation, with the criticism of the "cult of the personality" of Stalin. However, it continued to minimize the errors committed, treating them as abstract in character, and tried to limit its own self-criticism to the minimum possible, rejecting the idea of real coresponsibility. Thus the writer Claude Morgan, in an amendment to the theses, had demanded that the Congress

recognize that the PCF participated in the cult of the personality of Stalin and that the cult of personality in general had also developed in its own ranks and had led, from base to summit, to insufficient criticism and self-criticism.[26]

This had drawn a sharp response from Marcel Servin, then the organizational secretary of the Central Committee, in which post he had succeeded Auguste Lecoeur. Servin rejected the suggestion of instituting a secret vote—as had been done in Italy and in the Soviet Union since the Nineteenth Congress in 1952—for the election of the leadership organ. He also rejected Morgan's proposal to re-examine "the case of comrades against whom measures of expulsion have been taken or who were removed from responsible positions as a result of the Yugoslav affair." He stated categorically that the PCF was not a section of the CPSU: "There are matters which concern only the Communists of the Soviet Union and not the French Communists, and vice versa." And besides, even the Stalinist cult was not necessarily to be condemned in France, for

such matters have not at all the same significance in France as in the Soviet Union, because of the fact that here, in a capitalist country, Stalin was the symbol of the first socialist state.

The result was that these problems did not occupy a central place in the discussions preparatory to the congress or at the congress itself.

After the publication of Khrushchev's secret speech, this position became very difficult to maintain; and after June 17 it became completely impossible for the PCF leadership to keep silent about it. Not only did all conversations and discussions by PCF activists center around a document that their leaders did not even dare to call false (though in private they stressed all the more its "suspicious" origin), but Togliatti granted an interview to the magazine *Nuovi Argomenti*—published in the issue of June 16—that com-

[26] See Claude Morgan's letter and Marcel Servin's reply in "Tribune de discussion," *France Nouvelle*, June 2, 1956.

pletely authenticated from the international Communist point of view, as it were, the text of Khrushchev's secret speech. Moreover, Togliatti's interview did not limit itself to commenting on or paraphrasing the secret speech but contained some criticisms and daring propositions. The chief of the Italian Communist Party, though in very guarded terms, questioned the entire concept of the "cult of the personality" as utilized so far to describe the whole of the Stalinist phenomenon. Togliatti wrote:

It seems to us that undoubtedly Stalin's errors were tied in with an excessive increase in the bureaucratic apparatus in Soviet economic and political life, and perhaps, above all, in Party life.[27]

Clearly, this sentence referred to the de-Stalinizers in their capacity as members of the bureaucratic machineries, as well as to their predecessors, and the question was implicitly raised of their inability to clarify completely the nature of the phenomenon of which they had been participants. Togliatti did not evade the problem. Criticizing the attitude shown during Stalin's lifetime by his successors, Togliatti wrote:

At least they could have been more prudent in those public and solemn exultations of this man. . . . today, they criticize themselves, and this is to their great credit, but in this criticism they are losing without doubt a little of their own prestige.[28]

Going still further, Togliatti questioned the system itself:

The least arbitrary of the generalizations is the one which sees in Stalin's errors a progressive encroachment by personal power on the collective entities of a democratic origin and nature, and, as a result of this, the pile-up of phenomena of bureaucracy, of violation of legality, of stagnation, and, also, partially, of degeneration at different points of the social organism.[29]

Despite Togliatti's qualifications, this passage is strongly reminiscent of Trotsky's definition of the Soviet Union as "a degenerate workers' state."

Finally, and perhaps above all, Togliatti was not content to affirm that "the Soviet model cannot and must not any longer be obligatory." This had been said in almost identical words by Thorez himself as well as by several leaders of the people's democracies

---

[27] Palmiro Togliatti, "9 Domande sullo Stalinismo," *Nuovi Argomenti*, No. 20, June 16, 1956; quoted from *The Anti-Stalin Campaign and International Communism*, edited by the Russian Institute, Columbia University (Revised Edition; New York: Columbia University Press, 1956), pp. 97–139, at p. 121.

[28] *Ibid.*, p. 120.

[29] *Ibid.*, p. 103.

before the anti-Yugoslav campaign, which had underlined the similarities rather than the differences with respect to the Soviet model. The Italian leader added:

The whole system becomes polycentric, and even in the Communist movement itself we cannot speak of a single guide.[30]

Togliatti did not deny that in certain countries it might be possible in the future to arrive at socialism without the Communists being the leading party.[31]

Togliatti thus had questioned some of the fundamental dogmas on which the Communist movement had lived since the victory of Stalinism, and which the de-Stalinizers had tried to keep intact.

On June 18, it was the turn of the PCF Politburo to take a position on the problems raised by the "report attributed to Comrade Khrushchev." This expression, used then for the first time, was to become a favorite stereotype of the Communist press and literature in France. While echoing Togliatti's criticism with regard to certain points, the declaration of the PCF Politburo[32] was careful not to repeat the most imprudently extreme theses of the Italian leader. It seems, in fact, that the French Communist leaders were quick to profit as much as they could from the situation in order to consolidate their position in their own party and in the Communist movement in Western Europe.

After referring to the "legitimate emotion" aroused by the Khrushchev secret speech among PCF members, the Politburo declaration began with a compliment to the Soviet leaders:

The creditable effort of the leaders of the CPSU to undertake the correction of errors and faults connected with the cult of the individual emphasizes the strength and unity of the great party of Lenin, the confidence which it enjoys among the Soviet peoples, and its authority in the international labor movement.[33]

Then, after expressing regret about the conditions in which the bourgeois press had been "able to publish facts of which the French Communists had been unaware," the Politburo declaration contained a critical passage:

---

30 *Ibid.*, p. 139.

31 "In the rest of the world there are countries where we wish to start socialism although the Communists are not the leading party," *ibid.*

32 "Statement of the Political Bureau of the French Communist Party," *L'Humanité*, June 19, 1956; *Cahiers du Communisme*, Vol. 32, No. 8–9 (Aug.–Sept. 1956), pp. 926–927; all quotations from *The Anti-Stalin Campaign and International Communism, op. cit.*, pp. 168–171.

33 *Ibid.*, p. 168.

The explanations given up to now of Stalin's errors, their origin, and the conditions under which they developed, are not satisfactory. A thorough Marxist analysis to determine all the circumstances under which Stalin was able to exercise his personal power is indispensable.[34]

However, contrary to Togliatti, the PCF limited itself to demanding a "thorough Marxist analysis" without trying to put forth one itself. No explanation was given except that Stalin alone could not have been responsible and that the other Soviet leaders shared his responsibilities:

It was wrong, while Stalin was still living, to shower him with dithyrambic praise and to give him the exclusive credit for all the successes in the Soviet Union. . . . Today it is wrong to blame Stalin alone for every negative act of the CPSU.[35]

Then followed a ritualistic passage on Stalin's merits "during an entire historical period," plus a justification of Stalinism:

The development of this cult was facilitated by the position of the Soviet Union, for a long time exposed alone to the undertakings of a world of enemies. This necessitated an extreme test of the people's strength, an iron discipline, and strict centralization of power of the proletarian state.[36]

The Politburo declared that knowledge of these circumstances "help[s] to explain" the development of the cult "without justifying Stalin's activities, however," which the declaration condemned in more vigorous terms than had all prior PCF documents.

Contrary to Togliatti, the PCF Politburo made no allusion whatsoever to "polycentrism" but declared that it was "aware of the prominent role of the Soviet people, pioneers of socialism, and in close solidarity with the CPSU." It praised the work of the Twentieth Congress in lyrical terms as "the Congress of the brilliant balance sheet of the Soviet Union which, having achieved the construction of socialism, has started on the road to a Communist society,"[37] and which "emphasized the possibility of avoiding wars in our lifetime and of achieving socialism by new means," and "brightened the prospects of the working class's march to unity."[38]

In conclusion, the PCF Politburo demanded from the CPSU the text of Khrushchev's secret speech, a fact suggesting that the PCF leaders themselves had had no knowledge of this document before its dissemination by the State Department. Even though this as-

34 *Ibid.*, p. 169.
35 *Ibid.*
36 *Ibid.*, p. 170.
37 *Ibid.*
38 *Ibid.*

sumption appears highly improbable, the demand was quite clever, for up to a point it disarmed those activists who reproached their leaders for having hidden from them facts that they themselves had known. Accused of being accomplices, the leaders took on the role of victims.[39]

In fact, the June 18 declaration already seemed to contain the germ of a deal made some days later in Moscow by a PCF delegation sent there for that purpose. Moderating their criticism, tempering it with eulogies, avoiding the audacious heresies of Togliatti, the PCF leadership hoped to make Moscow appreciate its *sang-froid,* its deliberativeness, its sense of responsibility, and its loyalty. Under these conditions, the deal consisted in negotiating the PCF's unreserved alignment with the CPSU in return for the CPSU's unreserved support for the leading group in Paris and its policies with respect to the Algerian problem and against those PCF opposition elements who demanded a more rapid translation into practice of the "ideas of the Twentieth Congress."

The PCF delegation, composed of Étienne Fajon, Waldeck Rochet, and Marcel Servin, left on June 26, 1956 for the Soviet Union and returned with a long draft by the CPSU Secretariat (after conversations with Khrushchev, Pospelov, and Ponomarev), which was eventually published as the "Resolution of the CPSU Central Committee of June 30, 1956."[40] This text, which was termed "a more profound Marxist analysis," gave enough satisfaction to the PCF leaders so that the Central Committee, in its session of July 6, could

warmly approve the resolution of the CPSU Central Committee, which shows how the cult of the personality of Stalin has been overcome in the Soviet Union.[41]

On all points where the PCF and Togliatti disagreed, the Soviet document ruled against the latter, explicitly or implicitly, while it quoted the June 18 PCF Politburo declaration, that is, made it an example for other parties. In its enthusiasm, the PCF Central Committee celebrated on July 6 "the complete harmony of view of the

[39] This assumption is made even more improbable by the fact that the Yugoslavs themselves had received word of the text. *Borba* was the first to publish an extremely significant summary of the report—even before it was released by the State Department.

[40] Published in *Pravda,* July 2, 1956 under the title "On Overcoming the Personality Cult and its Consequences"; English translation in *Current Digest of the Soviet Press* (hereafter cited as *CDSP*), Vol. VIII, No. 24 (July 25, 1956), pp. 3–8. See also André Stil, "Un texte capital," *L'Humanité,* July 4, 1956 (reprinted by *Pravda,* July 6, 1956).

[41] *Cahiers du Communisme,* Vol. 32, No. 8–9 (Aug.–Sept. 1956), pp. 928 ff.

two parties—French and Soviet—on the whole range of questions posed by the Twentieth Congress"[42] and called the Soviet resolution an "invaluable document for the international workers' movement." The activists were requested to "study seriously" and "disseminate widely" this document, which had completely relegated to oblivion the PCF's demand, formulated a few days before, for the text of the secret speech "attributed to Khrushchev."[43]

When the PCF's Fourteenth Congress opened at Le Havre on July 18, its leaders did not need to worry. Their opponents had not been able to pass the obstacle of some departmental ("federal") conferences which had carefully excluded them from the delegations to the congress. As for those who could have attended the opening of the congress in order to unveil their batteries, they were made to understand, by a *Pravda* editorial greeting the congress under the title "The Fighting Vanguard of the French Workers"[44] and by the presence of a delegation led by Mikhail Suslov, that Maurice Thorez had once again been invested with Moscow's full confidence.

The International Scene

But what had happened in the meantime in Moscow? The PCF's moves were certainly made in the sense of Stalinist opposition to Khrushchev, who in turn was trying to limit the damage in the Soviet Union. Had the pressure of the French party been solicited by certain elements in the Kremlin who thought that Khrushchev had gone too far? The first signs of the disintegration of the monolithic character of the international Communist movement seemed to prove them right. Both the PCF and the PCI under Togliatti's leadership, each in its way and without accord, were more or less declaring that, after all, if they have already gone that far, why not further?

On the other hand, the Chinese Communist Party, without publicly expressing its reservations,[45] seemed hardly more satisfied with

---

42 *Ibid.*

43 In a speech of July 2, 1956 to the party militants of Paris at the Maison des Métallos, Étienne Fajon declared that the Resolution of June 30 "relegates the report attributed to Khrushchev to the background, except perhaps for a few comrades here and there who aspire to fish in troubled waters." (Editor's translation.) (*L'Humanité,* July 12, 1956.)

44 *Pravda,* July 18, 1956 (reprinted in *L'Humanité,* July 19, 1956).

45 In "The Origin and Development of the Differences Between the Leadership of the C.P.S.U. and Ourselves," *Jen-min Jih-pao* and *Hung Ch'i,* Sept. 6,

the course taken by de-Stalinization. More than by the repudiation of Stalin, the CCP seemed shocked by the fact that, without having consulted the other fraternal parties, Khrushchev had proceeded to demolish a myth that concerned the entire movement and that the Chinese had not found easy to implant in their own country. Khrushchev's principal error was to have acted in an irresponsible fashion, forgetting that he was not only the head of the CPSU but also, by virtue of this fact, the head of the international Communist movement. Basically, one could almost say that the Chinese criticized Khrushchev's procedures as being Stalinist in character, including his denunciation of Stalin: When the Soviet Union decided something, the entire world had to follow suit. This claim to govern and rule the world Communist movement in a sovereign manner, to expect all parties to align themselves upon a wave of the "baton," revealed the very "great-power chauvinism" that was soon to become, in subsequent Chinese documents, Peking's principal grievance against the CPSU—and was to be retroactively applied to Stalin's policies. Thus, in a certain sense, the reservations of the PCF and of the CCP converged in their results, which were to criticize the method followed by Khrushchev but were opposed to each other in their motives. The former particularly feared the possible consequences of de-Stalinization on the discipline, cohesion, and organization of the movement, as well as the implantation in it of ideas of doubt and criticism; it almost rebelled against the fact that the CPSU had given other parties the desire and the means to escape from under its aegis. The CCP, which had already succeeded under Stalin, and without public notice, in refusing to submit to him, was even less ready to bow before Khrushchev.

Nevertheless, at that time all these signs of resistance aided the numerous Stalinist elements inside the CPSU who were pushing Khrushchev to call a halt to de-Stalinization, as became apparent

---

1963, the Chinese explained their attitude. "It needs to be said, of course, that *for the sake of unity* against the enemy and out of consideration for the difficult position the leaders of the C.P.S.U. were then in, we refrained in those days from open criticism of the errors of the 20th Congress, because the imperialists and the reactionaries of all countries were exploiting these errors and carrying on frenzied activities against the Soviet Union, against communism and against people, and also because the leaders of the C.P.S.U. had not yet departed as far from Marxism-Leninism as they did later. *We fervently hoped at the time that the leaders of the C.P.S.U. would put their errors right.* Consequently, we invariably endeavoured to seek out positive aspects and on public occasions gave them whatever support was appropriate and necessary." (Quoted from *Peking Review*, Vol. VI, No. 37 [Sept. 13, 1963], p. 9 [our italics].) Reprinted in full in Griffith, *The Sino-Soviet Rift, op. cit.,* pp. 388–420.

after the liquidation of the antiparty group. In the last three days of June 1956, the Poznań rising provided additional arguments to these Stalinist elements. (The French Communist press, falling in line with the Soviet press, attributed the origin of the Poznań incidents to *"agents provocateurs,"* while the Chinese, the Yugoslav, and the Italian Communists seemed ready to accept the Polish interpretation[46] that the authorities had been responsible.)

Still, the resolution of June 30, 1956 was a success for the PCF leaders. By reaffirming their loyalty to the "center" of the international Communist movement, they acquired an even greater weight vis-à-vis that center, all the more so because Togliatti was forced to shift into reverse and to recant—a fact that did not increase his prestige, at least not for the time being.

The PCF's Fourteenth Congress, in this situation, was merely a demonstration of unanimity, a ceremony rather than a congress. The delegates' speeches were limited to embroidering the themes developed in Thorez' report to such a point that the journalist Raymond Barrillon, in the July 21 *Le Monde,* could speak of a "litany of approval." With regard to all the problems of de-Stalinization, Thorez in his report limited himself to hiding behind the Soviet document of June 30, which he was content to paraphrase. (A discreet allusion was made to Togliatti: "The hysterical campaign launched by the bourgeoisie did not succeed in making trouble, despite some errors of interpretation committed in certain countries.") The essential point was perhaps contained in this sentence:

The criticism of the cult of the personality created around Stalin and of the consequences of that cult can in no event be mechanically applied to our party, which did not have to suffer similar deficiencies.

Thorez added that the Central Committee had already "revealed and eliminated those traces of the cult of the personality which even so were able to appear in our ranks."[47] In sum, for the PCF the question was settled, and the affair over and done with.

The Soviet message of greeting to the Congress read by Mikhail Suslov gave Maurice Thorez a resounding endorsement:

The glorious French Communist Party rightly occupies a place of honor and enjoys the profound respect of the Communist and workers' parties

46 See *Trybuna Ludu,* July 7, 1956, where the Polish Communist Party and the trade unions are charged with responsibility for the riots.

47 Thorez' report to the Fourteenth Congress of the PCF, *L'Humanité,* May 19, 1956.

of all countries. The leaders of your party, your Central Committee, and our comrade, Maurice Thorez, who is also for us a very dear friend, are enshrined for us in a love and a respect that they have earned in battle.[48]

The only discordant note in the concert of approval and praise for Thorez was expressed by Giancarlo Pajetta, the PCI delegate, who slipped in some poisonous allusions, for example: "The unity with our Socialist comrades was left undisturbed." All that followed was designed to imply, without any direct attack, that the PCI's success was due to its correct policy of "the Italian road to socialism." With respect to the Twentieth Congress, Pajetta said that

the comrades of the CPSU . . . advance and call upon the entire socialist camp to advance. There is no question as to our response or your response to this appeal.[49]

The Yugoslavs, who had just accepted in principle an early meeting with PCF representatives, as Thorez himself announced to the congress, had not sent a delegation.

The ovations and eulogies that Maurice Thorez received during the entire congress were crowned, during the elections for the leadership, by his re-election to the position of Secretary-General, after Étienne Fajon had introduced him as "the leader who is the first in action as he is the first in the heart of every Communist and in the impotent hatred of the enemies of the working class. . . ." Thus Maurice Thorez, who had had reason to feel threatened in May, emerged in triumph from this congress in July.

But at the same time, the June 30 Soviet resolution, on which this triumph was built, was vigorously challenged by the rapid developments in Eastern Europe. There, the Central Committee of the Hungarian Workers' Party, which met at the same time as the PCF's Fourteenth Congress, replaced Rákosi by his faithful second-in-command, Gerő. But this half measure, far from pacifying the opposition of the intellectuals, who had taken the temperature of popular discontent in the course of the stormy sessions of the Petőfi Circle, only inflamed them further. Anxious to dam up and channel the stormy developments throughout their East European outposts, Khrushchev and Mikoyan had recourse to Tito's services. In a series of conversations that took place in Yugoslavia and in the Crimea during the last two weeks of September, Khrushchev tried to organize with Tito some patching up in order to reduce the ferment in the people's democracies. The support of the leader of Yugo-

48 See *Le Monde,* July 21, 1956.
49 *L'Humanité,* July 21, 1956.

slavia, whose resistance to Stalin had made him very popular in all of Eastern Europe, seemed indispensable to Khrushchev in his efforts to stabilize the situation in Poland and particularly in Hungary. But it was already too late to prevent the explosions of October.

CHAPTER SEVEN

THE PCF, THE OCTOBER 1956 EVENTS, AND THEIR SEQUEL

It is unnecessary here to review in detail the events in Poland and Hungary, concerning which there exists a considerable amount of literature. Let us simply recall that the PCF was in the forefront of those who encouraged the Soviets, in Poland as in Hungary, to use the greatest possible firmness in intervention and repression.

To register their dissatisfaction with the solution arrived at in Poland—a solution that the Soviets finally accepted, in part under pressure from Peking—the PCF leaders simply decided to censor Gomułka's Eighth Plenum speech. In his speech of November 2 to the activists of Paris assembled in the Maison des Métallos, Étienne Fajon was unable to hide the fact that he and his colleagues still considered Gomułka a dangerous "Titoist." A great number of activists in many cells, as well as the majority of Communist intellectuals, had objected to the systematic omission in *L'Humanité* of all news items and declarations emanating from foreign Communist parties not in harmony with the PCF's line. To these objections Fajon replied that if *L'Humanité*

were to do what some comrades ask, it would sow disorientation and doubt and demobilize from instead of arm for battle. *L'Humanité* did not publish Comrade Gomulka's report because several of its passages are in contradiction with the theses democratically formulated at our Congress.

If Fajon were to be believed, only those activists who had followed *L'Humanité*'s presentation of the events exclusively had "the exact facts with . . . their Marxist explanation."[1]

Formally, Fajon definitely acknowledged a difference between Poland and Hungary, namely, that the Communist party remained in power in Poland; but Thorez himself, presiding at the Novem-

1 *L'Humanité*, Nov. 3, 1956.

ber 2 meeting, stressed that "the events in Poland have shown the intervention of identical elements [that is] antisocialist, chauvinist, and anti-Soviet."[2]

For the French Communist leaders Gomułka's "national communism" was as grave a heresy as Nagy's "revisionism." On this point Thorez was aligned with the Bulgarian, Czechoslovak, Albanian, Romanian, and East German Communist parties, while Mao Tse-tung was ready to encourage in Eastern Europe the tendency to break free from Soviet tutelage, on the condition that the political hegemony of the respective Communist parties was not jeopardized. On October 31 the Chinese government warmly endorsed the declaration in which the Soviet government on October 30 had proclaimed its intention to respect in the future the principle of equality and sovereignty of nations in its relations with socialist countries.[3] Peking took advantage of this to condemn severely "great-power chauvinism" for the first time in a public document.[4] (Thorez and Fajon saw signs of chauvinism only on the part of the Poles and the Hungarians.)

Isolated in the international Communist movement, with allies whose positions in their own countries could change from day to day if the Soviet promises of October 30 were kept, the PCF leadership seems to have done what it could to encourage the Soviets to crush the Hungarian insurrection. How else can one interpret the accusations leveled by Étienne Fajon on November 2 against Nagy —and Kádár—whom he accused of "covering up the slaughter of Communists by Hungarian fascists," or his refusal to open an exchange of views with the new leaders of Communist Hungary on the ground that "the retreat of the people's power before the reactionary revolt was not conducive to discussions between Marxist workers' parties"?[5] If the problem was no longer fit for discussion,

2 *Ibid.*

3 "Declaration by the Government of the USSR on the Principles of Development and Further Strengthening of Friendship and Cooperation Between the Soviet Union and Other Socialist States, October 30, 1956," *Pravda*, Oct. 31, 1956; *CDSP*, Vol. VIII, No. 40 (Nov. 14, 1956), pp. 10–11; and Paul E. Zinner, ed., *National Communism and Popular Revolt in Eastern Europe* (New York: Columbia University Press, 1956), pp. 485–489.

4 "Statement by the Government of the People's Republic of China on the Declaration of the Soviet Government on Relations among Socialist States, November 1, 1956," *Jen-min Jih-pao*, Nov. 1, 1956; *Survey of the Mainland China Press* (hereafter cited as *SCMP*), No. 1405, Nov. 1, 1956; and Zinner, *National Communism and Popular Revolt, op. cit.*, pp. 492–495.

5 *L'Humanité*, Nov. 3, 1956. Fajon expressed his opinion of Kádár in these terms: "We note that Kádár, after becoming first secretary of the Hungarian Workers' Party, has, quite simply, just left the ranks of that party, taking Nagy

it had to be solved by force. Ultimately, whether spontaneously or under pressure from the Soviet leaders, the PCF called upon the Soviet Army to intervene.

The fact that the two equally heretical currents, "national communism" and "revisionism," converged in the person of Imre Nagy seemed to the Communist leaders in Paris almost a providential windfall. Peking, too, immediately reversed itself and, if one gives credence to the Chinese version disseminated *a posteriori* in "The Origin and Development of the Differences Between the Leadership of the CPSU and Ourselves,"[6] incited Khrushchev to put down Nagy by force of arms.[7] Once again the enemy took on a clear outline, and in view of the almost unanimous applause of the Communist world for the fire of the Soviet tanks directed at the people of Budapest, the heretics in Warsaw and Belgrade seemed isolated in their reserve or silence.

To be sure, this unanimity was neither complete nor without some reservation. In Italy Togliatti, like Tito, approved the second Soviet intervention as a sort of necessary evil, with a tone of regret in marked contrast to the indecent cries of triumph in *L'Humanité*. But the principal Communist leader of the Italian trade-union movement, Di Vittorio, had made some statements between the two interventions which clearly favored the Hungarian insurgents. The unity of the PCI with the Nenni Socialists, which had endured during the entire period of Stalinism and the Cold War, did not survive the test of Budapest, and some small West European Communist parties, such as those of Belgium and Norway, did not accept what became the official thesis of the "crushing of the counter-revolution" in Hungary.

In France itself there were also some defections from the PCF, spectacular because of the reputation of those involved, but without much importance on the political plane. After the resignation of Aimé Césaire, a deputy from Martinique and a poet of talent, the writers Claude Roy, Roger Vailland, Jacques-Francis Rolland, and Claude Morgan, and the jurist Gérard Lyon-Caen joined in a protest by the fellow traveler Jean-Paul Sartre against the Soviet inter-

---

with him. . . . It has become manifest that these individuals only talked of 'liberalizing' the party in order to disguise their real aim of destroying it."

[6] *Jen-min Jih-pao* and *Hung Ch'i*, Sept. 6, 1963; *Peking Review*, Vol. VI, No. 37 (Sept. 13, 1963), pp. 7–23.

[7] For a more detailed discussion of the events of this period, see François Fejtö, *Chine-U.R.S.S., la fin d'une hégémonie: Les origines du grand schisme communiste, 1950–1957*, Vol. I (Paris: Plon, 1964), in particular, Chapter 7, pp. 159–171.

vention. They were punished by a temporary expulsion of one year from the PCF. Most "progressives," like Emmanuel d'Astier de la Vigerie, and the writer Vercors, remained aloof. Those Communist intellectuals who had taken the initiative in collecting signatures for a message of solidarity to be sent to Gomułka, before the outbreak of the insurrection in Hungary, and who had received several hundred signatures in a few days, now accepted the demand made to them by the clever Laurent Casanova (who mixed intimidation and blandishments) to delay the sending of the message until after a meeting with the Politburo, scheduled for mid-November.[8] The telegram was never sent; rather, in an ostensible concession, the Politburo promised to edit Gomułka's report for internal dissemination only. At the same time, Servin issued a grave warning to the "oppositionists":

We will not tolerate, and the working class will not permit us to tolerate, the action of termites who try to undermine the party from within. Nor will we tolerate that obscure little Petőfi Circles work to split our party.[9]

Servin's warning was understood; the opposition, although not as negligible[10] as has often been said, began to disperse in various directions. Most, particularly workers, simply left the party, with which they no longer could agree; the internal struggle and the moves against the "termites" were deeply repugnant to them. Those who remained were for the most part intellectuals: teachers, students, physicians, particularly writers, who were divided on what tactic to follow. After the *Tribune de Discussion* was launched in the spring of 1956 by a group composed of Communist students at the Sorbonne, metal workers, and Trotskyites of the Fourth International who applied their infiltration tactics to the PCF, some well-known intellectuals launched a new clandestine bulletin, *L'Étincelle* (The Spark), whose first issue was dated September 1956. (The initiative for this bulletin came from the same activists who

---

8 Information from a private source, confirmed, however, *inter alia*, in *Le Monde*, Nov. 13, 1956 and in the clandestine bulletin *Tribune de discussion* (mimeographed), No. 6, p. 11.

9 *L'Humanité*, Nov. 12, 1956.

10 At the assembly of party militants held on November 2, 1956 at the Maison des Métallos, the resolution approving Fajon's report was accepted unanimously, barring five abstentions, according to eyewitnesses. Now only the votes of those militants chosen in advance were counted, and this voting could have taken place inside the room well in advance of the meeting. Most of the opposition who challenged and interrupted Fajon during his speech were in the entrance hall or the courtyard. It was only from a corner of the courtyard that some forty votes against the resolution were counted, contrary to all usual procedures at this type of meeting.

had made the abortive attempt to send a message of solidarity to Gomułka.) These two bulletins were the successors of two other, older ones, *Le Communiste,* founded by a defector from the Fourth International, Michèle Mestre, and *Unir,* whose origin has always remained a mystery, although it dates back to 1952; its anonymous editors have always remained completely clandestine. For his part, Pierre Hervé moved closer to Auguste Lecoeur, and their group, *La nation socialiste,* moved toward joining the SFIO at just the moment when the capture of Ben Bella's and his companions' airplane and the unfortunate Suez expedition had brought profound discredit upon Guy Mollet's party.

The most important initiative of the intellectual opposition was a letter composed at the end of November 1956 and signed by ten eminent Communist intellectuals which protested in the name of "revolutionary honesty" against the attitude manifested by the Central Committee and *L'Humanité* since the Twentieth Congress and against the "interpretations given to the events in Poland and Hungary." The letter spoke of "confusion" and "a deep and extensive malaise in the entire party," and it demanded "the convocation of an extraordinary Congress with the least possible delay."[11] Distributed to all members of the Central Committee[12] by one of its ten signatories, the writer Hélène Parmelin (who at that time still had a column in *L'Humanité*), it carried among others the signatures of Pablo Picasso, the painter, Édouard Pignon, the writers Georges Besson, François Jourdain, and Paul Tillard, the professors Marcel Cornu, Henry Wallon, and René Zazzo, and a scientific researcher, Dr. Harel. *L'Humanité* withheld these names except for that of Hélène Parmelin, whom it declared guilty of the gravest breach of discipline because she had taken upon herself the distribution of the "Lettre des Dix" even though she was a party functionary. Without quoting the text, which the activists had not been able to find anywhere except in *Le Monde,* Laurent Casanova replied, in *L'Humanité* of November 30, that there was no reason to call an extraordinary congress because events had only confirmed the decisions of the Fourteenth Congress, that there had been plenty of time to discuss these problems during that

11 The text of this letter was published in *L'Étincelle,* No. 2 (Jan. 1957). One of the more scandalous articles to appear in *L'Humanité* was André Stil's "Le Sourire de Budapest," written after the suppression of the Hungarian Revolution. As late as November 24, André Stil described Rákosi with pity as "the old militant who had spent fifteen years of his life in prison."

12 At the November 20–21, 1956 Central Committee meeting.

Congress, and that no "factional" activity could be tolerated. The principal result of this affair, which at the time seems to have worried the Politburo considerably, was that the PCF leaders increased their pressure on Picasso to obtain a retraction from him. When they failed to obtain one, they contented themselves with the publication, on the first page of *L'Humanité*, of a photograph showing Picasso side by side with Maurice Thorez, Jeannette Vermeersch. and Laurent Casanova, on the occasion of an opening of an exposition in Nice. The event seemed symbolically out of date.

Eventually the PCF was to emerge from this crisis weakened but less seriously shaken than the majority of the other parties in the West. To be sure, the Soviet model of socialism had been seriously compromised in the minds of the faithful. In practice, this was manifested particularly in a sizable loss by the CGT, which had, however, been careful not to take a position in favor of the Soviet intervention in Hungary, in the various elections of factory delegates in the course of the winter of 1956–57 and the following spring. Yet the PCF's cadres and *apparat* remained practically intact.

How is it to be explained that the PCF, like the KSČ (Czechoslovak Communist Party), was able to withstand this blow, or at least that its armor held so well? One may assume that the leaders of the two parties were strongly helped by their appeal to the traditional reflexes of the workers, expressed in this simple argument: Since the Poles and Hungarians are applauded by the bourgeoisie, they must be traitors to communism. The violent demonstrations that took place in France, as in the rest of the world, during the first days of November 1956, and during which there appeared traditional anti-Communist elements of the extreme fascist right, reinforced this type of argument.

Even inside the PCF itself, the fact that the theses of the opposition had been formulated principally by intellectuals, many of whom did not participate at all, or at least very little, in the concrete and unrewarding tasks of daily activism, also allowed the leaders to play on the old anti-intellectual worker reflexes and to represent the opposition as an expression of "petit bourgeois doubts," the result of class influence.

Finally the political context (particularly the Suez expedition) gave a certain probability in the eyes of the activists to the thesis of a vast international conspiracy, in which the Franco-British aggression in Egypt and the "counterrevolution" in Hungary were two episodes separated geographically but coordinated by imperialism at the summit.

It must be noted, however, that faced with the necessity of defending the PCF's cohesion against the consequences of the Hungarian uprising, the party proceeded to make some changes in its internal policies. Since the SFIO had showed itself particularly aggressive in its condemnation of the Soviet intervention in Hungary, propaganda for unity of action once again made way for vehement denunciation of the Social Democratic leaders. This exclusively verbal vehemence (for the PCF abstained from all violent or spectacular action, which, moreover, might have revealed the measure of its weakness and isolation) satisfied the old sectarian instinct of the activists. For if the latter were just barely able rationally to accept unity with the Socialists, they continued to feel a strong emotional antipathy for their "fraternal enemies."

Post-1956 Positions within the International
Communist Movement

During those last days of 1956 the international Communist movement was still a long way from Thorez', Novotný's, and Ulbricht's dream of reconstructing the monolithic unity of the Stalinist epoch around the Soviet center. The PCI Eighth Congress, meeting from December 8 to 14, 1956, undoubtedly represented a retreat from criticism of Stalin as compared to Togliatti's audacious statements in his interview with *Nuovi Argomenti* six months earlier.[13] But the fact that some discussions took place even in plenary sessions, the re-election to the Central Committee of men like Fausto Gullo, who had gone so far as to criticize Togliatti publicly in person, and the re-election of the leadership organs by secret vote were all factors that combined to give the PCI congress a very different appearance from the vast meeting of unanimity that the PCF had held at Le Havre. Moreover, on certain points Togliatti continued to express highly original positions. For example, a new step was made toward the concretization of the "Italian road to socialism," the definition of which was in accord with the claim for some degree of nationalization and structural reforms. In practice, this "Italian road" revealed itself more and more as peaceful and reformist, despite all references to classical doctrinaire

[13] See Chapter 6, footnote 27.

orthodoxy. Finally, without repeating his adventurous formulations on "polycentrism," Togliatti nevertheless renewed the attack by declaring: "There is neither a guiding state nor a guiding party."

For its part, the Chinese Communist Party published in *Jen-min Jih-pao* on December 29, 1956, at the conclusion of an enlarged session of its Politburo, a new article entitled "More on the Historical Experience of Proletarian Dictatorship."[14] This article did not clash head on with the Soviet interpretation, but it unmistakably tried to provide a Marxist explanation for the entire problem of Stalin and the events connected with de-Stalinization. Implicitly, the idea permeating the entire article was that neither the Twentieth Congress itself nor the famous Soviet resolution of June 30 had furnished such a Marxist analysis. Actually, except for some quotations from Engels and Lenin, the only theoretical references in the new Chinese text referred back to the preceding *Jen-min Jih-pao* article of April 5[15] devoted to the same subject. This silence indicated courteously—but it could not have been made more clear —that the entire literature that had in the meantime appeared on the subject was questionable or without value.

But the *Jen-min Jih-pao* article was extremely ambiguous in its contents. On the one hand, it spoke at length of Stalin's "merits" and even objected to the very term "Stalinism" and to the tendency to create a cleavage between Stalinists and non-Stalinists; on the other hand, it tried to deepen the analysis of the phenomenon of "contradictions among the people," that is, ultimately, the social and historical roots of "Stalin's errors." On the one side, the article polemicized, although in a moderate tone, against the speeches made by Tito and Kardelj on the Hungarian affair,[16] and more generally against the danger of "revisionism"; but, on the other side, it developed a vigorous criticism of "great-power chauvinism." On the one hand, it reaffrimed that "the Soviet Union during these past thirty-nine years has been the center of the international Communist movement"; but, on the other hand, it immediately added

14 "More on the Historical Experience of Proletarian Dictatorship," *Jen-min Jih-pao*, Dec. 29, 1956; *Current Background*, No. 433 (Jan. 2, 1957), pp. 1–20.
15 "On Historical Experience Concerning the Dictatorship of the Proletariat," *Jen-min Jih-pao*, Apr. 5, 1956; NCNA Peking, Apr. 5, 1956; *Current Background*, No. 383 (Apr. 9, 1956).
16 "Address by the Secretary General of the Yugoslav League of Communists, Tito, before a Meeting of League Members, Pula, November 11, 1956," *Borba*, Nov. 16, 1956; in Zinner, *National Communism and Popular Revolt*, *op. cit.*, pp. 516–541, and Kardelj's speech at the Federal People's Assembly, December 7, 1956.

that "this circumstance is not the result of anyone's arbitrary decision, but the natural outcome of historical conditions."[17] In short,
the Soviet Union had received its responsible position from history
and not from any particular abilities of its leaders. What is to be
read between the lines here is that if the Soviet leaders do not have
the necessary capacity to exercise their role of being the "center,"
it will be up to others to help them eventually to discharge their
responsibility.

Should the Communist parties maintain relations of equality among
themselves and reach common understanding and take concerted action
through genuine, and not nominal, exchange of views, their unity will
be strengthened. Conversely, if in their mutual relations, one party imposes its views upon others, or if the parties use the method of interference in each other's internal affairs instead of comradely suggestions
and criticism, their unity will be impaired.[18]

Here the allusion to the Chinese dissatisfaction with the manner
in which the Soviet Communist leaders carried out de-Stalinization
is transparent. Furthermore one of the principal theoretical theses
of the Twentieth Congress—that of the possibility of "peaceful
roads to socialism"—was indirectly contested in the *Jen-min Jih-pao*
article, which isolated five basic principles, over and beyond national particularities, as "universal truths of Marxism-Leninism
which are generally applicable."[19] But the second of these principles
was formulated as follows: "The proletariat, under the leadership
of the Communist party, rallying all the laboring people, takes
political power from the bourgeoisie by means of revolutionary
struggle."[20]

Without further pursuing the exegesis of this very long document,[21] the reader will note that it, in fact, confirms the résumé
given in the Chinese article of September 6, 1963 of the 1956
"errors" of which the Soviet Communist leaders were accused:
complete lack of a total analysis of Stalin, lack of self-criticism,
and lack of prior consultations with the other fraternal parties.

The ambiguity of the article in *Jen-min Jih-pao* explains how it
could be used in France in different ways. The PCF leadership
reproduced it not only as a pamphlet but also in its biweekly

---

[17] "More on the Historical Experience of Proletarian Dictatorship," *op. cit.*,
p. 16.
[18] *Ibid.*
[19] *Ibid.*, p. 5.
[20] *Ibid.*
[21] For analysis, see Fejtö, *op. cit.*, pp. 174–177.

France Nouvelle.[22] The party leadership could use the article to the extent that it contained an explicit criticism of Tito, to whose rehabilitation Thorez and his friends paid only lip service, and, by its condemnation of revisionism, furnished some support for the polemics then being directed by the PCF against the PCI, in connection with the theses of the latter's Eighth Congress.[23] One may even assume that, if Thorez was effectively allied with the "Molotov group" in the Soviet Union, the implicit criticism by the Chinese of the fashion in which Khrushchev had carried out de-Stalinization did not displease Thorez. Conversely, the CCP's refusal in fact to accept the "peaceful road" and its insistence on the duty of solidarity with the "oppressed nations" of Asia, Africa, and Latin America contradicted the essentials of the PCF's concrete policies.

Thus at the beginning of 1957 we can already see the development of one of the great contradictions that the Twentieth Congress produced in the PCF. This contradiction opposed the PCF's centralizing tendencies, in internal as well as international affairs, to its reformist, opportunist tendencies—in fact, even to its conservative policies in the internal French context. The PCF tried to escape this contradiction by avoiding in every possible way the transformation of its practice into theory. To translate its practice into theory would have meant for the PCF placing itself resolutely at the side of the PCI, but it meant at the same time taking the road toward the dissolution of centralism in party organization as well as in the international movement. To make a stand clearly, together with the CCP, in favor of a renaissance of a centralized structure of the international Communist movement would also have meant accepting the fundamental requirement of proletarian internationalism, which in fact underlay this claim by the Chinese —that is, to condemn a policy of prudent *attentisme* with respect to wars of national liberation of the Algerian type and also to replace simple campaigns of peace petitions by more violent forms of action.

Furthermore, the opposition was plagued by the same contradictions. Tempted to begin an all-out struggle against the PCF leadership, it very much counted on the help of foreign Communist parties to deal the decisive, finishing blow against the Thorez clique, and even the spectacular support which that clique had

22 *France Nouvelle*, Jan. 10, 1957.
23 See the articles by Roger Garaudy in *Cahiers du Communisme*, Vol. 33, No. 1 (Jan. 1957) and the supplement to *France Nouvelle*, Feb. 7, 1957.

received from Suslov at the PCF Fourteenth Congress had not entirely disabused them of such hopes.

For this reason the publications of the opposition, whose arguments were repeated in PCF cells and sections by oppositional activists, used systematically the arguments furnished them by Italian as well as by Chinese declarations in their struggle against the PCF leadership.

There are striking examples of this in the opposition bulletin *Étincelle,* whose issue No. 2 of January 1957 devoted three pages out of a total of ten to the PCI Eighth Congress, and whose issue No. 4 of April 1957 treated at length the "remarkable text" of the December 29, 1956 *Jen-min Jih-pao* article. In the first issue of the ephemeral *Étincelle-Tribune de Discussion,* born in May 1957 out of the fusion of the two bulletins, the principal article, entitled "La Chine nous donne une grande leçon," termed the *Jen-min Jih-pao* article and other articles published in Peking during the spring of 1957, in the framework of the "hundred flowers" campaign, "fundamental texts . . . that in our opinion herald a new stage in the history of communism."

In fact, despite the profound differences of opinion on fundamentals, the PCF leadership found itself in 1957 provisionally in the same camp as the Chinese Communist Party with regard to the exercise of pressure in favor of re-establishing a certain unity in the international Communist movement, which had been only incompletely and artificially pieced together, after the shock of the Twentieth Congress, by the approval of Soviet repression in Hungary. It is very possible that this offensive of "centralist elements," coordinated on a global scale, was initially synchronized with the action conducted at that time inside the Soviet Union by the "anti-party group" that rallied around Molotov to overthrow Khrushchev.

The establishment of this 1957 "centralist bloc," to which the PCF belonged, rested on an equivocal basis and on a great strategic maneuver by Mao Tse-tung. During the course of the journey Chou En-lai made in January 1957, which led him to Moscow, Warsaw, and Budapest, after stops in various capitals of Asia, he endorsed the Soviet intervention in Hungary; nevertheless he took care to insist that the Soviet Union had not acted "as a great power" but had merely done "its duty dictated by internationalism." In other words, because the Soviet action had not this time been decided unilaterally but had been the result of a consultation in which Peking believed it had played a decisive role, its nature was by this very fact changed. Chou En-lai exercised pressure on

Gomułka to have him accept this point of view, but without receiving more than partial satisfaction, in the form of an assurance by the Polish leader of his "support" for the Kádár government. On the other hand, however, in the communiqués that he signed in Moscow and Warsaw, Chou En-lai had inserted an endorsement of his conception that relations between socialist countries should be "founded on principles of respect for their sovereignty, and non-interference in their internal affairs, and equality and mutual benefit."[24] As a protagonist of the re-establishment of discipline around the Soviet "center," China thus hoped to earn Soviet gratitude, while as protector of the small socialist states against Soviet imperialist tendencies, it was entitled to gratitude from these states. Such a position was designed to permit China in effect to substitute itself for the Soviet Union in the leadership of the movement, because ultimately both the Soviet role of "center" and the independence and equality of other socialist countries would be recognized by all, thanks only to the intervention of China.

However, the Chinese conception of international centralism was tied to one of global strategy, in which the relationships between countries were "subordinated to a superior interest, that of a victory to be won in the general battle against imperialism" (1957 Moscow Declaration). The important thing was that this "superior interest" was no longer confounded with the interests of the Soviet state, and that thus one moved away considerably from Stalinist orthodoxy.

On internal affairs, too, China was at that time completely breaking away from Stalinist orthodoxy. With the campaign of the "hundred flowers" in full bloom, on February 27, 1957 Mao Tse-tung delivered before the Supreme State Conference his major speech "On the Correct Handling of Contradictions Among the People," which went much further with regard to rectification than did the Twentieth Congress.[25] Also, despite the tactical alliance that tied the PCF to the CCP in connection with the centralist campaign, the PCF leaders felt a certain reluctance to echo Peking's heterodox policy positions. The articles devoted by *Jen-min Jih-pao* to the rectification campaign in April 1957, though reproduced by *Pravda*, were printed only in brief excerpts in *L'Humanité* and

24 Sino-Polish declaration signed in Warsaw, January 16, 1957. See also Fejtö, *op. cit.*, pp. 177–178.

25 Delivered by Mao Tse-tung at a closed session of the Supreme State Conference in Peking, February 27, 1957, released by NCNA on June 18, 1957. For excerpts see Roderick MacFarquhar, *The Hundred Flowers Campaign and the Chinese Intellectuals* (New York: Praeger, 1960), pp. 265–273.

other PCF publications. Moreover, Yves Moreau, under the pretext of discussing China, essentially had to prove in *L'Humanité* of May 9, 1957 that in any case there was nothing to rectify in the PCF.

It was more with the Albanian, Bulgarian, Romanian, East German, and especially the Czechoslovak leaders that the leaders of the French Communist Party therefore felt themselves in full agreement.[26] At the same time that Chou En-lai became the traveling salesman of the Chinese version of centralism, the Czechoslovak Communist Party, which had just had consultations with the Hungarian, Romanian, and Bulgarian parties,[27] received a PCF delegation, thus opening a whole series of meetings between centralists of the more classically Stalinist orientation. The declaration published at the end of the conversations between the leaders of the French and the Czechoslovak parties stressed the perfect identity of views of the two parties.[28] The two found themselves in accord in condemning at the same time national communism, revisionism, and polycentrism, in their criticism of Yugoslavia, and in their insistence that the struggle against the cult of Stalin served as a pretext for attacks on the party and Marxism. Both parties seemed to favor the restitution of an institutional form of international Communist organization, to succeed the Third International and the Cominform. They endorsed Kádár but were reserved with respect to Gomułka's regime. (In this they deviated from the Chinese position, toward which they had veered by their common hostility to revisionism.)

Franco-Czechoslovak Affinities

That the attitude of the French and Czechoslovak Communist parties coincided perfectly in this respect, one may add, was not just an accidental phenomenon. Throughout their entire history, deep affinities may be found between the two parties, which may legitimately be attributed to "a certain parallelism of their historical destiny and their structure."[29]

26 Raymond Guyot had already revealed the actual direction of the PCF's line at the Central Committee meeting of November 20, 1956, where he attacked Tito "whose position [with regard to the Hungarian Revolution] is worthy of Horthy's," cited the Albanian Party of Labor as an example of firmness, and eulogized the KSČ.

27 In Budapest, January 1–4, 1957. (The Soviets were represented at these discussions.)

28 The text was published in *L'Humanité*, Jan. 22, 1957.

29 Fejtö, *Chine-URSS, la fin d'une hégémonie, op. cit.*, p. 188. For a parallel between these two parties, see *ibid.*, pp. 188–190. See also Fejtö, "Le parti communiste français et le polycentrisme," *Arguments*, No. 25-26, 1962.

At the beginning of this parallelism, which we have already mentioned, we must note that, like the PCF, the KSČ developed in an advanced industrial country (the only East European party to do so) and under conditions of legality (until the 1938 Munich agreement, as far as the KSČ was concerned). Both inherited from the pre–World War II period many activists, a working-class base, and solid roots in the trade unions. In France, as in Czechoslovakia, the Communist Party distrusted intellectuals, whom it confined to a marginal and decorative role, while its leadership was composed of *apparatchiki* of working-class origin, trained in the mold of the Comintern. The Gottwalds and Zápotockýs were the same type of men as the Thorezes and Frachons. They were all administrative types, which earned them Stalin's favor, and shared the same indifference, indeed suspicion, with regard to theoretical debates, for which they were personally little gifted. The entire *apparat*, strongly bureaucratized, was in both parties impregnated with this deliberate "practicism," and it strictly respected the hierarchical principle.

The two parties, authoritarian and centralized in their internal functioning, had nevertheless an essentially democratic and parliamentarian experience in concrete politics, at least until 1939. After 1935, both parties had crowned this experience by participating in a popular front, which intensified the opportunist, nationalist-democratic, and nonrevolutionary aspects of any policy designed to introduce the party over a long period into the framework of bourgeois institutions.

The parallels continued during the Resistance, which did not produce armed actions on a large scale, at least not in Bohemia, where the Communists appeared perhaps even more than in France as the principal coherent organized group from the beginning of the German attack against the Soviet Union. Immediately after Liberation the two parties engaged in moderate policies, in conformity with the Stalinist strategy of that era, and participated in coalition governments. But if the destinies of the French and Czechoslovak parties began to diverge with the outbreak of the Cold War, this divergence was by no means ideological. On the contrary, it was the result of their common and scrupulous respect for the partition of the world as decided by Stalin and his wartime allies. As long as this alliance retained a semblance of existence, the Czechoslovak and French parties based their policies on the hypothesis of taking power by parliamentary means. In preparation, they attempted to infiltrate cells into as many organs of power as possible, in order to seize control of a certain number of levers of command. While cooperating in the application of a program of democratic and social reforms, they opposed workers' tendencies that might hamper the rebuilding or further development of the national economy and thus participated in the administration of a state that by classic Marxist criteria, remained formally bourgeois, however great the nationalized sector in Czechoslovakia was.

But while the Yalta agreements tacitly authorized the Czechoslovak Communists to carry through to the end their plans to take power, they made this an illusory objective for the French Communists, to the extent that the PCF's infiltration in the police, the army, and the administration, so effective in Czechoslovakia, was systematically undone in France. Communists who had been placed in the important machinery of the state were quickly neutralized, marked, and eliminated (or corrupted) soon after the breakup of the coalition. But by rebelling against its exclusion from the government and by trying to duplicate the Prague coup in Paris, the PCF would have disobeyed Stalin and adopted the attitude that incurred for Tito the beginning of his troubles with the Kremlin. Thus the transformation of Czechoslovakia into a people's democracy, while the PCF again became a party of opposition, failed to jeopardize the affinity of the two parties since their different development stemmed ultimately from the same rigorous respect for international discipline.

Intense "internationalism" was another common trait of the two parties, in the sense that it represents in France, as in Czechoslovakia, an attachment to the Soviet Union strong enough to guarantee unconditional obedience. This sympathy for the Soviet Union was supported, in the case of the Czechs, by pan-Slav sentiment, very widespread in all strata of Czech society even long before World War II and reinforced by the Soviet attitude at the time of the Munich agreements, when the "Great Slav Brother" had been the only power to oppose, at least verbally, the breakup of the Czechoslovak state. In France, as we have seen at the beginning of this study, the "myth of the Soviet Union" had more complex origins and more ambiguous roots: In addition to the appeal of the emotional shock of the October Revolution it follows an old internationalist tradition, while at the same time it feeds on patriotic sentiments—the absence of antagonism between France and Russia and the tradition of Franco-Russian alliances against Germany.

Moreover, in both parties this internationalism apparently serves to camouflage a specific form of centralist and paternalist nationalism. In Czechoslovakia, where the unevenness of economic development underlined and accentuated the lack of national unity, Czech—or Prague—centralism tended to use Soviet support to contain and restrain Slovak national aspirations. (Thus in 1952, during the Slánský trial, Slovak "bourgeois nationalism" was indicted together with "cosmopolitan Zionism.") In France the PCF has often brandished its internationalism, which is closely tied to defending the superior interests of the Soviet Union, in order to control parties that had been placed under its aegis in the old French Colonial Empire and that smarted under a tutelage frequently used to subordinate struggles for national emancipation to the imperatives of policies conducted in the metropole. Thus in both cases centralist internationalism had the function of protection against centrifugal tendencies and thus corresponded to internal necessities. Both parties have a sort of "ultramontane" heritage that allows them to overcome internal tensions by transcending them and projecting them internationally. This affinity contributes largely toward ranging the two parties in the same camp, with very similar attitudes, in moments of great crisis when the international Communist movement has to make decisions.

After the seizure of power by the Czechoslovak Communists in 1948, following a "peaceful revolution" obviously of Soviet inspiration but executed by the KSČ alone with the help of a technique relying at the same time on a putsch and on classic methods of mass mobilization,[30] analogies between the two parties continued despite the difference in their situations. The PCF militants, disappointed by their successive failures in 1936 and 1945–1946, had to fall back entirely on their own party, which came to constitute for them a universe apart, with its own value system, its faith, its laws, its rites, its literature, its science, its art, its administration, and its hierarchy, leading a life independent from that of the rest of the nation. In Czechoslovakia the victorious Communist Party,

[30] According to Paul E. Zinner, *Communist Strategy and Tactics in Czechoslovakia 1918–1948* (New York: Praeger, 1963), Soviet assistance did not play an essential role in the 1948 takeover by the Czech Communists. "Much has been made of the assistance rendered by the Soviet Union to Communists in Czechoslovakia and elsewhere in Eastern Europe. . . . In Czechoslovakia, direct assistance was marginal. . . . To assert that the threat of Soviet intervention, possibly of a military character, decided the outcome of the clash in 1948 is *ex post facto* rationalization on the part of those who lost the struggle. There is no certainty that Russian troops would have moved across the border, and there were none inside the country. In any event, the intentions of the Soviet Union were never tested." (pp. 229–230.)

placed at the head of a country completely dependent on Soviet aid because of the brutal redirection of its trade pattern, and forced to orient its policies to serve Soviet interests, also came into a position of opposition to the rest of the population. As the opposition party in France and the nucleus of the state machinery in Czechoslovakia, the Communists found themselves driven into a sort of ghetto in both countries. The fanatical fervor with which both parties abandoned themselves to the cult of Stalin and to the pursuit of heresies was, in large part, a result of this situation. In both countries "vigilance" became a paroxysm bordering on hysteria during the last months preceding Stalin's death, with the Slánský-Clementis trial in Prague and the Marty-Tillon affair in Paris.

Thus it is not surprising to find in both countries, after the Twentieth Congress, the same reservations with regard to the debunking of Stalin, the same delay and repugnance with regard to resuming good relations with Titoist Yugoslavia, and the same protracted refusal to rehabilitate the domestic victims of Stalinism. This period was to last in Czechoslovakia until December 1962; and even then certain "juridical" rehabilitees like Slánský were only partially cleared, with reintegration into the party, symbolic because posthumous, still denied them. In France no rehabilitations occurred at all. Both parties persevered in their efforts to maintain the same leaders and the same leadership methods after de-Stalinization, by limiting themselves to the sacrifice of a few scapegoats. In this fashion, one after another, Lecoeur, Casanova, and Servin in France, and Barák in Czechoslovakia, men out of favor or in political disagreement with the leadership, were retroactively charged with all its mistakes.

Still, in their silent opposition to Khrushchev at the beginning of 1957, when the meeting between the French and Czechoslovak parties took place, these Stalinists still had a certain prudence. Thus the conversations that had been planned for more than a year between the PCF and the League of Communists of Yugoslavia, delayed by the tension created by the policy positions taken by Tito and Kardelj on Hungary, took place in the spring of 1957 in Belgrade. In the communiqué, published on March 28 at the end of the meeting, mention was made of the desirability of increased exchanges between the two parties, of instituting a spirit of "brotherly criticism, based on mutual respect," and of "criticism in principle, based on comradeship." The Franco-Yugoslav text, as though it had been inspired by the December 29, 1956 *Jen-min*

Jih-pao article, noted the three elements that needed to be taken into account in order to attain true cooperation: "the fundamental teachings of the great October Revolution, various experiences in the building of socialism, and the national peculiarities of each country."

To be sure, these contacts with Belgrade were a concession by the PCF leadership not only to Khrushchev but also to the impatience of its activists, who were surprised at the long postponement of the conference announced over a year before. But at the same time, one may ask whether this meeting, so long delayed, was not partly the result of the tension that existed at the time in the Soviet Union between Khrushchev and his opponents in the "antiparty group." Soviet publications and other testimony tell us, in fact,[31] that Malenkov, Molotov, Kaganovich, and their allies had greatly intensified their offensive against Khrushchev in the spring of 1957, and it seems at least probable that they tried to coordinate this with the support in the international Communist movement of which they had assured themselves.[32] It is therefore possible that by resuming relations with Tito just at that moment the leaders of the French Communist Party, in a maneuver coordinated with the "Molotovists" in the Soviet Union, simply wanted to deceive Khrushchev; on the other hand, one might suppose that Khrushchev had asked Tito to renounce his preconditions, which had slowed down the resumption of relations between the two parties.

The fact remains that this Belgrade communiqué had few practical effects on PCF policies. At the end of June 1957 a PCF delegation departed for Albania and at Tirana, together with the representatives of the Central Committee of the Albanian Party of Labor, signed a declaration, published on July 2, 1957, that is, on the eve of the announcement on the outcome of the June CPSU Central Committee plenum, which saw Khrushchev's triumph over the "antiparty group."

Curiously enough, in an entirely different context, in November 1960, on the occasion of his speech in the name of the French delegation at the conference of the eighty-one Communist parties in Moscow, Maurice Thorez recalled in great detail the existence and

31 With regard to the "antiparty group's" offensive in the spring of 1957, see the Italian Communist journalist Giuseppe Boffa, *Inside the Khrushchev Era* (New York: Marzani & Munsell, 1959), in particular, pp. 110–111.

32 At the time of the Twentieth Congress of the CPSU the press had emphasized that the only praise publicly accorded to Thorez at the actual sessions of the Congress was by Lazar Kaganovich, who referred to the Thorez articles on "pauperization," implicitly rejected in, for example, Mikoyan's speeches.

content of the declaration signed in 1957 at Tirana.[33] It confirmed the "universal validity" of Soviet experiences, called the CPSU "the rich common source of experience of all Communist and workers' parties," warmly approved the Soviet intervention in Hungary as conforming to the "principles of proletarian internationalism," and condemned "national communism" as well as "the idea that several centers of the international Communist movement could exist"—that is, polycentrism. When this declaration was signed, its wording corresponded perfectly to the position of the "centralist" bloc created by the alliance of the PCF and the Stalinists of Eastern Europe with the CCP. Tito, Togliatti, Gomułka, and above all Khrushchev had been the targets of the Franco-Albanian document. But in 1960 Thorez, referring to this text, which he did not repudiate, let it be understood that by then only the Chinese (and the Albanians) were guilty of "national communism" and of denying, in fact, its role as "center" of the movement to the Soviet Union. Yet at the same time his renewed reference to this document meant that the PCF would continue to distinguish itself from Yugoslav revisionists ("national Communists") and Italians ("polycentrists"), while at the same time finding itself in the same camp as those two in condemnation of the CCP.

To return to the summer of 1957, it really seems that the news of Khrushchev's triumph over the Molotov group threw the PCF leaders into considerable confusion. It was even said that Maurice Thorez had already prepared to send a congratulatory message to the victorious Molotov.[34] However, contrary to what had happened the day after the CPSU Twentieth Congress, the PCF lost no time in making a 180-degree turn and in approving without reservation the liquidation of the "factional," "conservative" group. Maurice Thorez himself—still according to the same sources of information, which speak of a message to a Molotov who had "come back" at the last moment—completely changed the indictment against Khrushchev that he had planned to read before the Central Committee into charges against the "antiparty group" and into a speech of allegiance to Khrushchev.

However that may be, from July 1957 on, it seems that the PCF,

---

[33] See *Problèmes du mouvement communiste internationale* (Paris: PCF, Jan. 1963), pp. 40–41. See also Maurice Thorez' speech in Alexander Dallin, ed., with Jonathan Harris and Grey Hodnett, *Diversity in International Communism* (New York and London: Columbia University Press, 1963), pp. 830–845, particularly pp. 840–841.

[34] Private information. See Fejtö, *Chine-U.R.S.S. la fin d'une hégémonie*, *op. cit.*, p. 190.

like the KSČ and its allies in Eastern Europe, lost hope of seeing
Khrushchev quickly overthrown by more traditional elements, and
it began to try to adapt itself to Khrushchevism and to develop,
after a fashion, in the Khrushchev framework, without giving up
its tenacious passive resistance to de-Stalinization within the PCF.
For years thereafter the PCF's policy was to give constant support
to Nikita Khrushchev and to follow the twists of Soviet policies all
the more painstakingly and firmly because Thorez, like Novotný
in Czechoslovakia, had received Khrushchev's support and his consent for the maintenance in France of an antirevisionist course, as
well as an *immobilisme* that might be called neo-Stalinist. In
return the PCF represented a certain support for Khrushchev because it was a guarantor of the Soviet party's orthodox internationalism and thus protected Moscow's flank from Chinese attacks
on this point.

It seems that the efforts made later in France by Laurent Casanova
and Marcel Servin, and in Czechoslovakia by Rudolf Barák, to
persuade the Soviets to withdraw their support from Thorez and
Novotný, on the grounds that these two had never really accepted
the consequences of the Twentieth Congress and were therefore
uncertain allies in the struggle with Peking, were definitely condemned to failure after the considerable services that the leaders
of the French and Czechoslovak parties rendered Khrushchev in
November 1960 by their speeches at the Moscow conference. After
January 15, 1961, in fact, Casanova and Servin were charged and
condemned by the PCF Central Committee; and in Czechoslovakia
Barák was gradually eliminated, first from the Ministry of the
Interior in June 1961 and then from the KSČ Politburo in February 1962, at which time he was also arrested.

The PCF and the Conference of 1957

When the international conference met in Moscow in November
1957, on the occasion of the Fortieth Anniversary of the October
Revolution, one month after the launching of the first Soviet sput-
nik on October 4, the situation in China had undergone profound
changes. The rectification campaign had disappointed Mao Tse-
tung, and it had been necessary to end the campaign suddenly
because it threatened to turn into a disaster. Abandoning the liberal line in domestic affairs in order to prepare the "great leap
forward," Mao Tse-tung, further pursuing the maneuver he had
begun at the opening of the year, made himself the chief of the

bloc of "antirevisionist centralists" in the international Communist movement. In this connection, it must be remembered that China had just scored important successes that had encouraged Mao to believe, in his famous formula, that from here on "the east wind would prevail over the west wind." Shortly after the Soviet success in intercontinental missiles, the Soviet government signed with Peking on October 15, 1957 an "accord on modern technology of national defense," whose existence became known only six years later,[35] and which created for China the opportunity of joining the ranks of nuclear powers. Not only did Mao celebrate in the most lyrical terms the changed power ratio between the socialist camp and the capitalist camp, but he also anticipated a change of power relationships inside the socialist camp. Soon China's superiority, already undeniable in the realm of numbers and in the domain of theory, was to rest on a military infrastructure.

We shall not go into details here about the discussions and the conclusion of the Moscow conference.[36] According to the Chinese article of September 6, 1963,[37] which is the principal source of information concerning the debates at the 1957 conference, the Chinese delegation presented and gained acceptance for a whole series of amendments to the draft initially presented by the CPSU leadership. The content of the statements there by the French delegates is not known, but there is every reason to believe that they found themselves frequently on the side of the Chinese, including the decison to make revisionism enemy number one and to condemn "opportunism"; yet it seems probable that on the so-called question of "peaceful transition to socialism" Thorez sided with Togliatti and Khrushchev to prevent the adoption of the Chinese theses, which were completely different from the PCF's and PCI's practice for many years.

The 1957 Moscow Declaration was only a compromise. Its verbal content remained ambiguous, for the same words did not have the same meaning for the different signatories, as became clear later when, after the polemics between the Soviet and Chinese parties

[35] "Statement by the Spokesman of the Chinese Government—A Comment on the Soviet Government Statement of August 3—August 15, 1963," *Peking Review*, Vol. VI, No. 33 (Aug. 16, 1963), pp. 7–19; in William E. Griffith, *The Sino-Soviet Rift* (Cambridge, Mass.: The M.I.T. Press, 1964), pp. 340–353.

[36] For the text of the 1957 Moscow Declaration, see G. F. Hudson, Richard Lowenthal, and Roderick MacFarquhar, *The Sino-Soviet Dispute* (New York: Praeger, 1961), pp. 46–56.

[37] "The Origin and Development of the Differences Between the CPSU Leadership and Ourselves," *op. cit.*

had become public, each began to accuse the other of being unfaithful to the Moscow Declaration.

There can hardly be any doubt, for example, that when the PCF endorsed the condemnation of "opportunist trends," it thought of Tito, Gomułka, and Togliatti, while the Chinese—and the Italians too—could very well be thinking of the PCF's Algerian policy. Similarly, the concept of the Soviet Union as the "center" of the international Communist movement, reaffirmed by the 1957 Moscow Declaration, which made the Soviet Union the "head" of the socialist camp, had a different meaning for Mao than that which Thorez and other ex-Stalinists attributed to it.

If one tries to draw up a balance sheet of the mutual concessions that led to the final text, the compromise appears to be, roughly speaking, favorable to the CCP. The Moscow Declaration was signed by the twelve Communist parties in power, Yugoslavia being excluded—which showed the failure of Khrushchev's patient efforts to reintegrate Yugoslavia into the "socialist camp," a failure hardly camouflaged by the presence of the Yugoslav signature at the bottom of the "Peace Manifesto" side by side with the signatures of the parties of the capitalist countries. But, above all, as the Chinese article of September 6, 1963 was to stress, Mao derived his principal satisfaction from the fact that "the conference . . . rejected and rectified . . . on an important range of questions of principle the erroneous views of the Twentieth Congress." But—and the author apologizes for quoting himself—

by adopting theses which modified the decisions of the Twentieth Congress, which had been defended by the Soviets, the meeting implicitly established an all-party conference, where the influence of China was as an authority considerably superior to the CPSU, and as the only valid authority for the movement as a whole.[38]

If the CPSU, the "center" and "head" of the movement, was bound to accept the decisions of the international conference, then it was enough for China to acquire a majority in the conference in order to exercise in fact the leadership of the entire movement.

Thus the November 1957 Declaration already contained the germ of the whole subsequent Sino-Soviet conflict, but the contradictory positions were still sometimes juxtaposed and sometimes camouflaged in ambiguous formulations. Yet in appearance the year that had begun with a situation of crisis and division ended with a striking manifestation of cohesion and unity of the international Communist movement.

[38] Fejtö, *Chine-URSS, op. cit.,* p. 207.

CHAPTER EIGHT

DEVELOPMENTS WITHIN FRANCE IN 1958: A YEAR OF DEFEATS

Beginning in 1958, the fragile façade of unanimity began to show dangerous cracks. For the French Communists it was a year of great defeats, which seem to have contributed to the diminution of the PCF's international role. The party's weakness in French internal politics accentuated its subjection to the Soviet Union, and this subjection in turn influenced it to tolerate in fact the accession of de Gaulle to power and to fight him only with words.

On the one hand, the PCF paid the price for its long opportunism in the Algerian affair. This opportunism had been a source of discontent for the partisans of "French Algeria," for whom the PCF, despite all its precautions, remained the accomplice of the enemies of France, and also for the partisans of an independent Algeria, who did not understand the PCF's timid attitude or its respect for the most inoffensive legal actions, such as petitions, delegations, or symbolic demonstrations of limited duration. In a document disseminated at the beginning of 1958, following in the wake of articles that appeared in the official organ of the FLN, *El Moudjahid,* on the same subject and that had been partially reprinted by the leftist weekly *France-Observateur,*[1] the French Federation of the FLN severely criticized the PCF's attitude on Algeria and its theoretical justification and derided its tactical zigzags.[2] Sensi-

---

[1] *France-Observateur,* Dec. 26, 1957.

[2] "Bulletin d'Information No. 4" (entitled "Le P.C.F. et la révolution algérienne"), by the Fédération de France du F.L.N., dated February 15, 1958, was reprinted almost *in toto* by *La voie communiste,* No. 3, Apr.–May 1958. Mohammed Harbi was mainly responsible for the text (according to private information). A few years later, in behalf of the FLN, which had become the sole and official party of Algeria, he signed on October 19, 1964 a joint communiqué with the PCF which declared that "the Algerian delegation have expressed their recognition of the support shown to Algeria by the PCF during the war of liberation."

tive to such criticism, a certain number of Communist activists participated in the formation of a network giving direct aid to the Federation of France of the FLN. Without going that far, numerous sympathizers turned away from the PCF, particularly students, who were doubly sensitive because of the danger of having to go to Algeria for military service, and intellectuals, who were indignant over the more and more systematic use of torture by French troops in Algeria. This current benefited organizations of the left, such as the UGS (Union de la Gauche Socialiste), which included quite disparate elements: leftist Christians, neutralists, Socialist dissidents, ex-Trotskyites, and defectors from the PCF. It also aided the activity of a certain number of committees, quite active despite their limited number of followers but usually with only an ephemeral existence.

The PCF leadership seemed to be suffering from myopia. When on March 13 the Paris police demonstrated before the National Assembly shouting slogans of the "protofascist" extreme right, and when the preparation of a coup against the Fourth Republic was already anticipated and commented on by all observers, the Communist press obstinately insisted that the signature on a petition against the installation of launching pads for missiles in France must take first priority over all other objectives. In *L'Humanité* of March 14, Laurent Casanova deplored the meagerness of the results obtained but drew no conclusions from it! "The decisions of the Central Committee," wrote Casanova, "are law for the party, a law that everyone must apply."[3] To be sure, this priority corresponded, as always, to that of Soviet diplomacy, but the proposed campaign appeared at that moment so completely untimely and so completely unrelated to French reality that the activists lost interest in it.

When the "ultras" and the army took power in Algeria on May 13, 1958, the PCF tried to profit from the disturbance created by the fear of a landing of parachutists in France to conclude an alliance with the defenders of the Fourth Republic. In its concern to show its good will, it voted for special powers to Pflimlin's MRP (Mouvement Républicain Populaire) government and for a law instituting a state of emergency which primarily forbade street demonstrations.

The slogans running contrary to the real concerns of the masses,

---

[3] In Paris, party members were expelled just for maintaining, *at party meetings,* that the campaign against the war in Algeria should take precedence over "the campaign against launching sites" (private information).

the routine noises emanating from PCF propaganda texts, larded with slogans of an anesthetizing optimism ("unity is on the march," "victory of popular action," and so forth, formulas systematically employed on the occasion of relatively insignificant and local events), the memory of past failures, and the malaise that remained in spite of everything in the wake of the Twentieth Congress and the Hungarian repression—all these factors had contributed toward softening the power of resistance of the PCF to a violent offensive and toward weakening the impact of its slogans on its customary clientele. The indecision of the PCF after May 13, in arranging for demonstrations and then calling them off at the last moment in order to reassure its new allies in the Pflimlin government, disconcerted both activists and sympathizers. These groups were equally bewildered to see the PCF limit itself to the defense of the Fourth Republic, which it had attacked so violently for many years, and in practice to act the same as the parties against which it had ceaselessly struggled, at the very moment when these parties and the parliamentary regime itself were completely discredited among the majority of the population.

On May 28, 1958 the PCF succeeded in mobilizing its forces in Paris for a demonstration, in which the SFIO participated. But all the spectators of the procession agreed that it resembled a funeral. On June 1, the day of General de Gaulle's investiture, only small groups of PCF activists, pushed around by the police, often "armed" with simple bouquets of flowers which they wanted to deposit symbolically on the statue of the Republic, provided an "honor guard" in the streets of Paris. Meanwhile, the SFIO had agreed to participate in de Gaulle's government, and the PCF's hopes of attaining at least unity of action with the Socialists disintegrated again, just as they had after the electoral "victory" of January 2, 1956.

Handicapped by the defeat, a defeat without a real battle, badly served by the excesses of a propaganda that had likened de Gaulle to fascism and that were to be refuted by the first few months of the Gaullist government, and incapable of presenting an alternative to those who already vaguely saw in de Gaulle the only man capable of arriving eventually at a peaceful solution of the Algerian problem, the PCF leadership began its campaign for the constitutional referendum of September 28 under very unfavorable conditions. The negative vote requested by the Communists not only seemed destined to entail, if it should be in the majority, the re-establishment of the old constitution but also seemed to be a show of solidarity with the totality of the regime that had just failed and with men and political moves that recent years had completely discredited. Moreover, the PCF could not permit itself to go beyond certain limits in its opposition to de Gaulle, because the General's declared desire, even before his return to power, to practice a more independent foreign policy and to move a certain distance away from the United States had evoked a favorable response from the Soviets. (Of the Soviet ambassador in Paris, Vinogradov, it was often said that he was a fervent "Gaullist.")

In fact, the referendum, which resulted in close to 80 per cent of the votes for the Gaullist Constitution, was a disaster for the PCF. The "no" vote that had been advocated, along with the Communists, by a group of the Radicals, the SFIO dissidents of the *"Parti socialiste autonome,"* and the *Union des forces démocratiques* (a sort of electoral cartel in which, side by side with the UGS and the autonomous Socialists, there were personalities like Pierre Mendès-France and François Mitterrand) received one million votes less than the Communist Party had obtained by itself in January 1956. The legislative elections of November 23 and 30, 1958 confirmed the extent of the catastrophe. The number of Communist votes dropped from 5,532,000 in 1956 (25.7 per cent of the total vote) to 3,882,000 in the first poll in 1958 (18.9 per cent). Thus in less than three years the PCF had lost 1,650,000 votes, or 30 per cent of its voters. The percentage of Communist votes was barely higher than that in 1936 for the whole of the country, but it was clearly less in certain industrial citadels of the PCF. The electoral law amplified the effects of this loss of votes. The Communists retained no more than 10 seats as compared with 145 in 1956. It should be noted that in the same year, on May 25, 1958, the PCI gained close to 600,000 votes in the legislative elections and somewhat bettered its percentage, attaining with 22.7 per cent of the votes cast a result superior to all previous elections.

The absence of a display of energy by PCF leaders against the preparations for a coup in Algiers, their pusillanimous attitude during the time between this coup and de Gaulle's coming to power, the rather unexciting and essentially conservative character of the Communist slogans chosen to carry on a campaign against de Gaulle which the PCF clearly did not expect to win, the feeling of total ineffectiveness of the sacrifices made to gain possible allies, who, nevertheless, continued to slip away, and, finally, the shock experienced as a result of the extensive defeat and the bitter rancor felt by the most devoted and disciplined activists toward a nation that had massively rallied to Gaullism—all these factors contributed to creating a new situation of internal crisis in the PCF.

The opposition had split in 1957: the old guiding spirits of *Étincelle* had decided, after the elimination of the Molotov group in the Soviet Union, to suspend their "factional" activity, which in their opinion might be harmful to the democratization and de-Stalinization of the PCF, now inevitable because the Soviet allies and protectors of the Thorez leading group had been beaten in Moscow.[4] In January 1958 a new opposition bulletin, *La voie communiste*, was founded by those in the amalgamated *Étincelle-Tribune de Discussion* group who did not share the optimism of the founders of *Étincelle* concerning the automatic consequences of the Moscow events for the PCF. Moreover, three months later, the intellectuals who had formed the nucleus of *Étincelle* enlarged it by several people, including non-Communist fellow travelers, to publish a review of essentially theoretical orientation, *Voies Nouvelles*, whose first issue appeared in April 1958, with articles by the philosophers Henri Lefebvre, Jean-T. Desanti, Maurice Caveing, Jean-Pierre Vernant, and the writer François Jourdain. Other well-known Communist intellectuals, economists, and historians contributed to later issues under transparent pseudonyms, side by side with non-Communist personalities such as Jean-Paul Sartre or university professors J. J. Mayoux and Louis Gernet. The PCF leadership reacted vigorously against this new wave of organized opposition, all the more dangerous because in the spring of 1958 there was a risk that it would merge with spontaneous manifestations of bad humor, that is, "sectarianism," particularly against the abstentions in favor of the Socialists in regional elections, and the tendency in the CGT unions to subordinate all large-scale actions, even those purely for higher wages, to the attainment of the unity "at the summit" between the two centers. In his report to the Central Committee, published on April 19 in *L'Humanité*, Marcel Servin expressed the concern of the PCF leadership:

Some comrades approach this audacious policy of unity gingerly . . . and the "buts" accumulate in such numbers that all concrete application of the line becomes impossible.

Furthermore, numerous expulsions from the PCF were carried out in May–June 1958, of which some were "definitive" and others "temporary." Particularly affected was the philosophy circle of the Union of Communist Students, which during the May crisis had

4 *L'Étincelle-Tribune de discussion*, No. 18, July 1957 (special issue).

disseminated a text written jointly with the Socialist and UGS students against voting for special powers for the Pflimlin government. The philosopher Henri Lefebvre, the physicians Michel Sapir, Bernard Abramovitsch, and Angelergues, and five students of the Communist cell of the *Antony Résidence Universitaire* fell victim to this wave of expulsions. In Montreuil, Jacques Duclos's fief in the working-class suburbs of Paris, the leaders of the Communist section and of the local metallurgical union were censured and sent back to the "base."[5]

After the failure in the referendum the dissatisfaction of the activists expressed itself particularly in the resolution of the "Sorbonne-Lettres" cell of the University of Paris, dated October 10, 1958. This resolution was strongly critical of the responsibility of the PCF leadership for the defeat and analyzed at length the "very grave errors" committed by the PCF leadership in its Algerian policies, its conception of the policy of unity, its resistance to a "genuine Marxist analysis of the French situation," and its shirking of the problem of "French roads to socialism," which "had never been seriously taken up." Finally, the "Sorbonne-Lettres" cell accused the PCF leadership of rejecting all criticism against it by declaring it to be inspired by the "enemy."[6] The document had double importance: on the one hand, it was a resolution adopted by a regular organ of the party; and the fact that the members of this cell were essentially professors, the most eminent Communist specialists in various disciplines, gave this basic organization a particular weight. On the other hand, the resolution of the "Sorbonne-Lettres" formulated a set of criticisms that might unite the "rightist" (or "revisionist") and "leftist" oppositions against the PCF leadership. Widely known within and outside the party, the declaration of the "Sorbonne-Lettres" could have profoundly influenced the entire section of the Fifth Arrondissement of Paris, where most of the university members of the PCF were to be found. Moreover, persistent rumors circulated[7] according to which certain members of the Cen-

5 See *La voie communiste*, No. 5, July 1958, and *Le Communiste*, No. 45, June 1958. The principal animating spirits of the Montreuil-oriented opposition of the Metal Unions, Pierre Folgalvez and Simon Blumenthal, were ultimately to be expelled from the PCF. They later emerged as leaders of the "Amicale des ancients membres du PCF," set up by *Unir*, and as editors of *Le débat communiste* and *La voie communiste*.

6 The full text of this resolution appeared in a special supplement to *Voies Nouvelles*, Nov. 1958.

7 See especially the editorials "Les difficultés de la Direction du PCF," *Le Communiste*, No. 41, Feb. 1958, pp. 3–4; "Les dangers du bonapartisme," *ibid.*, No. 42, Mar. 1958, p. 4; "Se préparer pour la bataille due XV° Congrès," *ibid.*,

tral Committee, like Laurent Casanova, Waldeck Rocket, Jean Pronteau, and some others, were not unhappy to see a hostile atti- tude toward the principal leadership group develop in university circles. The inferred intention of these Central Committee mem- bers, who incidentally proceeded very cautiously, was to conjure up a "division" in the party in order to offer themselves as arbiters and to stress the necessity of properly managing the university circles, whose importance was great from the viewpoint of a unitary leftist coalition. The PCF therefore proceeded with surprising moderation in taking steps against the "Sorbonne-Lettres" cell. Its moves extended over several weeks and ended with simple "suspensions" and retractions on the part of militants of the section committee of the Fifth Arrondissement.

The resolution of the "Sorbonne-Lettres" incident was followed by a letter from Professor Marcel Prenant of the Faculty of Science, former member of the Central Committee, who had been expelled from it for having expressed reservations on Lysenko's theories on biology in the midst of the Zhdanov period, when the duty of dis- cipline and solidarity with regard to the Soviet Union also included a "proletarian science," which could only be Soviet science. Vio- lently attacked by Maurice Thorez, who called him a "crybaby" without naming him specifically, Prenant, whose arguments were quite similar to those of "Sorbonne-Lettres," did not have to suffer censure, for he did not renew his party card in 1959.

It is interesting to note where Maurice Thorez saw the principal danger at that time. At the meeting of the Central Committee at Ivry on October 4, 1958 he stressed that

it is important not to make concessions to those who have tried and will try again to criticize us from the left, for example in connection with our vote of March 12, 1956.

Without limiting himself to the already classic justification of the PCF's prudent policies on the subject of Algeria, Maurice Thorez blamed the FLN for being partially responsible for the PCF's elec- toral defeat. (At the end of August 1958 the FLN Federation of France had launched a series of military operations on metropolitan territory.) Thorez declared:

The methods used by the FLN in France have not served the just cause of the Algerian people; we must say this quite clearly. That cause always

---

No. 43, Apr. 1958; and "Quatre questions à la Direction," *La voie communiste,* No. 3, Apr.–May 1958, p. 8, which was already taking notice of the hint of change among the leadership of the party.

had the benefit of the understanding and political support of the French revolutionary workers. . . . If the FLN thinks it can mobilize public opinion, it is wrong. It will direct that opinion against itself. Far from gaining sympathies, it loses them. Such methods provide easy ammunition against the Algerians. Moreover—these things must be said to the Central Committee—such methods open the door to all types of provocations against us.[8]

Maurice Thorez' reasoning was entirely typical of the PCF's paternalistic opportunism, in which the Algerians saw evidence of the penetration of colonialism into the French workers' movement. Addressing the Algerians, Maurice Thorez seemed to admit that they could have no objective other than to "gain sympathies" in French opinion. He counseled them to renounce their military tactics so as not to offer their flank to provocations against the PCF. He clearly placed the electoral interests of his party in France over the needs of the war of liberation of the Algerian people. It is important to stress this fact, for the PCF has rarely so candidly affirmed the concept of a one-way proletarian internationalism, which it followed in its relations with the "colonies": In their struggle for national emancipation, Communists or national movements of the countries of the old Empire had to subordinate their tactics to the requirements of domestic politics at home. To safeguard a certain number of seats in the French Parliament took precedence over the war of the Algerians for their independence. This "Eurocentrism" (or "great-power chauvinism") was in flagrant contrast to the Chinese version of proletarian internationalism, which had not yet been systematically developed but which, on the contrary, tended to consider that the principal immediate task for Communists in capitalist countries was to support national and colonial revolutions in the Third World, and to subordinate everything to their success.

The frankly opportunist orientation chosen by the PCF Secretary-General emerged even more clearly from his speech on the adoption of the new Constitution, one week after the referendum:

. . . We shall take into account the fact that it exists. We will not let ourselves be turned away from our theses of 1946, confirmed ten years later by our Fourteenth Congress, on the possibility of peaceful roads toward socialism, or on the role that a true parliament can play, a true expression of popular sovereignty, based on the masses. . . . We believe in our theses on the eventual peaceful transition to socialism. And on this demo-

8 "Discours de clôture de Maurice Thorez, Session du Comité Central du PCF, Ivry, 3 et 4 octobre 1958," supplement to *Cahiers du Communisme*, No. 11 (Nov. 1958), p. 30.

cratic terrain we are ready to meet with all republicans who do not share our opinions on the necessity and certain coming of socialism in France, but who understand and admit that we have the legitimate ambition to lead the working class and the people of our country one day to this goal.[9]

Thus Thorez did not even limit himself to a profession of faith in the possibility of "peaceful transition"; he implored the bourgeois "republicans" to understand that in the immediate future this "peaceful transition" was nothing but a "legitimate ambition," without any actuality and relegated to an entirely indeterminate "one day." No more diametrically opposite position to the theses defended by Mao Tse-tung and the Chinese delegation in November 1957 at the Moscow Conference could have been taken.

While the PCF was primarily occupied with the deterioration of the political situation in France, clouds began to gather over the international Communist movement. The publication of the program of the League of Yugoslav Communists, at the April 22–26, 1958 Ljubljana Congress, gave the signal for a new and extremely violent offensive against "Yugoslav revisionism." Launched by Peking, this second anti-Titoist campaign, enthusiastically welcomed in Tirana and Sofia, was taken up by Khrushchev in his turn, although less sharply, when he proclaimed at the Seventh Congress of the Bulgarian Communist Party in June 1958 that it had been correct to adopt the first resolution of the Cominform in 1948 "because it corresponded to the interests of the revolutionary movement" and accused Yugoslavia of having made of its embassy in Budapest the seat and asylum of the Imre Nagy group of "traitors and defeatists" during the autumn of 1956. Imre Nagy, incidentally, was executed on June 16, 1958 with three of his comrades after a trial behind closed doors, whose circumstances have remained partially a mystery.[10] The PCF was unusually discreet when announcing the news of the execution of Nagy, which seemed very inopportune within the context of the internal French policy of that time. L'Humanité merely reproduced, without comment, the official communiqués from Budapest. The official Communist weekly, France Nouvelle, published an anonymous article approving the executions. Maurice Thorez himself was laconic. In his report to the PCF National Conference at Montreuil on July 17, 1958, he only

9 Ibid. p. 32.
10 With regard to Imre Nagy, see Tibor Meray, Imre Nagy, l'homme trahi (Paris: Julliard, Collection "Temps Modernes," 1960), and Documents of the "Tribune Libre," La vérité sur l'affaire Nagy (Paris: Plon, 1958). See also Albert Camus's preface and François Fejtö's conclusion in ibid.

touched on the trial in connection with questions asked by certain non-Communists in antifascist committees:

In this respect our position is clear: We unreservedly approve the acts in the defense of proletarian democracy against those who plotted for its destruction.

He added immediately:

It is true, however, that not everybody in the committees shares our view.[11]

From this it might be concluded that in Thorez' view, the less talk about the matter the better. On the other hand, Thorez seemed to consider the resumption of the anti-Yugoslav campaign almost as a personal triumph:

We can therefore state that the evaluations formulated at our Fourteenth Congress have been confirmed. . . . We decided to establish new relations with the Communist organization of Yugoslavia in conformity with the interests of the international workers' movement and of peace. But we have continued to think that the basis of the judgment of 1948 was correct, and the facts confirm this view.[12]

In other words, it was Thorez who had been clairvoyant, rather than Khrushchev.

Although everyone seemed to agree in the Communist movement (except for the noticeable reticence on the part of the Poles and the Italians) on attacking Tito, the new Chinese policy of the "great leap forward," officially launched on May 5, 1958 by the report of Liu Shao-ch'i before the second session of the CCP Eighth Congress, was received in Moscow without enthusiasm. Moreover, it seemed all the more heterodox since it was accompanied by the rediscovery of the theory of the "permanent revolution," a formula dear to the Trotskyites and therefore hated by the Stalinists. However, it does not seem that in this first period of China's forced march "toward communism" the PCF press was as hostile as the Soviet press with respect to news from Peking. *L'Humanité* mentioned China relatively little and always in very positive terms.

The August 1958 Peking meeting between Mao and Khrushchev did not end the Sino-Soviet tension. Moscow gave only moral support to China in the latter's attempt to conquer by force the islands of Quemoy and Matsu, in the course of the summer of 1958.

---

11 Maurice Thorez, *Union et action de tous le républicains pour le "Non" au référendum-plébiscite* (Report on the National Conference of the PCF, Montreuil, July 17–18, 1958), pamphlet published by the PCF, p. 23.

12 *Ibid.*, p. 27.

In part as a reply to being abandoned in this fashion, Mao in September turned the entire Chinese economy onto the road of integralist militarization (people's communes of giant size and small open-hearth furnaces in the villages). The silence observed at the time by the Soviet press with respect to these developments revealed the dissatisfaction that Soviet officials no longer concealed in private conversations. The PCF press became more and more laconic and less and less laudatory about China: It devoted itself essentially to routine proclamations of solidarity in the Quemoy and Matsu affair without the slightest concrete manifestation of such solidarity.

CHAPTER NINE

THE PCF FIFTEENTH CONGRESS AND ALGERIAN DEVELOPMENTS

1959

Originally planned for the summer of 1958 and twice postponed as a result of disturbing developments in internal French politics, the PCF Fifteenth Congress was held at Ivry from June 24 to 28, 1959. Compared with the period immediately following the 1958 double electoral defeat, the atmosphere among the activists had become somewhat more serene and thus more favorable to the leadership. The municipal elections of March 8 and 15 had been marked by a very definite recovery of the Communist vote, particularly in urban centers and industrial regions, and between the two elections by the conclusion of a certain number of electoral alliances with the SFIO. The PCF's electoral resurgence can be explained primarily by the unpopularity of the anti-inflationist economic measures taken by the French government. The electoral alliances of the "new popular front" in certain towns, despite the watchful eyes of the SFIO leadership, had only limited objectives and were not supported everywhere by the voters. At least, however, the new tension in the relationship between Communists and Socialists that had followed the participation of Guy Mollet and several SFIO ministers in de Gaulle's government had begun to abate.

The discussion preparatory to the congress was much duller than the one that had preceded the congress at Le Havre. Since then, expulsions and resignations had removed from the PCF a great number of opposition elements or even of simple critics. The agitation among the intellectuals over the affair of the cell "Sorbonne-Lettres" had died quickly. The theses presented by the Central Committee to the Fifteenth Congress contained some concessions to the positions of the PCI, with whom the PCF on December 23, 1958 had signed a joint declaration, admitting the positive character in certain respects of structural reforms (nationalization, democratic control of planning, and so on) in the perspective of the struggle for socialism by "democratic development," and envisaging, moreover, the development of common policies by Western Communist parties. (The traditional reference to the sole "center" of the international Communist movement was notably absent from the French-Italian communiqué.)

This rapprochement with the "revisionist" Italians corresponded, without doubt, to the necessity to establish vis-à-vis the Chinese a certain common front by partisans of the "peaceful road to socialism" and "peaceful coexistence," since the conflict that had broken out on the first of these two points in November 1957 in Moscow had spread to the second in 1958, during the international crises in the Middle East and Formosa.

However, the last weeks of 1958 and the first months of 1959 had seen a détente in Sino-Soviet relations. The CPSU Twenty-First Congress (January 27 to February 5, 1959), principally devoted to the adoption of the Soviet Seven-Year Plan, seemed politically a retreat from the 1956 Twentieth Congress. It had much more to say about the condemnation of "Yugoslav revisionism" than about de-Stalinization; Khrushchev, in an allusive and veiled form, had barely permitted himself some criticism of the Chinese "great leap forward," and Chou En-lai had left Moscow with a loan of $1,250 million granted to China by the February 7 Sino-Soviet economic cooperation treaty.

This temporary détente, however, was already much compromised when the PCF met for its congress. (On June 20, 1959 the Soviets announced in Peking that they would not furnish to China the atomic assistance promised two years earlier.) In a parallel fashion, the relations between East and West, after the crisis that Khrushchev had provoked in November 1958 by his ultimatum on West Berlin, seemed again to be improving. The six-month delay had passed, his threat of signing a separate peace with East Germany had not been carried out, and peaceful coexistence again became the great theme of the day.

The "theses" of the PCF Fifteenth Congress, which reproduced the draft presented by the Central Committee without important modifications, had various internal contradictions: The affirmation of the "peaceful road," all the more vigorous because the political situation in France seemed to make the "peaceful road to socialism" in France a faraway, utopian hypothesis, forced the PCF to take up again certain of the reformist formulas dear to the PCI. Thus a program of constitutional reforms, of nationalizations, and of control of economic life by the workers was sketched out. Quite clearly inspired by Togliatti's "Italian road," Point 30 read:

The struggle for socialism thus is located within the perspectives of the struggle for democracy and its continual progress, the struggle to give a concrete answer to the great questions which events pose to France.

All this sounded very "Italian." Yet the PCF did not hesitate, in Point 9 of the same theses, to condemn "the falseness of neo-capitalist and revisionist theories," to deny the "pretended modifications in the nature of capitalism," and to reaffirm "the trend toward pauperization of the working class."

If in the circumstances of the summer of 1959 Maurice Thorez resigned himself to revive certain revisionist formulations, he was nevertheless not at all disposed to the slightest self-criticism and even less to yield his place to those who in France could have claimed to have anticipated him. On the contrary, in his report to the congress, the PCF Secretary-General declared:

. . . The revisionists have been defeated along the whole front. Honest Communists who had let themselves be influenced by them have come back to the proper positions. A small handful of enemies of the party, corrupt and demoralized men, have left our organization. By cleansing itself of such foreign and hostile elements, the party has strengthened itself.[1]

In any event, due to the party's default, Maurice Thorez emerged strengthened from the Fifteenth Congress. Once again Suslov had come to support him with his presence. He delivered a message of greeting remarkable for its emptiness, contenting himself with repeating the principal decisions of the CPSU Twenty-First Congress and the broad Soviet policy lines, and characterized by its diplomatic treatment of Gaullism. One of the rare members of the Central Committee known for his opposition to Maurice Thorez' line, André Pierrard, was expelled from that body. Marcel Servin limited himself to timid criticism of the inability of the party to carry out concrete moves: "One must speak and act, and not just say in general what should be done." These words were to be

[1] For texts concerning the Fifteenth Congress of the PCF and its preparation, see "Tribune de discussion," *L'Humanité*, May 15, 1959, and following issues. The most interesting letters are those of the "Marat" cell of the d'Orsay section (Seine-et-Oise) and the "Henri Martin" cell of Tarascon (Bouches du Rhône) which appeared in the issues of May 19 and 25 respectively. These are the only letters that neither approve nor echo the authorized interpretation of the official theses. *L'Humanité* published Thorez' report on June 25, the other speeches between June 26 and 29, and the final version of the theses on July 4.

quoted against him later, but at the time the cohesion of the leadership group seemed undeniable.

De Gaulle's declaration of September 16, 1959 recognizing the principle of self-determination for Algeria caused considerable trouble for the PCF Politburo. The next day, September 17, the Politburo condemned what it considered a simple maneuver on the part of the General to shift onto the FLN the responsibility for the conduct of the war. Maurice Thorez, who had been on vacation in Moscow when the Politburo declaration was published, reiterated this viewpoint shortly after his return in a speech made at Martinet before the miners of Gard: "De Gaulle's recent declaration takes us still further away from a solution of the Algerian problem. Under these conditions the promise of self-determination is only a maneuver."[2]

A few days later, Khrushchev, pursuing vis-à-vis France his great offensive of smiles, whose most recent expression had been the conversations at Camp David with Eisenhower in mid-September, gave a positive evaluation of de Gaulle's declaration on self-determination. On October 23 the President of the French Republic announced that Nikita Khrushchev had been invited to visit Paris. Thereupon, on October 26, L'Humanité published an editorial by Maurice Thorez calling de Gaulle's recognition "of the right of the Algerian people to self-determination" a "fact of cardinal importance."

Before the PCF Central Committee met on November 2–3, 1959 at Choisy-le-Roi, Maurice Thorez did not hesitate to forget his own declarations at Martinet and to accuse his colleagues in the Politburo of having displayed political blindness in his absence.

After my return, I had formulated some observations on the declaration of the Politburo of September 17. I had found it hasty, precipitous, and therefore incomplete and inexact. Now I must say even more: there was already in it another line, another evaluation of the situation.[3]

In fact, Maurice Thorez defended himself against Moscow by thus attacking his colleagues and by letting it be clearly understood that in his absence they could only commit "political errors." In his cynicism, Thorez did not even hesitate to reproach a member of the Central Committee, Roland Leroy, for not having shared his disagreement with the Politburo!

However, Thorez and the PCF Politburo changed their line too

[2] *Ibid.*, Sept. 28, 1959.
[3] This declaration was not published except by *L'Humanité*, Nov. 11, 1959.

late to be able to play an active role in French politics, now more and more dominated by the Algerian crisis. When at the end of 1960 the "conspiracy of the barricades" erupted in Algeria, the PCF could only leave entirely to de Gaulle the initiative in repressing the movement of the "ultras," and its only intervention in the crisis consisted in participating, on February 1, in a "national work-stoppage" of one hour—not even called a strike—at the moment and in the form desired by de Gaulle in order to make it a manifestation of support for his regime.

The day after the suppression of the "conspiracy of the barricades," de Gaulle multiplied his concessions to the army that had supported him against the civilian rebels. The repression of the Algerians became stronger, in turn, on both sides of the Mediterranean. A group around Francis Jeanson, who had organized a network of support for the FLN, were arrested. The PCF, completely occupied with preparations for Khrushchev's visit to France in April, hardly reacted at all. In the Midi, the Communist municipal council of the town of Sète (Hérault), had decided on February 16 not to receive de Gaulle on the occasion of his trip to the region. But its mayor, Pierre Arraut, was ordered by the Politburo to reverse this decision and to receive the chief of state personally. Incidentally, Arraut discharged this mission with poor grace.[4]

The Double Menace of 1960

Khrushchev had hardly left France, carrying with him only a communiqué drafted in generalized, protocol phrases, when the Chinese Communist Party, on the occasion of the ninetieth anniversary of Lenin's birth, published three articles, which were later published in a pamphlet under the title of one of them, "Long Live Leninism," and soon translated into many languages. The CCP had been hit in rapid succession by Soviet disapproval of the September 1959 Sino-Indian conflict, by Khrushchev's diatribe against "comrades trying to test by force the stability of the capitalist regime" (on the occasion of the ceremonies of the CPR's Tenth Anniversary, in October 1959 in Peking), and by the offensive against the "great leap forward," more or less steered by Moscow and mounted in the CCP Central Committee by P'eng Teh-huai. Counterattacking, "Long Live Leninism" violently criticized the policy of peaceful coexistence and the thesis of peaceful transition to socialism. Al-

[4] See *ibid.*, Feb. 24 and 29, 1960.

though only the Yugoslav leaders were attacked by name, it was difficult to mistake the identity of those merely called "modern revisionists."

From May 1960 on, the brochure "Long Live Leninism" began to be distributed in the PCF, particularly among the activists. Its distribution was not extensive, but was partly ensured later by the initiative of oppositional groups. But the Chinese pamphlet, which denounced any orientation based on legal, peaceful, and parliamentary struggle—that is, the PCF's fundamental domestic orientation—was particularly dangerous at a moment when from all sides and even from within the leadership the very mediocre results of this orientation in France provoked discontent and intrigues that threatened Maurice Thorez.

Apparently in those first months of 1960 several members of the Central Committee, without making common cause in the beginning, reacted more or less simultaneously and in different forms against the autocratic regime imposed by Thorez and his wife. Marcel Servin, sensitized by his functions as secretary of the organization of the Central Committee, had already on several occasions indicated what could have led him to pose such political issues: his statement concerning the PCF's loss of members, not compensated by new ones, the lack of activity on the part of the cadres, and the general lack of attendance at internal and public meetings organized by the party. In short, the PCF's political impotence could not be reduced to mere faults, of a more or less localized character, within the organization. On the occasion of a meeting of the Central Committee in the spring of 1960, Maurice Thorez attacked a young member of the Central Committee, Jean Pronteau, director of the magazine *Économie et politique,* which despite successive changes in editorship[5] had always distinguished itself from other PCF publications by its openness to certain forms of research and its tendency to reject pure dogmatism. But since Thorez had falsified Pronteau's statements in order better to attack them, Servin succeeded in having Pronteau's recorded statements played back to the Central Committee.[6] Frustrated, Thorez took revenge by dis-

---

[5] Professor Jean Baby, the first editor of this review, was expelled from the PCF in the spring of 1960, after he had published his *Critique de base* (Éditions Maspero), in which he criticized in particular the economic policy of the PCF.

[6] This incident has never been made public; however, it has been confirmed by several private sources. For allusions to the affair, see *Unir,* No. 88 (May 1960), p. 1; *ibid.,* No. 90 (July 1960), p. 8; and *ibid.,* No. 91 (Aug. 1960), p. 7. See also an anonymous pamphlet (probably published by *Unir*) entitled *La vérité*

covering in the analyses of *Économie et politique* grave "errors," such as statements giving credit to the idea of contradictions between "national" capitalist milieus more or less represented by Gaullism on the political plane and more "traditional" capitalism on the American pattern, of which the former Minister of Finance of the Debré government, Antoine Pinay, out of office since January 1960, had been the exponent. Jean Pronteau had to make self-criticism of his errors in an editorial of *Économie et politique* of June 1960. According to Thorez, the incriminated analysis, by insisting on internal contradictions of French capitalism and suggesting the possibility of a will to "national independence" on the part of big capitalists, ran the risk of justifying a policy of support of Gaullism.[7]

Servin published in *L'Humanité* of April 1960 an article entitled "On the Subject of the Engineer Bakhirev," which, under cover of literary criticism of the Soviet novel of that title by Galina Nikolaeva, was a barely disguised attack against Maurice Thorez. (Servin did not seem to have appreciated the organized campaign for a solemn celebration of Thorez' sixtieth anniversary at which, furthermore, he was not present.)

At the same time, Laurent Casanova and a certain number of intellectuals who had grouped themselves around him, particularly the writer Louis Aragon, the physician Jean-Pierre Vigier, and the publicists André Stil and Jean Kanapa, all members of the Central Committee who were greatly compromised from the Stalinist epoch by the out-and-out sectarianism that they had shown in imposing the dogmas of Zhdanovist orthodoxy in letters, arts, and sciences, concocted a small plot. Its essential strategic idea seems to have been to profit from the Sino-Soviet dissension in order to ruin Thorez' credit with Khrushchev.

Since he represented the PCF in the World Peace Council, Laurent Casanova was in a good position to maintain international contacts and to slip into Soviet ears rumors of Thorez' pro-Chinese sympathies. Casanova also seems to have used his good relations with the Soviet ambassador in Paris, Vinogradov, the principal architect of the rapprochement between the Soviet Union and de Gaulle, to accuse Thorez of sabotaging, by his systematic opposition

---

sur l'affaire Servin-Casanova, p. 13 (reprinted in *La voie communiste*, No. 21 [Mar. 1961], pp. 8–9). See also *ibid.*, No. 20 (Feb. 1961), p. 5.

[7] The criticisms made at the Central Committee session of May 23 in Pronteau's article were merely alluded to in the official minutes of the debate published in *L'Humanité*, May 27, 1960.

to Gaullism, all possibilities of a "national" policy for France, instead of encouraging de Gaulle's meritorious efforts to solve the Algerian problem and to detach France from American tutelage.

Louis Aragon, who frequently published the contributions of Gaullist and rightist writers in his biweekly *Les lettres françaises,* was also vice president of the international Lenin Prize jury, and in this capacity he saw to it that in 1960 the Lenin Peace Prize went to his friend Laurent Casanova. The latter also exercised considerable influence on the leadership of the Union of Communist Students, the UEC (Union des étudiants communistes), whose organ, *Clarté,* discreetly echoed Casanova's line. On his part, Jean-Pierre Vigier more or less controlled the PCF's university sector, which was much concerned with the "struggle against fascism," that had come to the surface after the "affair of the barricades" in Algiers, thus confirming its political importance.

Another member of the Central Committee, Maurice Kriegel-Valrimont, editor-in-chief of *France Nouvelle,* tried, with some success, to give this PCF central weekly a new appearance and tone. Pierre Courtade, who had already been criticized several times by Thorez since 1956 for his impulsive speeches at Central Committee sessions, continued to make himself conspicuous by his insufficiently conformist statements. Kriegel-Valrimont and Courtade had been part of the group around the paper *Action* at the time of the Liberation, where they had hobnobbed with Pierre Hervé, expelled in 1956, and Victor Leduc, known since the Twentieth Congress to be among the inspirers of the intellectual opposition. This whole group, all from the Resistance, had been viewed with very strong suspicion for many years by the PCF Secretariat-General.

A total of 10 to 15 members of the Central Committee (out of more than 90) were suspected of participating in this "conspiracy," which without doubt was never really synchronized, even if some connecting links were possibly established by simple conversations between one or the other of the "conspirators." While waiting for the end of this affair, which was to see the elimination of Servin and Casanova in January 1961, efforts were made not to advertise it, and Maurice Thorez limited himself to moving against some of its important personalities: Pronteau was humiliated by public self-criticism, Courtade was transferred from *L'Humanité* to Moscow as its permanent correspondent, and Kriegel-Valrimont was discreetly removed as editor-in-chief of *France Nouvelle.* Thus the menace seemed to have been partially removed in the early summer of 1960, when a conference of Communist and workers' parties opened in Bucharest, a prelude to one in Moscow in the autumn.

All these events inside the PCF are very important in order to understand the outstanding role that Maurice Thorez was to play in the preparation and course of the great Communist council that the representatives of eighty-one parties were to hold in November 1960. In the interim, moreover, the international situation had presented difficulties for Khrushchev. After the U-2 incident and the failure of the May summit conference in Paris, Khrushchev's attitude, which combined a harder line vis-à-vis the United States with increasingly open hostility to China, induced him to seek the support of old militants like Thorez, for it was now necessary for him to prevent all the elements that had remained Stalinist in the leadership of the CPSU and of other Communist parties from slipping into the Chinese camp. As he had in June 1956, Thorez knew how to take advantage of this situation cleverly.

CHAPTER TEN

THE PCF AND THE NOVEMBER 1960 MOSCOW CONFERENCE

The PCF was for the first time called upon to align itself with the Soviets against the Chinese in Peking between June 4 and 9, 1960, on the occasion of the meeting of the General Council of the World Federation of Trade Unions (WFTU). The principal French delegate, Benoît Frachon, present in his capacity as Secretary-General of the CGT, was a member of the PCF Politburo. There the Chinese delegates, addressing themselves particularly to Communist trade unionists, tried to win them over to their concept of world revolution by using the U-2 affair and the failure of the summit conference to proclaim the failure of the policy of peaceful coexistence. The French and Italian delegates, who in the WFTU as well as in other Communist-controlled international organizations shared the essential responsibilities of the *apparat*, thus had to take the lead against the Chinese attack, which had significant repercussions among the delegations from Asia, Africa, and Latin America. The French Communist press did not print a word about these incidents which were made public by *L'Unità* on June 19.[1]

The signing on June 26, 1960 of the so-called Declaration of Bucharest by the delegates of the twelve Communist and workers' parties of the socialist countries represented at the Congress of the Romanian Workers' Party, after a turbulent meeting,[2] did not lead

---

[1] The course of these debates can be approximated from the speeches made by the French delegation to the eighty-one-party meeting in Moscow. See *Problèmes du mouvement communiste international* (Paris: PCF, Jan. 1963), especially Thorez' speech, p. 36, and the Declaration of the French delegation, pp. 44–46. Excerpts in Alexander Dallin, ed., with Jonathan Harris and Grey Hodnett, *Diversity in International Communism* (New York and London: Columbia University Press, 1963), pp. 830–845 and 861–862, respectively. All quotations from Thorez' speech (hereafter cited as Thorez, *Speech*) and the Declaration, except for those cited in notes 10, 14, and 15 are taken from this source.

[2] For the text of the final declaration of the Bucharest Conference see *CDSP*, Vol. XII, No. 26 (July 27, 1960), p. 14. For a Chinese account of this

by any means to a détente in Sino-Soviet relations. On the contrary, tension reached new heights with the Soviet decision in July to withdraw the Soviet technicians working in China.

The PCF Central Committee, which met at Ivry on July 1, 1960, was confidentially informed of the incidents in Peking and Bucharest, but the resolution adopted, which "disapproved the positions expressed by the comrades of the Chinese Communist Party" and "approved the position of the Communist Party of the Soviet Union, clearly in conformity with the principles contained in the Declaration and Manifesto for Peace adopted in Moscow in November 1957, principles that are reaffirmed by the international Communist and Workers' Movement in the recent Declaration of Bucharest," was not made public until January 1963![3]

To prepare for the conference of the eighty-one Communist parties, the PCF leadership formally decided on a blackout. While the PCI had informed its federal secretaries on June 21 of the informational circular letter of the CPSU Central Committee, which set forth the Soviet grievances against the CCP and which was made known to all the parties present at Bucharest, whether they were signatories of the declaration or not, the greatest discretion was recommended in France to the members of the Central Committee.

The PCF leaders doubtless preferred to avoid the additional commotion that the divulging of the international Communist crisis might have provoked in the ranks of the party, within which, as a result of the war in Algeria and its repercussions in France, a sense of political failure was becoming apparent. Actually, despite the failure in early summer of negotiations at Melun with the emissaries of the provisional government of the Algerian Republic, a development which created the best conditions for antigovernmental agitation, the PCF lost more and more the initiative in the campaigns against the war in Algeria, while a numerically smaller group, the PSU (Parti Socialiste Unifié), showed a certain dynamism in this respect. The PSU, founded in the spring of 1960 by the fusion of "autonomous Socialists," SFIO dissidents, the *Union de la Gauche Socialiste,* and a small group of old Communist oppositionists who in 1958–1959 had published the bulletin *Tribune du*

---

meeting, see "The Origin and Development of the Differences between the Leadership of the CPSU and Ourselves." *Jen-min Jih-pao* and *Hung Ch'i,* Sept. 6, 1963; *Peking Review,* Vol. VI, No. 37 (Sept. 13, 1963), pp. 7–23; in William E. Griffith, *The Sino-Soviet Rift* (Cambridge, Mass.: The M.I.T. Press, 1964), pp. 388–420.

[3] In the pamphlet *Problèmes du mouvement communiste international, op. cit.,* pp. 3–9.

Communisme, was joined by a certain number of young people, particularly students, who were particularly concerned with action against the war in Algeria. Only feebly rooted in the working-class milieu, which it could reach only through a few leftist-Christian nuclei, it nevertheless exercised an undeniable effect on students, professors, and instructors. Its influence was reinforced by the fact that some of its guiding spirits or important adherents, on the one hand Mendès-France and on the other Claude Bourdet and Gilles Martinet, reached a considerable public through their weeklies *L'Express* and *France-Observateur.* But the new party united very heterogeneous elements, from *Mendèsistes* representing the liberal left of the Radical Party all the way to Trotskyites, with anticlerical Freemasons, Catholic militants, and close PCF sympathizers of the crypto-Communist variety.

It was the trial of Frenchmen accused of helping the FLN, the so called Jeanson network, accompanied by the simultaneous publication of a manifesto by 121 intellectuals, among them Sartre and several PCF members, that revived the dormant campaign against the war in Algeria. The "Manifesto of 121" publicly endorsed the insubordination of young soldiers who refused to go to Algeria as well as participation in networks supporting the FLN. Without going quite that far, the PCF, which had until then vigorously denounced such actions under the pretext that they were contrary to Leninist orthodoxy and had systematically expelled those of its members who were implicated in military insubordination or support for the FLN, modified its position and pronounced itself in favor of the "Defense of the 121" and of those who, like them, "fought in their way" for peace in Algeria. A "national day of action against the war in Algeria," organized by the National Union of French Students, UNEF (Union Nationale des Étudiants de France), strongly influenced by the PSU, was set up by a group in which the CGT was represented side by side with three other trade-union centers: CFTC, *Force Ouvrière,* and Federation of National Education (autonomous). The date was set for October 27, 1960. However, since the principal demonstration planned for Paris on that day had been forbidden by the government, the PCF persuaded the CGT to withdraw at the last moment from the group of organizers, who had just obtained authorization to hold a central meeting at the Mutualité. The meeting nevertheless took place, with a large crowd overflowing into the neighboring streets, and the participants clashed violently with the police, while the disciplined Communist activists attended small, scattered, short, and almost unnoticed demonstrations around the mayors' offices in Paris and in the outskirts.

In fact, in those few weeks, and particularly those few days preceding October 27, the PCF leadership demonstrated a hesitant and incoherent attitude, largely because there were contradictory "lines" within it.[4] Marcel Servin, Laurent Casanova, and Jean-Pierre Vigier were in favor of participating in the general demonstration even if it was prohibited. Maurice Thorez, who on October 14 had spoken at a Central Committee plenum of "regrettable leftist tendencies" on the part of the UNEF,[5] Étienne Fajon, and Waldeck Rochet, who used in his report to the same Central Committee the argument that later served as a pretext for the defection of the Communists and the CGT (". . . Our Party will never consent to be only a supporting force"),[6] were from the beginning hostile to participation.

The problems arising from this dispute at the PCF summit, which were not known until after the publication of the Servin-Casanova "dossier" by the Politburo, were very directly linked to those that were beginning to be discussed on the international Communist level. Servin and Casanova argued that the unity attained in the preparation for October 27 should not be broken at any price, thus profitably resuming their offensive against Thorez and his group, who applied "in a restrictive fashion" the line set by the Fifth Congress (more particularly, in their view, the aspects of that line inspired by the PCI). Thorez and Rochet replied that the PCF was threatened by being "pushed to the left" by the PSU and that it was necessary to avoid "provocations" that might throw the party back into illegality. Thus they appeared to be the defenders of the "peaceful road," while Servin and Casanova fell into "leftism," considered in Moscow as enemy number one at the moment.

While thus defending his position on the international level, Thorez maneuvered skillfully by abandoning the other organizers of the Paris demonstrations at the last moment; the retreat of the PCF and the CGT left the PSU alone with the Socialist and Christian organizations. Suddenly Communist propaganda accused the "leftists" of the PSU of having tried to restore the fortunes of the

[4] For an account of this indecisiveness, as manifested by *L'Humanité* in its October issues, see *La voie communiste*, No. 18 (Nov.–Dec. 1960), pp. 4–5.

[5] *L'Humanité*, Oct. 19, 1960.

[6] *Ibid.*, Oct. 15, 1960.

friends of Guy Mollet by giving them a platform. Thus on the interior plane, the PCF's withdrawal was presented as a manifestation of revolutionary purism!

Few cadres at that point suspected the game that was being played in the international Communist movement. During the summer of 1960 Maurice Thorez had gone again to Albania, and *L'Humanité* of August 5 had carried extracts of a speech that he had made at the Stalin Textile Combine there, with a front-page photograph that showed him and his wife side by side with Enver Hoxha. In his speech, Thorez spoke of successes

due above all to the merits of the Albanian people, the Party of Labor, and of its Central Committee led by Comrade Enver Hoxha. They were also accomplished thanks to the fraternal help of the great Soviet Union and the other countries of the socialist camp, whose power grows with every day.

Is it possible that after the violent dispute between the Albanians and the Chinese in Bucharest, Thorez, accompanied by another member of the Politburo, Léon Mauvais, and the latter's mistress, Juliette Dubois, member of the Central Committee, tried to bring about a Soviet-Albanian reconciliation? In any event, thirteen days later, on August 18, he met with Khrushchev at Yalta. And on September 2, *Pravda* published an article by Arzumanyan and Korionov, "The Last Confessions of a Revisionist," which violently criticized Kardelj's *Socialism and War* and defended China against "slanderous" accusations of "aggressiveness."

During the entire autumn session of the United Nations, *L'Humanité* continued to push Khrushchev's proposals and reported as a great accomplishment the affair of Khrushchev's pounding the desk with his shoe.[7] Therefore, by the opening of the November 1960 eighty-one party conference Khrushchev knew that he could count on Thorez as one of his staunchest allies.

From the beginning of his talk at the conference, Maurice Thorez left no doubt on the position of the French delegation:

From the very beginning we want to state our deep and unreserved agreement with the high-level speech delivered here by Comrade Khrushchev on behalf of the Communist Party of the Soviet Union. However, we state our absolute disagreement with the ideas put forth by Comrade Teng Hsiao-p'ing on behalf of the Chinese Communist Party.[8]

Compared to the 1957 conference, there was by 1960 a sort of reversal of alliances: The "centralist" coalition had disappeared,

7 *Ibid.,* Oct. 14, 1960.
8 See Thorez, *Speech*, pp. 830–831.

and one now found together on the same side those Communist parties which had remained the most Stalinist (French, Czechoslovak, Bulgarian, and East German) and the Polish and Italian "revisionists," all rallying around the "de-Stalinizer" Khrushchev. To make the confusion complete, "centralism" was verbally defended by the Chinese, who, however, in fact openly refused to endorse decisions by the alleged "center," while Khrushchev refused to have the "leading role" of the Soviet Union mentioned in any declaration—in order to be able to continue to exercise it in practice! But in the new anti-Chinese coalition, nuances were perceptible between the French and Italian Communist parties, particularly as their common opportunism in domestic politics converged to oppose Chinese "leftism." By comparing the roles played by Maurice Thorez and Luigi Longo[9] at the conference, one can see quite a few traces of these nuances.

Even the tone used by Thorez showed the difficulty experienced by the French leader in shedding the habits of the Stalinist epoch. He called Khrushchev the "incomparable propagandist of the great ideas of communism," who "in the eyes of the masses has been the incarnation of the calm force of victorious socialism" and "whose Leninist style has left its imprint on the entire fruitful work for peace."[10]

While approving the policy of peaceful coexistence, Thorez denounced, in passing, China's policy in its conflict with India and welcomed "the political wisdom of the Soviet Union in this question." In the long passage of his speech devoted to the crumbling of the colonial system in the world, Thorez made a veritable plea for the anticolonial activity of his party—ground on which he felt himself to be very vulnerable. (It was the "fraternal party" of France that the PCI delegate had in mind when he asked the Conference to "reconfirm . . . the criticism of all opportunist hesitation that may manifest itself on this score.")

On the question of the peaceful road to socialism, Longo replied to the Chinese that

> We answer, with firm confidence, that our own PCI has long acted on this belief, which best fits the Italian situation, and that so far it has had undoubtedly significant successes.

It was obviously much more difficult for the PCF delegate to find

9 *Interventi della delegazione del PCI alla Conferenza degli 81 Partiti communisti e operai* (Rome: Sezione centrale di stampa e propaganda della Direzione del PCI, Jan. 15, 1962); in Dallin, *op. cit.*, pp. 845–861 and 863–867.
10 *Problèmes du mouvement communiste international, op. cit.*, pp. 20–21.

in the reality of French politics recent convincing proofs of the "success" of the peaceful road. Strangely enough, Thorez wriggled out of this by disinterring the interview that he himself had given to the London *Times* on November 18, 1946 and by complaining that at the time he had not been "encouraged" but had been charged with "opportunism and parliamentarianism" by the Yugoslav delegates to the First Cominform Conference, whose "attitude later on showed adequately the value of such a claim."[11] By thus recalling that recent Chinese charges of opportunism regarding "the peaceful road" had followed the attacks made by the Yugoslavs shortly after the war against the French and Italian Communist parties, Thorez put himself in the position of being the precursor of the correct political line and of simultaneously justifying his persistent hostility to Tito and opposing on this point the conciliatory attitude of the PCI.

On this point the PCF diverged the most from its allies across the Alps: It insisted "that the struggle be energetically pursued on two fronts, against revisionism, the principal danger and against dogmatism and sectarianism."[12] Thorez did not find it at all troublesome to make concessions to the Chinese by making sharper the denunciation of Yugoslav revisionism. The Italians, on the other hand, whose revisionism in fact went much further than Tito's, disagreed with this definition of the "principal danger" and in a letter to the conference expressed reservations with respect to the repetition, in its final document, of the anti-Titoist formulations of the 1957 conference:

We should like here to point out a fact that often escapes some comrades who do not work in capitalist countries. The tone in which we speak of our quarrel with the Yugoslav Communist League is one of the units of measurement by which the Social Democratic parties and unions, and public opinion in general, evaluate the sincerity of our unity policies, and our capacity for collaboration with groups ideologically and politically foreign to us.[13]

In short, the PCI, which in its concern for international unity subscribed to the condemnation of Yugoslav revisionism, tempered its allegiance with reservations that it justified by cleverly hiding behind interpretations of "anti-Titoism" by allies of the Communists in Western countries. The implicit reference to the Nenni Italian Socialist Party was transparent in this connection and un-

11 Thorez, *Speech,* p. 837.
12 *Ibid.,* p. 843.
13 *Interventi della delegazione del PCI,* from Dallin, *op. cit.,* p. 866.

doubtedly sprang from a real concern, one nonexistent in the PCF, since Guy Mollet's SFIO did not represent a dangerous competitor in the labor movement itself. However, aside from such tactical considerations, the PCI made the barely veiled accusation against the PCF of not giving proof of "sincerity" in its policy of unity (with the SFIO) and of not being able to collaborate with other political forces. In its turn, the PCF insinuated that the PCI had forgotten the necessity of the "dictatorship of the proletariat." Maurice Thorez said:

Efforts of opportunists and revisionists, in France *as elsewhere*, consist in effacing this necessity of the revolutionary act. They interpret the manifold forms of transition from capitalism to socialism as a possibility to make and not to make revolution, to establish and not to establish the dictatorship of the proletariat.[14]

The two great Western Communist parties opposed the Chinese attempt to delete from the final resolution all reference to the international effects of the CPSU Twentieth Congress, which they had accepted in 1957. But while the Italians stressed the denunciation of the cult of the personality, Thorez was practically silent on the subject and even declared in his second speech that his party had "based itself on the theses of the Twentieth Congress in order to combat revisionism."[15]

In connection with the question that led to the most violent controversy in the course of the conference, a debate fundamental in its implications despite its entirely Byzantine appearances, Thorez pointed out very clearly that his denunciation of the "centralist" formulations of the Chinese did not imply support for the "polycentrist" heresy of the Italians:

We reject any position which might tend to weaken the unity of the socialist system and the international Communist movement by considering that they might have several centers. Our party has fought this erroneous point of view already.[16]

Finally, the concept defended by Thorez triumphed at the conference: "recognition in acts and in words of the vanguard role played by the Communist Party of the Soviet Union," but rejection of the formula, proposed by the Chinese, placing the CPSU "at the head of the international Communist movement," a formula that

14 *Problèmes du mouvement communiste international, op. cit.,* pp. 30–31. (Our italics.)
15 *Ibid.,* p. 42.
16 Thorez, *Speech,* p. 839.

"may be prejudicial to the extent that it furnishes a pretext for the calumnious bourgeois propaganda against the [Communist] parties," and "under the cover" of which "attempts are being made to injure the prestige of the CPSU and the authority of its leadership, in particular that of Comrade Khrushchev."[17] In brief, the Communist parties had, in fact, to bow before the authority of the CPSU, instead of treacherously accepting this authority in declarations in order to contest it all the more in their acts, as did the Chinese. Thorez was opposed to any resurrection of a formal international organization[18] because "the unity that we need is the voluntary but *real unity,* of all the detachments of our movement *around the Communist Party of the Soviet Union.*"[19] The passages we have italicized indicate with sufficient clarity that the positions defended by Thorez were the opposite of polycentrism.

In order to prove more clearly the CCP's bad faith, Thorez evoked with undoubtedly sincere indignation the attitude of the president of the Chinese delegation at the Conference of the International Association of Democratic Jurists that had just taken place at Sofia. Actually, the latter had criticized, before two French delegates, of whom one was a non-Communist, the "systematic and unconditional alignment" of the PCF with the CPSU.[20] Thorez declared:

We are accustomed to this parody of the close bonds that have always united the French Communists with the Soviet Communists. But until now it issued only from our opponents—reactionaries and socialist leaders. This is the first time that it has been picked up by comrades.[21]

In reality, Thorez was all the more sensitive to this criticism as the Chinese jurist had put his finger on an open wound when he attributed to this "systematic and unconditional alignment" the PCF's failure in the support of the Algerian struggle. The French delegate violently denounced "petit bourgeois elements . . . using leftist phrases" who had "claimed of late to be drawing the partisans of peace into a test of force with the Gaullist government," and whose "adventurous attempts" had "disorganized the alignment of the largest possible mass against its war policy." As one can see, Thorez

17 *Ibid.,* p. 840.
18 It is not known for certain whether the proposal to create a permanent committee or secretariat, which Thorez rejected, as did Luigi Longo, was put forth by the Chinese delegation, but in any case the Chinese inspired the proposal. See Griffith, *op. cit.,* p. 19.
19 Thorez, *Speech,* p. 840.
20 *Ibid.,* p. 843.
21 *Ibid.*

did not neglect the exigencies of the internal struggle inside the PCF: By comparing the Paris demonstration of October 27 to the leftist tendencies of the Chinese, he discredited those who had favored participation in this demonstration, that is, Casanova and Servin, and asked Khrushchev for carte blanche for their early elimination.

It is important to stress the vigor with which Thorez defended, against the Chinese delegates, the necessity of reaffirming in the text of the declaration "the denunciation of factional activity." (However, he was not to receive satisfaction on this point.)

It is known that the capacity for action characteristic of a Communist Party derives precisely from its refusal to permit any factions whatsoever within itself. In the same fashion, there would no longer be a unitary international Communist movement if groups could form or factions crystallize. The concept according to which this movement might accept the presence within itself of a permanent and organized minority . . . threatens the unity of the movement.[22]

With such words Thorez expressed not only the anxieties that he felt because of the "factional" activities already undertaken by the CCP, either in the leadership of certain African parties dependent on the PCF until this time or in the PCF itself; he claimed for himself the right to stand on a document of the international Communist movement thus preventing any minority opinion in the French party from crystallizing into a tendency.

Even though the 1960 Moscow Declaration was again a hybrid product like that of 1957, juxtaposing contradictory theses within it, the role Maurice Thorez had played during the debates unquestionably raised once again the international prestige of the PCF and the personal prestige of its Secretary-General.

22 *Ibid.*, p. 841.

CHAPTER ELEVEN

FROM THE PCF SIXTEENTH CONGRESS TO THE CPSU TWENTY-SECOND CONGRESS

The PCF Congress

The prelude to the PCF Sixteenth Congress, scheduled for May 1961, took place in January of that year. Having secured his position in Moscow, Maurice Thorez felt that he could go on to liquidate the internal menace that had given him trouble in 1960. The condemnation of Marcel Servin and Laurent Casanova by the Central Committee meeting of January 13, 14, and 15 was made known only on January 25 by the "bourgeois" papers and confirmed on January 26 by *L'Humanité*.

One month before this session of the Central Committee, on December 13, 1960, Laurent Casanova had been awarded a Lenin Peace Prize in Paris by Skobeltsin, President of the International Jury and President of the Soviet Academy of Sciences, who made the speech at the prize-giving ceremony, which took place in the presence of Soviet Ambassador Vinogradov but in the absence of Maurice Thorez, who was "excused." However, this support did not suffice to dissuade Thorez, who merely let the campaign of the referendum (January 8, 1961) pass before taking action. The new deviationists, summoned to make their self-criticism, never had a chance to explain their deviations to the activists; these deviations thus became known only through the indictments made by Thorez and Waldeck Rochet, supplemented by several more or less anecdotal variations, and rounded out with indiscretions. Only Maurice Kriegel-Valrimont refused to make any self-criticism at all, which brought him a more severe penalty than that reserved for the other accused (expulsion from the federal committee of Meurthe-et-Moselle before the holding of the congress, in violation of party statutes). We shall not return here to the injustices done to Casanova, Servin, Kriegel-Valrimont, Pronteau, Vigier, or Kanapa, because they have already been mentioned with respect to the period

126

of their "factional" activity.[1] Suffice it to say that for the first time since the Liberation, and in contrast to the Marty-Tillon and Lecoeur affairs, where the dossiers of the indictment were spurious, the indictments in this case rested on a solid basis: This time there really had been, if not a factional group, at least an attempt by several members of the Central Committee, and even of the Politburo, to work together to put an end to Maurice Thorez' autocratic regime.

Apparently, however, feeling that the Soviet support on which they had counted was slipping away, the "opponents" in the Central Committee lost all their courage. The development of events in France would really have permitted them to counterattack: They were accused among other things of having "overestimated the Fascist danger," and a few weeks later, on April 22, the military coup d'état in Algiers, with solid support by the army in France and Germany, had confirmed the existence of this danger. The PCF showed itself hardly more dynamic on this occasion than it had in January 1960; it again participated in a "national work-stoppage" of one hour, encouraged by de Gaulle, and during the entire crisis simply appeared as supporting the General—but this time it was impossible to make Servin's and Casanova's "parallel line" responsible.

The PCF Sixteenth Congress, held at Saint-Denis from May 2 to 15, 1961 was intended primarily to legalize the elimination of Servin, Casanova, Pronteau, Kriegel-Valrimont, and Jean-Pierre Vigier, who were not re-elected to the Central Committee. (Casanova's mistress, Claudine Chomat, was also expelled from the Central Committee.) But the matter was settled before the opening of the congress, and none of the activists affected could defend himself, or wanted to do so, in plenary session. Aside from the necessary action of replacing Servin and Casanova in the Politburo (by George Marchais and Roger Garaudy respectively, both old candidate members) and the nomination of a new candidate member, Paul Laurent, leader of the Communist youth movement, the principal innovation of the congress was the designation of a "Deputy Secretary-General" to assist Maurice Thorez, in the person of Waldeck Rochet. This man, who, as the reader will remember, had for some time in 1956 been the focus of the hopes of the partisans of de-Stalinization in France,[2] thus received his reward for the loyalty with which he had aided Thorez, particularly in 1960. A sick man,

1 See Chapter Four of this study.
2 See Chapter Six of this study.

the Secretary-General from then on entrusted his deputy with current affairs. Finally, together with Servin's successor, Georges Marchais—a protégé of Thorez who had made his career in the Fédération Seine-Sud, directly controlled by the Secretary-General—another young man, Roland Leroy, entered the party secretariat.

At the congress no word was said about the Sino-Soviet divergences; the speakers referred to the 1960 Moscow Declaration as though it had truly and lastingly re-established the unity of the international Communist movement. Yet during the period of Sino-Soviet "truce," which was to last until the CPSU Twenty-Second Congress, the PCF was not completely inactive on the international front. For example, a candidate member of the Politburo, Gustave Ansart, attended the Congress of the Albanian Party of Labor, from February 13 to 21, 1961. L'Humanité reported the events at the Albanian Congress in brief articles. However, Ansart did not publish his own report until nine months later,[3] after the CPSU Twenty-Second Congress had given the signal for the offensive against Albania.

In his speech at the CPSU Twenty-Second Congress, Maurice Thorez did not hesitate to present himself as the champion of the Twentieth Congress, which had "written an essential page . . . in the rich history of the workers' movement . . . and elaborated new theses of exceptional importance." He condemned the "factional activity of the antiparty group, which delayed the application of the line set by the Twentieth Congress," and "the sectarian and adventurous attitude" of the leaders of the Albanian Party of Labor.[4]

This time, by aligning himself instantly with the CPSU and by not repeating in October 1961 the hesitation and silence of the spring of 1956, Thorez hoped to prevent the reappearance of such PCF internal struggles as had followed the Twentieth Congress. Besides, during the five years thereafter, the voluntary or enforced departure of numerous opponents, the systematic elimination of cadres that had at one point or another shown critical tendencies, and, finally, the humiliating self-criticisms imposed on Servin and Casanova had profoundly modified the situation in the party, par-

---

[3] In France Nouvelle, Nov. 15, 1961. On the Fourth Congress of the Albanian Party of Labor, see William E. Griffith, Albania and the Sino-Soviet Rift (Cambridge, Mass.: The M.I.T. Press, 1963), pp. 68–72.

[4] "22e Congrès du P.C.U.S.," Cahiers du Communisme, No. 12 (Dec. 1961), special issue, pp. 528–532.

ticularly since it was accompanied by a partial change among the PCF activists, joined during those five years by young people for whom the Stalinist period was mere history and not living experience.

Toward the end of 1961, moreover, the struggle against the war in Algeria revived and took on a new vigor. The police had decided to impose a curfew on the Algerian workers in Paris and, under the pretext of making them respect this curfew, had resorted to extremely violent methods: brutality, maltreatment, and summary executions. The Federation of France of the FLN replied with large street demonstrations, very spectacular despite their violent suppression (October 1961). As a negotiated Algerian settlement seemed near, moreover, the PCF lifted the veto that it had long exercised against all street action, and permitted young Communists to organize in Paris, together with the PSU youth and the students of the UNEF, a demonstration on November 18, 1961 that inaugurated a series of similar actions. Even though it continued to hide behind "mass organizations," youth organizations, CGT unions, or the peace movement, in order to avoid giving a reason for repression against the PCF itself, the PCF leadership in autumn 1961 accepted and even encouraged what it had refused and sabotaged in the autumn of 1960. This satisfaction given to the desire for activity and combativeness of the activists actually effectively contributed to limiting their interest in the consequences of the CPSU Twenty-Second Congress.

The Struggle on Two Fronts

One cannot help being struck by the contrast between the considerable political emotion and activity that the Twenty-Second Congress provoked, from base to summit, in the PCI and the sluggishness that seemed to incapacitate the cadres of the PCF. This state of affairs permitted the PCF leaders to resume in November 1961 the "struggle on two fronts": against the "leftism" of the Albanians on the one hand—for publicly the Chinese were still being spared—and against the polycentrist and revisionist theses emphatically reaffirmed in Italy on the other.

Even though the only discordant voice raised at the Central Committee meeting at Ivry (November 25–27, 1961), at which the report of the PCF delegation to the Twenty-Second Congress was presented, had been that of Giovoni, who disagreed with the public denunciation of the Albanian Party of Labor,[5] the main stress during this early period was placed by the PCF leaders on the refutation of the daring Italian interpretations. In the speech by Maurice Thorez, which inspired the resolution adopted by the Central Committee, the relationship between the "two fronts" was presented thus:

While struggling against revisionist and opportunist currents, we cannot neglect the sectarian and dogmatic deviation, which could become the greatest danger if we ceased to struggle against it.[6]

As it merely "could become" the principal danger, this meant it was not that as yet.

To show, however, that the new antirevisionist campaign by no means implied any complacency toward the Chinese theses, the PCF selected precisely this moment (November 1961) to make public the speeches of its delegates at the Moscow November 1960 Conference. The publicity given to them was limited, because this first brochure remained an "internal document" distributed only to party members.

The priority given to the struggle on the "Italian front" could doubtless be explained by the extent of the open debates in the PCI in November 1961, immediately after the Twenty-Second Congress. Togliatti himself was in danger of being outvoted at the session of the Central Committee, both from the right, by the offensive of the revisionists led by Georgio Amendola, a party secretary,

[5] See Waldeck Rochet's report and Maurice Thorez' speech in *Problèmes du mouvement communiste international,* (Paris: PCF, Jan. 1963); excerpts in Alexander Dallin, ed., with Jonathan Harris and Grey Hodnett, *Diversity in International Communism* (New York and London: Columbia University Press), pp. 476–495.

[6] *Ibid.,* p. 494. Note that the form is taken almost literally from the "New Program" adopted by the Twenty-Second Congress of the CPSU: "Dogmatism and sectarianism, unless steadfastly combated, can also become the chief danger at particular stages in the development of individual parties." *The New Soviet Society: Final Text of the Program of the Communist Party of the Soviet Union* (New York: New Leader Paperback, 1962), with annotations and introduction by Herbert Ritvo, p. 82. This was still nothing more than a warning.

The French Communists followed the "New Program" almost to the letter. Under the circumstances their adherence to the Soviet line seems to have been formal rather than otherwise, although the form of the new program did correspond somewhat to the French situation. As a matter of fact, the most obvious threat came from the revisionist intellectuals and the Italian example, but at that particular moment it was possible for the leadership of the PCF to have an inkling of the danger that could represent a new growth, of a more or less "Chinese" type, of a permanent "leftist" trend among the working masses, who were dissatisfied with rapprochement with the Socialists and with the increasingly reformist policy of the PCF.

and from the left, by the FGCI (Italian Federation of Communist Youth), whose central organ, *Nuova Generazione,* practically rehabilitated Leon Trotsky in its issue of November 10, 1961.

But Togliatti, finding himself in the middle, even then went much further on several essential points raised by the Twenty-Second Congress than did Maurice Thorez or Waldeck Rochet. The latter two contented themselves with endorsing the Twenty-Second Congress and tried to stick as close as possible to paraphrasing Khrushchev. They continued to state that the PCF had not had to suffer any consequences of the personality cult, that it did not share the responsibility for the "errors" and "crimes" of Stalin, and that it was sufficient to take some small steps, such as changing the names of some streets that had been called "rue Staline" on the initiative of Communist municipalities on the outskirts of Paris, particularly in Ivry, Thorez' suburb.

Togliatti, however, declared that the new revelations of the Twenty-Second Congress justified the "partial conclusions" that he had reached in his interview of 1956 with *Nuovi Argomenti* on the Marxist explanation of Stalinism.[7] Repeating the theses that the Soviets had forcefully disowned in June 1956, Togliatti declared that the theoretical analysis furnished by the Twenty-Second Congress was not "entirely satisfactory" and that it was in the interest of the Soviet people themselves to "pursue research and deepen analyses" in order to have a better guarantee that "such serious events would not repeat themselves."[8]

Contrary to Togliatti, the PCF repeated literally, in their Central Committee resolution, the restrictive Soviet interpretation, which refused to see the roots of Stalinism in the reality of Soviet society.

The cult of the personality resulted neither from the nature of the socialist system nor from the leading role played by the Leninist party. A further proof of this is the fact that the one and the other found the necessary strength within themselves to extirpate the phenomenon foreign to them. The cult of the personality and its consequences are in fact in contradiction to the principles of Marxism-Leninism itself, which show that the masses are the ones that make history. The cult of the personality and its consequences are defects inherited from the capitalist regime and bourgeois individualism.[9]

At least on two points, but points of very great importance, Amendola went much further than Togliatti. On the one hand, he

[7] See Chapter Six of this study, note 27.
[8] *L'Unità,* Nov. 11, 1961.
[9] *L'Humanité,* Nov. 27, 1961.

developed at length the coresponsibility of the Italian Communists
("therefore criticism of Stalin necessarily becomes self-criticism").[10]
On the other hand, Amendola indicted the principle of monolith-
ism and "fictitious unanimity" in the international Communist
movement as well as inside the PCI. The diversity of positions taken
by different parties was, according to Amendola,

a necessary and inevitable consequence of Communist advance in the
world. It leads to polycentrism, which does not weaken internationalism
but on the contrary constitutes a precondition of a no longer formal but
profound internationalism which must grow in the whole world.

He continued:

In our own party a discussion ought to take place, if it is necessary,
from time to time on the formulation of various problems by minorities
and majorities.[11]

Amendola and his comrades in spirit (Alicata, Trombadori, and
several others) did not limit themselves to placing the blame on
"deformation of the principles of democratic centralism," "bureau-
cratization," "arrested development of democratic life at the base
and the maintenance of personal leadership methods," or "the false
Stalinist conception of monolithic discipline and unity in the party,
which regards disagreement as a complete break and as treason."
They specifically attributed to Stalinism the failure of the PCI's
policies since the Liberation:

By virtue of the deceptive fashion in which the war of liberation ended,
our policies consisted in a sterile waiting for a liberation coming from
the outside, thanks to the growing strength of the Soviet Union. This
led to a permanent contradiction between the national conception of
Italian revolutionary strategy, which not only expressed the official line
of the party but also the real political will of the leaders, and daily
practices, based in large part on exalted propaganda in favor of the
socialist system and in passive waiting for its arrival.[12]

Purged of its jargon, this last sentence clearly meant that the dependence of the PCI on the Soviet Union had condemned to failure the reformist line chosen by the party.

Amendola and his friends did not receive satisfaction all along the
line, and their demand for an extraordinary PCI congress was rejected.[13] But their positions largely inspired the document of the

10 *Rinascita,* Dec. 1961.
11 *Ibid.*
12 *Ibid.*
13 For a more detailed account see Giorgio Galli, "Italian Communism," in

PCI secretariat, dated November 27, 1961,[14] that spoke for example of assuring in the party

free confrontation of opinion and open manifestation of any possible dissension, whether in discussions or in voting. . . . The custom and broad spirit of tolerance should obviate the possibility of divergences becoming grounds for breach or administrative measures.

On the problems of the international Communist movement, the document of the PCI secretariat repeated, with much more force than in 1956, the polycentrist theses shared by Togliatti and Amendola. Not only did the document stress that "there is not and cannot be a leading party or state, nor one or several instances of centralized leadership of the international Communist movement," and not only did it demand the "full autonomy of each party," but it proclaimed "that the international conferences of 1957 and 1960 did not satisfy the necessity of further development and theoretical and political elaboration" and that "one must always be on guard against that form of provincial presumption that consists in expressing at every moment hasty political judgments on all aspects of the policies of other parties." It would certainly seem that for the writers of this document Khrushchev's anti-Albanian declarations constituted one of these manifestations of "provincial presumption," since they carefully abstained from taking any position about it, except to say:

It must be admitted . . . within certain limits, that there should be expressions of disagreements and differences without this giving rise to irreconcilable conflicts or to political ruptures.

The document then expressed the view that "party organizations should be more fully informed of debates on the great political and ideological problems of the Communist movement."

All these positions appeared completely unacceptable and very dangerous to the PCF leaders. In his report of November 26 to the Central Committee Waldeck Rochet criticized the "opinions voiced in the Italian party by certain opportunist and revisionist elements." He accused them of questioning "the Leninist concept of the new type of party thus favoring the old Social Democratic concept of a party, based on the existence of divergent ideological tendencies," and he announced that "we will not allow such con-

---

William E. Griffith, ed., *Communism in Europe*, Vol. 1 (Cambridge, Mass.: The M.I.T. Press, 1964), pp. 301–383.

14 "Documento del PCI sul XXII Congresso," *L'Unità*, Nov. 28, 1961.

cepts to be developed in our party, in which we have defeated the opportunist and revisionist elements."[15]

Maurice Thorez was still clearer and more vehement without, however, naming the PCI leaders specifically:

What must be guarded as our most precious possessions are the bases of Marxist-Leninist principles, common to all parties, the universal rules that guide their activity. They are solidarity, confidence, and international unity. We on our part will continue to watch over them and to fight every factional spirit in the international Communist movement. In some quarters people persist in developing the theses of "polycentrism." This formula, we fear, strengthens the trend toward factionalism, and we are resolved to preserve international cohesion against this danger.[16]

According to Thorez, the very fact that there was no longer a Comintern or a Cominform and that

Each Communist party is fully independent, from the point of view of organization and of policy. That is precisely why the thesis of polycentrism causes surprise and concern. There is no longer a single center of direction; why talk of setting up several?[17]

To be sure, Togliatti had used an ambiguous formula by saying that the new situation imposed "a multiplicity of leadership centers."[18] In answer to Thorez, he stressed a little later that polycentrism did not consist in "demanding the formation of different regional centers"[19] but in affirming at one and the same time the "full autonomy of the parties" and the necessity of accepting differences between the policies of various groups of parties placed in different conditions. (These remarks of Togliatti seem somewhat hypocritical, since there is reason to think that Togliatti and his intimates really did dream of various regional centers, as did the Italian delegates to the October 1964 WFTU Executive Committee meeting, who envisaged the same for the WFTU. We shall return to this point at the end of this study.)

Thorez also accused the Italian Communists of denying "the universal validity of the Marxist-Leninist theory of revolution" by putting "exclusive value" on "national particularities" and by claiming that the "Twenty-Second Congress did not represent a step forward" on this question of "national roads to socialism." He

15 *L'Humanité*, Nov. 27, 1961; excerpts in Dallin, *op. cit.*, pp. 478–487, at pp. 486–487.

16 *L'Humanité*, Nov. 30, 1961, reprinted in *Problèmes du mouvement communiste international, op. cit.*, p. 67.

17 Quoted from Dallin, *op. cit.*, pp. 492–493.

18 *L'Unità*, Nov. 11, 1961.

19 *Ibid.*, Dec. 1, 1961; *Le Monde*, Dec. 3 and 4–12, 1961.

added: "The Twenty-Second Congress has also been presented as a sort of correction of the [November 1960] 81-Party Declaration, putting an end to 'fictitious unanimity.'" Finally, having expressed, after Rochet, his opposition to "the formation of a majority and a minority" in the party, Thorez gave free rein to his indignation:

A national organization of [PCI] Communist youth has just published a journal where we find the following title on one page: "The Degeneration of the Socialist State." They even talk of acknowledging Trotsky![20]

After that, he recalled at length that he had been present at the meeting of the Comintern Executive Committee in 1927 that had expelled Trotsky from its ranks, treating the latter as a "petit bourgeois who has wind in his sails only when things go well" and as an "unstable element . . . . neither Leninist nor Bolshevik." Thorez then recalled "his [Trotsky's] factional activity in the Soviet Union and the international Communist movement," but he was careful not to say a single word concerning the accusations against Trotsky at the Moscow trials.

The final resolution adopted by the PCF Central Committee on November 26 only repeated on all these points the themes and arguments developed by Waldeck Rochet and Maurice Thorez.

This time the PCI did not give in, as it had in 1956. It indulged in the luxury of publishing the essential passages of the PCF Central Committee resolution in *L'Unità* (contrary to *L'Humanité*'s current practice of criticizing texts without ever quoting them except in truncated form) and of adding an acid note to these extracts:

We consider it opportune to stress the polemical character of Waldeck Rochet's report on the subject of the debate in our party. Particularly where the critics do not have direct and sufficient information and do not refer to concrete cases, and where they speak of a debate that is still in process and where various ideas confront each other freely, a method of judgment consisting in hastily cataloging things and applying labels has neither foundation nor utility.[21]

Having thus rejected the labels of revisionism and opportunism with which Rochet had attacked the whole PCI leadership, *L'Unità* ironically declared that the PCF seemed at least to be in accord with the PCI in wishing that the debates between Communist parties should be public, "in view of the fact that it took the initiative of a public polemic with our party."[22]

20 *L'Humanité*, Nov. 30, 1961, and *Problèmes du mouvement communiste international, op. cit.*, pp. 67–68.
    21 *L'Unità*, Nov. 28, 1961.
    22 *Ibid.*

Togliatti himself, in moderate terms, accused the PCF leaders of bad faith:

The interpretation [of polycentrism] and thus the polemics of our French comrades surprise me particularly because they come from competent leaders who know how matters stand, in all details. . . . In 1956, during the Twentieth Congress, in the course of a meeting in which all representatives of the parties belonging to the Cominform participated, an organization of the regional type was proposed, that is, on the basis of closer informational contacts between parties operating in analogous situations. But it was not proposed by our party. The proposition was accepted experimentally and after some hesitation. Some efforts to implement it were definitely made, particularly by our French comrades and ourselves, but they attained no useful result; we gave it up and no longer talked about it, ever.[23]

In short, if one is to believe Togliatti, the PCF leaders pretended to fear that the PCI had the ambition of establishing one of those multiple "leadership centers," knowing perfectly well that there was nothing to it. Simultaneously, he revealed that it was very difficult to collaborate with the "French comrades."

Let us add further that during a press conference in Rome on December 1, 1961, a PCI secretary, Pajetta, maintained that in the preparations for a congress "other documents," opposed to those presented by the Central Committee, could be submitted when the latter were not "satisfactory" and that such texts were subjected to a full discussion. On the question of Trotsky, Pajetta declared that the latter was "a revolutionary who had not joined the imperialists in criminal acts against the Soviet Union" and that his "juridical rehabilitation" was already an accomplished fact but that there was no reason to rehabilitate him "politically."[24]

After his return from Moscow, where he had been accompanied by Giorgio Napolitano (a member of the Central Committee and a partisan of Amendola), Luigi Longo, Deputy Secretary-General of the PCI, confirmed in essence the positions taken by the PCI secretariat of the party the previous week:

We have informed our Soviet comrades of the lively interest and wide approval aroused by the decisions of the Twenty-Second Congress among the Italian Communists and the Italian workers' movement. But we have also presented to them the questions that were provoked by these decisions, and stressed the necessity, particularly for the Soviet comrades, to pursue and deepen the search for the causes of the cult of the personality.[25]

23 *Ibid.,* Dec. 1, 1961; *Le Monde,* Dec. 3 and 4, 1961.
24 *L'Unità,* Dec. 2, 1961.
25 *Ibid.,* Dec. 4, 1961.

It is probable, however, that the Italians, who had advanced their views in isolation, were told in Moscow to be more prudent with their public declarations, all the more so as the other front on which Thorez had declared himself ready to fight could not be forgotten. While the Soviet-Albanian tension led to a rupture of diplomatic relations on December 10, 1961, and Chinese support for Albania became more and more spectacular, a new international skirmish took place at the December 17–19 session of the World Peace Council at Stockholm.

Still defending the priority of national liberation wars and anticolonialist solidarity against the protagonists of "peaceful coexistence," the Chinese delegation opposed the convocation in 1962 of a world congress on such central topics as "general disarmament" and "the solution of the German question." Driven into the minority, the Chinese demonstratively withdrew, followed by the Albanian, Guinean, and—significantly—Algerian delegates. However, the Chinese delegation was able to assemble in a closed session the representatives of the "three continents," that is, the African, Asian, and Latin-American countries, but excluding all other members of the World Peace Council. On January 24, 1962 the PCF Politburo addressed a letter to the CCP Central Committee denouncing the attitude of the Chinese delegation in Stockholm as jeopardizing the unity of the international Communist movement, and asking the CCP to "adhere" to the November 1960 Eighty-One Party Declaration.[26]

At the same time, at the WFTU Congress in Moscow (December 1961), the French trade-union delegation found itself united with the Chinese, Albanians, and Soviets in rejecting the criticism of the CGIL, which found too schematic the positions on the Common Market taken by the majority which associated the Common Market with the "pauperization" of the working class.[27]

In domestic French politics, the last months of the war in Algeria were marked by a series of demonstrations, of which one, which

---

[26] "Lettre du P.C.F. au C.C. du P.C.C.," *Problèmes du mouvement communiste international, op. cit.,* pp. 72–75. See also "La controverse sur le désarmement," *La voie communiste,* No. 27 (Mar.–Apr. 1962), p. 117, and Griffith, *Albania, op. cit.,* pp. 125–143.

[27] See Giorgio Galli, "Italian Communism," *op. cit.,* and L. Romagnoli, "Pour une stratégie nouvelle du mouvement syndical mondial," *Bulletin pour l'étranger* (Paris: Central Committee of the PCF, Jan.–Feb. 1962). Romagnoli implicitly criticizes the passivity of the French GGT in the face of the Algerian war and is explicitly critical of the "pauperization" theory. See also *La voie communiste,* No. 28 (May 1962), pp. 14–15, and Griffith, *Albania, op. cit.,* pp. 123–125.

took place on February 8 and was violently suppressed, was particularly bloody. On February 13 the funeral of the eight victims brought an enormous crowd of people together in Paris. Even though the PCF had left the initiative for the demonstrations of December 1961 and January and February 1962 to the trade unions and had limited itself to "moderate," "antifascist union" slogans, it nevertheless derived a certain advantage from this resumption and violence on the part of the activists. (The demonstrators killed on February 8 were all PCF members.)

Inside the PCF, the only area where any opposition reappeared at that time was the university sector. On the initiative of Jean-Paul Sartre, Professor Laurent Schwartz (PSU), and Jean-Pierre Vigier (expelled from the PCF Central Committee by the Sixteenth Congress), an effort was made by leftist intellectuals, including those who had come to this milieu from the Communist opposition, to create a "League" designed originally to coordinate all "antifascist committees," but later only all action by "university and intellectual" committees. Mixing infiltration with intimidation, the PCF leadership at first succeeded in relegating this new organization to the "ghetto" of the intellectuals, which the latter were, in fact, trying to escape, and finally in making it fail altogether.[28] It should be mentioned, however, that the influence exercised on the UEC (Union des Étudiants Communistes) by the positions taken by the PCI dates back to this period of late 1961 to early 1962, when the many statements by Togliatti, Amendola, and writers in *Nuova Generazione* and other periodicals were circulated and discussed in the UEC "circles" under the benevolent eyes of its leaders.[29]

[28] See "Entretien avec Jean-Paul Sartre," *La voie communiste*, No. 29 (June–July 1962), p. 20.

[29] The FUA (Front d'Unité Antifasciste), which brought together Communist students, students belonging to the PSU, and students without any particular affiliation, was created despite the opposition of the PCF. The party was afraid, with good reason, of being unable to control the FUA, which was based on election by its members rather than on a cartel system among organizations. The FUA survived until the university vacation of 1962.

CHAPTER TWELVE

TOWARD A SINO-SOVIET SPLIT

The months preceding the storm that broke in the fall of 1962 were marked by a relative calm in international Communist polemics. In France, the signing of the Evian Agreement (March 1962) on the cease-fire in Algeria was followed by a referendum in which the PCF for the first time had to endorse the "yes" called for by de Gaulle. Meanwhile, the disintegration and the certain prospect of the disappearance of the OAS (Organisation de l'Armée Secrète) terrorist groups, whose base was formed by men from the European population and military formations in Algeria, created for the PCF the problem of devising a new strategy to supersede the "defense against fascism," which had become pointless.

At the Central Committee session of May 31, 1962, Maurice Thorez revealed that the formula used from 1958 until that time in all PCF propaganda, "Restoration and Renovation of Democracy," had led to a "malevolent interpretation of our party's program." In any event, according to Thorez, "this formula could appear, and has been exploited in this fashion with many Frenchmen, as though it simply meant a return to the past." However, the formula suggested by the Secretary-General, "true, real" democracy, was not much more exciting. On another subject Thorez severely criticized the Communist trade-union leaders for their "inadequate and poorly thought out demands," their search for "unity at any price and only at the summit," and, finally, their "too frequent violations of the rules of trade-union and workers' democracy."[1] Undoubtedly, Thorez gave way to some extent to the pressure of the Italians, whose innovating tendencies contrasted with the PCF's conservatism, when he repeated in his speech some of the arguments that "oppositional" bulletins had been expressing for several years.

However, the PCF's effort to adjust to the actual situation in France progressed very slowly. It had taken the party almost four

[1] *L'Humanité*, June 5, 1962.

years to discover that its propaganda led others to confuse it with other parties identified with the old and discredited institutions of the parliamentary Republic. It took the PCF even longer to modify some of its positions, for example, on the Common Market. The PCI, following the CGIL, had already begun to change on this question. In his report to the Central Committee, published in *L'Unità* of April 27, Luigi Longo had acknowledged that his party had "not properly understood" how to evaluate the consequences of

European integration measures on the Italian economy. It is a fact that European integration was an essential element in the Italian economic leap forward. . . . We must recognize that the economic integration process rests on the objective momentum of productive forces; but we must criticize the way in which this objective necessity was translated into institutional and political terms.[2]

Polemics surged up again, limited, however, to specialists, in the course of a conference of "Marxist researchers," meeting in Moscow in August 1962 and attended by Communist economists of twenty-two countries (with China absent) under the direction of Rumyant-sev, editor-in-chief of the *World Marxist Review* and member of the CPSU Central Committee. Two Frenchmen, Henri Claude and Henri Jourdain, the latter Jean Pronteau's successor as editor-in-chief of *Économie et politique,* tried to defend the positions of the PCF Fifteenth and Sixteenth Congresses, which had termed the Common Market a simple instrument "for the reinforcement of American monopolies in Europe," which would "increase the dependence on the part of the countries of Europe on the United States and the dependence of France on a revanchist and reactionary West Germany."[3] They were in the minority, despite support from the Soviet economist Varga. Another Soviet delegate, Arzumanyan, criticized the "subjective errors" of those who see in the Common Market only "the work of America's and West Germany's foreign policy" and accused them of "ignoring economic facts." The Italian delegates, Emilio Sereni and Eugenio Peggio, were especially frank. They declared in substance that Communist parties could no longer limit themselves to demanding the dissolution of the European Economic Community (EEC) and the denunciation of the Treaty of Rome because, on the one hand, the EEC had considerable vitality, and on the other, it had been based on the real needs

2 *L'Unità,* Apr. 27, 1962.

3 The first quotation is from Waldeck Rochet's report to the PCF Sixteenth Congress; the second is from the thesis of the Fifteenth Congress of the PCF in *Cahiers du Communisme,* July 1, 1959, p. 521.

of economic development.[4] Thus, in this important debate, the PCI had scored an undeniable victory over the PCF, which did not give any publicity to the obsolete positions its delegates had tried to defend. This discretion was all the more natural because, by admitting that the French monopolies were not "simple economic and political agencies of American monopolies,"[5] the PCF gave belated approval to what it had called, a year earlier, the "opportunist deviation" of Servin, Casanova, and Pronteau!

But this was not the moment for the PCF to insist on such subtleties; in the midst of an electoral campaign it traditionally suspended theoretical debates. On the occasion of the October 28 referendum, concerning the election of the President of the Republic by universal suffrage, and of the November 18 and 25 parliamentary elections, the main PCF slogan was: "Marching separately side by side, we shall strike together." War had been declared on "sectarianism," for the object was to seduce the greatest number of those who, having formed an opposition coalition from the Socialists to the Independents, found themselves "objective allies" of the PCF in the "Battle of the Referendum." Despite the latter's discouraging results—de Gaulle, with the sole support of the UNR (Union pour la Nouvelle République) and against the opposition of all other parties, obtained close to 62 per cent of all votes cast and more than 44 per cent of the registered voters—the PCF's entire electoral strategy, particularly between the two rounds, consisted in defeating the candidates of the Gaullist UNR even if one had to vote for MRP or rightist independent candidates.

On November 18, 1962 the PCF received 4,010,000 votes, that is, 140,000 more than in 1958. But a comparison with 1956 shows that close to 1,500,000 Communist votes of that period still had not been regained. However, the PCF leaders attributed great significance to the instructions given to Guy Mollet and the Executive Committee of the SFIO, who withdrew a certain number of their candidates between the two elections and asked their members to vote Communist in order to "defeat the Gaullist candidate." These instructions, moreover, were followed quite well on the whole by the Socialist electorate, a fact which allowed the PCF to quadruple its members in the Assembly. In return, the SFIO

4 See "Facteurs nouveaux de 'l'intégration' du capital monopoliste," *Nouvelle Revue Internationale,* July 1962; *L'Humanité,* Sept. 4–18, 1962; and *L'Unità,* Aug. 29 and Sept. 3–4, 1962.

5 As stated by the French delegate, Henri Claude, according to *L'Unità,* Sept. 16, 1962.

benefited from Communist abstention wherever it found itself confronted head on by the Gaullist candidate, and in certain cases, the PCF even withdrew in favor of a Socialist candidate who had been behind its own in the first vote. This "unitary" attitude allowed the SFIO to avoid a disintegration of its parliamentary representation. But even so, the new Assembly was dominated by a majority of the UNR and of the Gaullist "independents." By embroidering the actual facts a little, the PCF wanted to make the main point of this electoral campaign the fact that for the first time in many years "unity of action" between Socialists and Communists had been achieved. In fact, however, Guy Mollet had made it very clear that his was only a simple electoral tactic, with no obligation for the future.

In the midst of the electoral fever in France, a double crisis broke out in the fall of 1962: the Sino-Indian conflict and the Cuban missile crisis. The PCF's press and propaganda completely aligned themselves, from day to day, with the official positions of Soviet diplomacy.[6] Even more remarkable was the absence of any but purely verbal reaction on the part of the PCF during the entire crisis, except for some very small demonstrations of delegates outside the American embassy which stopped as soon as the Kennedy-Khrushchev agreement was reached and even before Castro had given his consent.

In the new phase of Sino-Soviet polemics (this time public) which opened at the Congresses of the Communist Parties of Bulgaria, Hungary, Italy, and Czechoslovakia in November and December 1962, and which continued in January 1963 at the SED (Socialist Unity Party of Germany), Congress in East Germany, the PCF played an active role, particularly through the speeches of its delegates at these meetings. The PCF speeches supported those of the other Khrushchevian parties, and were always on the same model: approval of the attitude of the Soviet Union, which had "saved the peace" in the Cuban crisis, and denunciation of the Albanian "dogmatists" and their supporters. Yet, for some months the Chinese spared Maurice Thorez. In fact, of the first eight polemical articles published in *Jen-min Jih-pao* and *Hung Ch'i* between December 15, 1962 and March 9, 1963, which constituted the first

---

[6] To such a point that one could read in *L'Humanité* of October 24: "The pretexts invoked by Kennedy to hide his actions of piracy are pure lies. Everybody knows that the only military base in Cuba is an American base—Guantanamo." And this on the eve of the day when Khrushchev officially recognized the presence of Soviet missiles in Cuba!

distinct series of public positions taken by Peking on problems of the world Communist movement, one article was dated December 31, 1962,[7] while the other article appeared only on February 27, 1963.[8] It may be supposed that this delay was due to a tactical calculation on the part of the Chinese, who may have felt entitled to expect that the openly revisionist theses of the PCI Tenth Congress would arouse a violent reaction on the part of the PCF and that Thorez would hesitate to align himself with Togliatti and Tito.

If this was indeed Peking's calculation, it proved false. At the Central Committee meeting at Malakoff on December 13–14, 1962, Maurice Thorez gave a new and almost caricatured demonstration of his ability to align himself quickly with Moscow. On December 12, 1962, in a long speech before the Supreme Soviet in Tito's presence, Khrushchev proclaimed that the Cuban crisis had shown that "dogmatism . . . represents at present the greatest danger." On December 14, Maurice Thorez told the Central Committee (as Raymond Guyot had already done the night before) that the "dangers of narrowness and dogmatism . . . actually constitute the principal danger for the workers' movement."[9] The Central Committee resolution echoed his words:

[The party] will combat without respite the danger of dogmatism and sectarianism, which has lately become the essential danger for the international Communist and workers' movement. It will do this in common with all fraternal parties, with the universally recognized vanguard of the movement, the Communist Party of the Soviet Union.[10]

However, Thorez did not completely abandon his hostility to revisionism, but he was willing to tone it down and soften it. The night before, Raymond Guyot had already endorsed

efforts by the Soviet comrades . . . to help the League of Communists of Yugoslavia to take its place again in the great Communist family. . . . We were never resigned and will never resign ourselves to Yugoslavia's being absent in the united struggle of the world revolutionary movement.[11]

7 "The Differences Between Comrade Togliatti and Us," *Jen-min Jih-pao*, Dec. 31, 1962; *Peking Review*, Vol. VI, No. 1 (Jan. 4, 1963), pp. 9–21; in Alexander Dallin, ed., with Jonathan Harris and Grey Hodnett, *Diversity in International Communism* (New York and London: Columbia University Press, 1963), pp. 706–729.

8 "Whence the Differences?—A Reply to Thorez and Other Comrades," *Jen-min Jih-pao*, Feb. 27, 1963; *Peking Review*, Vol. VI, No. 9, (Mar. 1, 1963), pp. 7–16; in Dallin, *op. cit.*, pp. 782–794.

9 *Problèmes du mouvement communiste international* (Paris: PCF, Jan. 1963), p. 90.

10 *Ibid.*, p. 95.

11 *Ibid.*, p. 85.

Thorez was a little less warm but came to the same conclusions:

We have fought against the erroneous positions of the principal protagonists of the revisionist deviation, the leaders of the League of Communists of Yugoslavia. But we have done so in the desire to re-establish links with the Yugoslav people and organizations.

And with some daring he adduced as proof of this "desire" his having sent to Belgrade "after 1957" a delegation led by François Billoux[12] as though nothing had happened in between!

Thorez also took good care to make clear that there was no question of supporting the PCI theses:

We have also lead the fight against other opportunist theses in the international movement, on reformist views regarding the transition to socialism, on polycentrism, on Leninist principles for the organization of parties of the new type, and on certain tendencies toward integration in the mechanism of the Common Market.[13]

By these allusions he condemned the entire orientation of the PCI Tenth Congress.

The PCF's campaign against the Chinese positions intensified considerably in January 1963 with the publication of two articles in *L'Humanité*, one an editorial by Raymond Guyot, and of two articles in *France Nouvelle* in the period between January 5 and 16, 1963. During the same month the PCF also published the texts of its speeches at the November 1960 Moscow Conference, until then known only to its activists, together with a number of letters, speeches, and resolutions designed to show the continuity of the PCF line since the summer of 1960 on all problems of the international Communist movement. Clearly, this PCF offensive seems to have been coordinated with the staging of the SED Congress in East Berlin (January 15–21) in the course of which the Chinese delegate was drowned out by stamping of feet and Khrushchev made his proposal to stop the polemics between fraternal parties. The PCF played its role in a concerted maneuver designed to obtain from the Chinese cessation of public debate by showing them that they were isolated.

From the beginning of 1963, moreover, the PCF charted its course in the crisis of the international Communist movement strictly in accordance with the alternation of phases of calm and resurgence of tension between China and the Soviet Union. For Maurice Thorez, the denunciation of the Chinese theses seemed

12 *Ibid.,* p. 90.
13 *Ibid.*

to pay off on the plane of domestic politics: By taking a position in favor of peaceful coexistence, the "peaceful road," and collaboration with the Socialist parties, the French Communists also hoped to neutralize the mistrust of the SFIO and other non-Communist forces, to whom they had proposed unity of action with redoubled vigor since the legislative elections. Anti-Chinese firmness also paid off inside the PCF, where it gave to the Thorez group a sort of guarantee of Khrushchev's support against new threats arising from the right, that is, from the revisionists.

These threats were particularly noticeable in two areas, of which the first was the student sector. The UEC Sixth Congress, which met from February 21 to 24, 1962 at Chatillon-sous-Bagneux, represented a serious defeat for the PCF leadership. The draft program submitted by the UEC National Bureau was inspired by the PCI theses and was, in any case, an effort to set an independent line and gain freedom from the PCF's tutelage. It was adopted by a more than three-quarters majority. This majority, moreover, became so massive only after the formation of a tactical alliance between the "left" and the "Italian right" around the themes of anti-Stalinism and organizational autonomy, that is, against the PCF Central Committee. In his speech the Italian delegate, Terzi, expounded the positions of the PCI on the Common Market, and was given a standing ovation by three quarters of those present, including those on the dais, while from all directions cries of "Stand up!" were directed at the three delegates of the PCF Central Committee, Roland Leroy, Louis Baillot, and Jacques Chambaz, who alone had remained seated. This was the first time the PCF leadership found itself publicly beaten in a national organization (the UEC had nearly 4,000 members) that the party itself had set up. The PCF's immediate reaction was relatively moderate, limited to launching a campaign against the principal leaders of the UEC, particularly against its Secretary-General Alain Forner, based on an attempt to exploit the prejudice of the workers against the students, whose deviations were attributed to the "petit bourgeois" milieu whence they had come and to the inexperience of youth.[14]

14 With regard to the Sixth Congress of the UEC, see *Clarté*, No. 15 (Mar. 1963); "La Direction du parti contre l'U.E.C.," *La voie communiste*, No. 33 (Feb.–Mar. 1963), p. 16; "Debout, debout," *Le Débat Communiste*, No. 13 (Mar. 15, 1963), pp. 3–5; and *Unir*, No. 125 (Apr. 1963), pp. 2–3. It is worth noting that during this period, in February 1963, the UEC organized an evening with the Soviet poet Yevtushenko at the Mutualité in Paris, which was a grand success. A few weeks later, on March 8, Khrushchev delivered his speech criticizing Soviet intellectuals, among them Yevtushenko.

The other sector of the revisionist offensive was the WFTU, where, after having opposed the delegate of the French CGT and WFTU Secretary-General Louis Saillant (a "non-Communist" but a perfectly docile *apparatchik*) in several successive meetings of the Executive Committee, the CGIL decided to open an office in Brussels to deal with the Common Market. This decision had been pushed through by Luciano Lama, one of the most gifted Communist labor leaders of Italy, after discussions officially described as "very animated." Unable to prevent the Italians from executing their project, the WFTU Executive Committee specified that the Brussels office of the CGIL would act "in accordance with other organizations of the WFTU."[15] At the conference of the six Communist parties of the Common Market countries held from March 5 to 7 in Brussels, no agreement could thus be reached between the participants on the question of an immediate withdrawal from the Common Market, as proposed by the Dutch. The final communiqué concealed the persistence of the differences, mainly between the French and the Italians, with a general formula about the necessity of arriving at "the greatest unity of action between the parties and workers' movements of the countries concerned."[16] This was an admission of defeat.

During the same period, the revisionist trend in France became manifest with the publication of a certain number of books: *La coexistence pacifique,* by Victor Leduc, still a member of the PCF; *Le marxisme de notre temps,* by Gilles Martinet, a PSU leader; and *Le parti démocratique,* by a group of Communist activists under the pseudonym of Jean Dru, in which could be recognized numerous ideas dear to the former Central Committee member Jean Pronteau.[17] Chinese activity consisted mainly in the extensive dissemination of the fiery documents published in Peking after December 1962, particularly of the "Reply to Maurice Thorez."

If one compares this last text ("Whence the Differences?" in *Jen-min Jih-pao,* February 27, 1963) with the article against Togliatti, for example, one can see that the tone and the point of attack of the Chinese polemic were very different. Togliatti was attacked as a revisionist, mainly on the level of theory. Thorez was attacked

15 See *Avanti!,* Jan. 31 and Mar. 15, 1963, and Giorgio Galli, "Italian Communism," in William E. Griffith, ed., *Communism in Europe,* Vol. I (Cambridge, Mass.: The M.I.T. Press, 1964), pp. 365–368, and William E. Griffith, *The Sino-Soviet Rift* (Cambridge, Mass.: The M.I.T. Press, 1964), pp. 126–127.

16 *L'Unità,* Mar. 8, 1963.

17 All three books were published by Éditions Julliard in Paris. The first appeared in 1962, the remaining two in 1963.

for his actions, particularly "his 180 degree turns under the Soviet baton" performed since 1959 and "too numerous to mention." The "baton" was not specified more precisely in the article, but the blind submission to the Soviet Union on the part of Thorez and the French leaders was violently stigmatized:

What someone else says, they repeat word for word. If someone else takes one step, they follow with the same step. Here there is all too much ability to parrot and all too little of Marxist-Leninist principle. Are "creative Marxist-Leninists" of this kind something to be proud of?[18]

Togliatti was attacked, to some extent, as one of those who shared responsibility for the revisionist line, and Thorez as a simple parrot of Khrushchev. The Chinese Communists seemed, after several months of hesitation, to have deliberately chosen to wound Thorez' pride. With this they had burned all possible bridges for a reconciliation with Thorez unless the move was so ordered by Moscow.

In the beginning of April 1963, a PCF delegation held talks in Moscow with the CPSU leadership. The final communiqué confirmed once again "the total unity of views and identity of judgment of the two Marxist-Leninist parties on all questions under discussion."[19] However, once again the PCF had just demonstrated its political impotence in France: Despite the exceptional opportunity furnished by a miners' strike that was conducted from March 1 until April 8 by the three trade-union centers in complete unity, the CGT showed itself incapable of organizing the solidarity of the other groups and eventually called for a return to work on the basis of a compromise that had already been suggested two

18 "Whence the Differences?," op. cit., p. 15.

19 L'Humanité, May 9, 1963. It may be of some interest to note the time at which this meeting took place, the end of the winter of 1962–1963—a winter that Khrushchev seems to have found difficult even with regard to the Soviet Union. One of the more striking aspects of his difficulties was the offensive unleashed, beginning with the December 1, 1962 Manège exhibition, against abstract art and the new currents in Soviet literature which drove Khrushchev almost to the point of rehabilitating Stalin's image in his speech of March 8, 1963 (footnote 14, supra). The text was reprinted in full in France Nouvelle, Mar. 20, 1963, but the PCF's approval was reserved in tone without going so far as to show open disagreement, as did Togliatti (in an interview with L'Express, May 23, 1963). It may be important to note that the PCF delegation led by Waldeck Rochet and Raymond Guyot had had talks in April 1963 not with Khrushchev but with Frol Kozlov (one of Kozlov's last public activities before his "disappearance" and the announcement of his illness), Mikhail Suslov, and Boris Ponomarev. The PCF became directly involved in the "ideological" dispute over art when French Communist painter Fernand Léger's exhibition in Leningrad and Kiev was canceled on April 19. It had been highly successful in Moscow, where it had opened January 17.

weeks earlier and that provoked keen discontent among the dynamic trade-union activists. In contrast to this negative example, the PCI scored a great success in the legislative elections of April 28, 1963, gaining more than a million votes and advancing from 22.7 to 25.3 per cent of the votes cast. This victory gave a new argument to the students in the UEC, who continued to resist all pressures exercised by the party delegates to make them return to the positions of the Sixth Congress.

The PCF Central Committee, meeting at Ivry from May 8 to 10, 1963, devoted a special point on its agenda to the UEC problem. Contrary to general expectations, no decision was taken in the sense of "liquidating" this oppositional center; on the contrary, Maurice Thorez permitted the continuation of the discussion but "in a fraternal and sensible spirit." On the problems of the international Communist movement the Central Committee published a long document paraphrasing Soviet texts almost word for word, after Waldeck Rochet had said in his report:

The comrades in the Chinese Communist Party considered it necessary to repeat in their turn an old slander aimed by capitalist reaction against the Communist parties of every country, by accusing us of obeying the "Soviet baton." We can only register our indignation at finding this reactionary slander in the mouths of Communists.

This did not prevent him from immediately adding that the PCF was "happy" to be in accord with the CPSU

on all questions of the international workers' movement. . . . For us, French Communists, the great Soviet Union remains the first socialist country in the world, and the glorious Communist Party of the Soviet Union, the party of Lenin, the most experienced and battle-hardened detachment of the world Communist movement.[20]

In brief, these men disclaimed the baton, but not their obedience. And as the CPSU favored the end of public polemics, pending an international conference to "reinforce the unity of the movement," for which "favorable conditions" had to be created, the PCF fell into step.

20 *L'Humanité*, May 9, 1963. Khrushchev appeared to have strengthened his position. Shortly after his speech of April 24, in which he alluded to the possibility of softening his position, the "ideological" session of the Central Committee was set for June instead of May. In Czechoslovakia the measures taken for Karol Bacílek's expulsion from the party, as well as the plans for rehabilitation and various other procedures decided upon by the Central Committee on April 3 and 4 (contrary to the decisions of the Congress in December 1962), were made public on May 14.

On the Brink of Schism

With the publication by the Chinese of the "Letter of 25 Points" of June 14, 1963,[21] the conversations arranged for July between the CPSU and the CCP hardly promised to create "favorable conditions" for the "reinforcement of unity." Omitting the reference—traditional until that time in earlier polemical articles—to the Moscow Declaration, Peking proposed as the agenda for the meeting a new political line, thus letting it be understood that acceptance of the "25 Points" was the minimum for reaching an accord. It is no exaggeration to say that the document of June 14 was a veritable "Manifesto of Split."[22]

Actually, shortly after the "suspension" of the bilateral Sino-Soviet negotiations, tension reached a point equivalent to a de facto schism. The signing by Moscow of the test ban treaty on August 5, 1963 (already initialed on July 25) put an end to all efforts at compromise. The PCF immediately joined the international Soviet-sponsored campaign presenting the treaty as a great victory for the cause of peace, for which they warmly congratulated Khrushchev. Federal and sectional committees were invited to vote resolutions to that effect and to denounce the hostile attitude of the Chinese Communists to the treaty by comparing their attitude to that of the Gaullists.

The French "Chinese"

The worries of the PCF leaders were to some extent justified by the first manifestations of "Chinese" influence not only within the party and its fringes but in attempts to assume more organic forms. Already on June 9, 1963 a small but tenacious opposition had made its appearance at the Congress of the Franco-Chinese Friendship Society, set up in 1952 and administered by PCF functionaries, who had tried to let it become dormant after 1960. By a slim majority the congress had decided to hear two Chinese correspondents from the New China News Agency, despite the contrary ad-

21 "A Proposal Concerning the General Line of the International Communist Movement—The Letter from the Central Committee of the Communist Party of China in Reply to the Letter from the Central Committee of the Communist Party of the Soviet Union of March 30, 1963—June 14, 1963," *Jen-min Jih-pao*, June 17, 1963; *Peking Review*, Vol. VI, No. 25 (June 21, 1963), pp. 6–22, reprinted in full in William E. Griffith, *The Sino-Soviet Rift* (Cambridge, Mass.: The M.I.T. Press, 1964), pp. 259–288.

22 André Renaud, "La lettre en vingt-cinq points ou le manifeste de la rupture," *La voie communiste*, No. 36 (June–July 1963), p. 16.

vice of the PCF Politburo, which asserted that foreigners should be refused the right to speak because the organization in question was "French." However, the decisions made at the congress practically amounted to a scuttling of the society, as the latter refused to disseminate, even for informational purposes, Chinese texts "of an ideological nature." Only four delegates out of sixty voted against this: Professor Charles Bettelheim, the journalist and sinologist Claude Cadart (staff member of *France-Observateur*), and the two delegates of the society's Marseille Committee.

Although it did not represent a particularly important political force, the Marseille Committee, which had always been one of the most active in the society, rested to some extent on a proletarian base. The attraction that China held for a certain number of militant Marseille workers was undoubtedly connected with the discontent provoked by the PCF's policy of unity with the Socialists. (The tension between militant Socialists and Communists was particularly strong in Marseille, where the SFIO, led by Mayor Gaston Defferre, recruited extensively from the ranks of the bourgeoisie and practiced a policy of alliance with the right.)

In a speech made at Moyeuvre-Grande, in Lorraine, on June 23, 1963, Maurice Thorez himself had revealed that "sectarianism, the principal danger on the international plane," manifested itself internally, as well:

For example, we have learned that several of our mayors in the Pas-de-Calais area refused to put the flag at half-mast at the death of Pope John XXIII. We will take issue with these comrades publicly. And we will tell them that the Communists of 1963 need not be belated anticlericals. Another spirit must prevail.[23]

In other words, resistance to the policy of "the outstretched hand to the Catholics" disturbed the PCF leaders all the more because it might make the activists susceptible to the themes of Chinese propaganda. To those who opposed him, Thorez said brutally:

. . . You have many merits, but don't think that history came to a halt with your last strike. . . . You live in your memories now.[24]

All in all, he tried to discredit these recalcitrants by comparing them to old fighters incapable of doing more than ramble on about past exploits.

Pro-Chinese propaganda also fell on interested ears, particularly in some departments of the Centre, among old Resistance fighters

---

23 *France Nouvelle,* No. 924 (July 3–9, 1963), p. 20.
24 *Ibid.*

(these were regions where the Maquis had been mainly composed of Franc-Tireurs and Partisans under Communist leadership), a great number of whom still felt that they had been deprived of the fruits of their victory in 1944 and that the failure of the "peaceful road" was evident enough.[25]

However, the organizing efforts of pro-Chinese allies and sympathizers in France did not succeed and are still not succeeding in making serious inroads into those strata of activists or ex-activists who had rebelled against the PCF line. It is true, moreover, that many of them have grown too old and have experienced too great disappointment for their dynamism not to have been exhausted.

Thus, the first "French Chinese" appeared among intellectuals and students. These must be carefully distinguished from old opposition groups trying to exploit the opportunity furnished by the crisis by leaning on Peking's theses for tactical reasons or by trying to acquire thus a prestigious patronage. The group *Le Communiste,* which had been able to assemble several PCF members around a nucleus formed by dissidents from the Fourth International (particularly its guiding spirit, Michèle Mestre), violently denied their Trotskyite origins and busily disseminated literature from Peking, which they pretended to endorse completely. The Chinese Communists did not seem to be grateful to them for it and continued to ignore these activists who had their origins in anti-Stalinism. While favoring the distribution of the CCP documents, *La voie communiste* tried on its part to conserve a critical attitude with regard to their content and rejected in particular the campaign in favor of Stalin's rehabilitation, a fact which alone would have been enough to render it suspect in the eyes of the Chinese authorities.

Nevertheless, in July 1963 the men behind *La voie communiste* took the initiative of setting up committees for the creation of a "People's Franco-Chinese Society" to make up for the default of the "Franco-Chinese Friendship Society," controlled and neutralized by the PCF *apparat.* At the end of autumn 1963, particularly after the first public meeting held in Paris on October 25, the organizing committee had grown considerably: The original nucleus set up by oppositional activists and Claude Cadart, one of the opposition in the "Franco-Chinese Friendship Society," had been joined by personalities such as the agronomist René Dumont, some

[25] Information received from private sources that, though various, are in agreement. My sources are connected with a number of Communist federations (Corrèze, Dordogne, Creuse, Haute-Vienne, Lot-et-Garonne, Allier, Cher, Loir-et-Cher, Saône-et-Loire, Nièvre, Gard, Hérault, and Basses-Alpes, in particular).

revisionist intellectuals such as Henri Lefebvre, and left-wing Catholics such as Jean-Marie Domenach. *L'Humanité* denounced this "astonishing mixture of revisionists, unrepentant Trotskyites, and renegades from our party" and expressed regret that "in this curious amalgam" there were some "intellectuals who no doubt were misled."[26] Even though this spectrum was actually much less wide and disparate than that of most "friendship" organizations supported by the PCF, which traditionally reserved places for moderate or rightist personalities, it seems that the argument carried some weight with the Chinese. Doubtless, the latter would have preferred a society with the support of personalities far removed from communism, that is, close to the government, to a movement with too many intellectuals and anti-Stalinists ("Trotskyites"[27] and "revisionists"), which could serve as a docile instrument. In any case, since Peking withheld its support, the projected society, which despite its limited means had about a thousand members in a few months, never became active.

The lawyer Jacques Vergès, a native of Réunion and an old functionary of the international Communist apparatus, who had quietly left the PCF in 1957 to place himself at the service of the FLN, had obviously received moral—and probably material—support from the Chinese to launch his magazine *Révolution,* the first issue of which appeared in September 1963. Jacques Vergès placed himself under Chinese discipline without reservation or restriction. His magazine, luxurious in appearance and presentation, had an English and later a Spanish edition. It appealed for the collaboration of various pro-Chinese groups and personalities, particularly in the uncommitted world, and for some time it seemed to be the channel chosen by Peking to make its ideas known in France. However, its readership did not seem to go much beyond students, professors, and intellectuals.[28] Even in the UEC, where a resolution condemning the Chinese theses, in terms inspired by PCI statements, received forty-six votes as against ten abstentions in the

26 *L'Humanité,* Feb. 7, 1964.

27 In fact, neither of the two main branches of the Trotskyite movement in France—the "Franck" group with its organ, *L'Internationale* and the "Lambert" group with its organ, *La vérité*—belonged to the Association des amités francochinoises.

28 See François Fejtö, "A Maoist in France: Jacques Vergès and *Revolution,*" *China Quarterly,* No. 19 (July–Sept. 1964), pp. 120–127: "Vergès, as he expounded his ideas to me with the fine phrases of a brilliant Sorbonne student, made me think of the Russian 'Decembrists' and Nihilists of the nineteenth century, of the starry-eyed conspirators, like Rajk, with whom I rubbed shoulders in my youth." (p. 127.)

National Committee meeting of September 14–15, this minority of ten abstentions contained only one pro-Chinese, a friend of Vergès'; the rest consisted of adherents of opposition groups.

For this reason the CCP seems to have limited the hopes it felt it could place in Vergès and transferred them to Communist activists who had been able to maintain themselves at the head of some local committees of the "Franco-Chinese Friendship Society" in Marseille, Bordeaux, and Clichy. Beginning with these isolated nuclei, the monthly *Bulletin d'information marxiste-léniniste* was started; its first issue appeared in January 1964. But the principal guiding spirits of this enterprise, which had tried to distinguish itself very clearly from other small opposition groups by attacking them violently, were publicly denounced by Raymond Guyot at the Central Committee meeting of March 25, 1964 and expelled from the party. A meeting held in the little town of Libourne by pro-Chinese militants from Bordeaux was even interrupted by hecklers. Meanwhile, in Paris, on the occasion of the fifteenth anniversary of the Chinese People's Republic in October 1964, thanks to the support of the Chinese Embassy's cultural attaché, a "Maoist" meeting scored a first great success by its large attendance.

So far, however, Chinese Communist efforts to implant the seeds of a faction within the PCF or to create the nucleus of a dissident party have been unsuccessful. The Chinese did not even attain the first result they sought—to detach an important group from the Central Committee, as they were able to do in Belgium and Switzerland. Many rumors have circulated about the existence of Chinese sympathies on the part of François Billoux, but it would be foolhardy to take them too seriously. Finally, the preference the Chinese have given to the small groups in Marseille, Bordeaux, and Clichy can be explained by the fact that the Chinese Communists find resemblances to their own masses in these simple and believing activists, often workers. But this audience does not satisfy them. They seem desirous of acquiring at least some marginal influence in milieus far removed from communism, and after Communist China's recognition by the French government[29] they had some noteworthy successes in that direction: *Le Monde, Le Figaro,* and French State Television have published or shown reports on the whole very favorable to China. The Chinese know how to make use of the anti-Sovietism of the bourgeois press quite cleverly and

[29] January 27, 1964. It is of interest to note that the Chinese press and the New China News Agency usually cite the UNR daily, *La Nation,* whose poor circulation gives it something of the nature of a confidential newsletter.

are rather pleased to find there indications of a symmetrical rebellion by the two powers, France and China, against an invading
protector: the United States on the one hand and the Soviet Union
on the other.

Among French intellectuals of the extreme left who, particularly
during the war in Algeria, strongly resented the deception created
by the PCF leadership's opportunist attitude, the influence of
the Chinese and Italian Communist parties often blend in a strange,
entirely negative fashion. Since the only common point of these
two contradictory influences is their tendency to arrive at an oppositional attitude, the PCF leaders have never failed to throw the
two together in order to emphasize all the more the insignificance
of PCF opponents. In reality, this susceptibility to contradictory
influences is proof of immaturity and an emotional rather than a
political character trait.

The PCF Calls for a New International Meeting

Despite the worries we have described, the fact that the Central
Committee meeting of October 5 and 6, 1963 at Ivry became a
spearhead in the international offensive against the Chinese cannot be attributed mainly to internal considerations. For the first
time the PCF did not limit itself to following the CPSU Central
Committee; rather, it anticipated the Soviets by demanding that
an international conference of Communist parties be held for the
purpose of denouncing the Chinese and obtaining their submission.
Of course, this French "initiative" had probably been discreetly
solicited by Moscow beforehand. There were some indications to
this effect, such as the publication in *Pravda* on September 25 of
a resolution by the (clandestine) Portuguese Communist Party proposing even then the convocation of an international conference.
Yet, considering its importance, one can say that the PCF appeared
to have launched the campaign for the holding of an international
Communist meeting.

The reports and speeches by Waldeck Rochet, Raymond Guyot,
and Maurice Thorez at the Ivry Central Committee meeting were
all characterized by extremely violent denunciations of Chinese
policy. The stage of ideological polemics was largely over. Rochet
accused the Chinese Communists of following an "adventurist and
nationalist policy" and of aggravating international tension, as
well as of promoting the nuclear arms race by their hostility to the
Moscow treaty, a hostility which "in the last analysis they shared

with the imperialist 'madmen' and partisans of the Cold War such as de Gaulle." Rochet further accused the Chinese of maintaining positions very close to such Trotskyite ones as "permanent revolution" and "exporting revolution," as well as of intending to "divide the united revolutionary front of all anti-imperialist forces" and of reducing the working class of the capitalist countries to an "auxiliary role" at the risk of provoking "disastrous consequences." Rochet also accused them of pursuing a "reprehensible splitting and dividing action" by "grossly violating the most elementary rules of relations between fraternal parties and by flouting the principles of proletarian internationalism." He even went so far as to insinuate that the CCP leaders were conniving with "the worst reactionaries," because "in Franco's Spain and Adenauer's Germany Chinese documents are widely distributed, while Communists and anti-Fascists in those countries are stifled." The old method of association was used by Rochet in order to group together with Adenauer and Franco "the worst renegades," "oppositionists of all kinds," and, naturally, the "Trotskyites" who were all "supporting" Mao Tse-tung. Waldeck Rochet did not even spare the CCP the accusation that it was seeking to "isolate Yugoslavia from other socialist countries and to drive her into the imperialist camp." Since the resumption of contacts (interrupted in 1957) by a PCF delegation led by Georges Thevenin and received by the League of Communists of Yugoslavia in March 1963, the tone of the PCF press had in fact become quite warm again with respect to the Yugoslavs.

Before presenting his proposition to convoke a world conference of Communist and workers' parties "with the least possible delay," Rochet clearly defined the objective of such a conference:

Between the correct line of the international Communist movement and the sectarian and adventurist line of the Chinese leaders, one cannot remain impartial or adopt a conciliatory position. The erroneous theses of the Chinese leaders and their splitting activity must be denounced and fought without hesitation.[30]

The phrase "no conciliatory position is possible" was taken up by Maurice Thorez in his speech when he accused the Chinese of being more belligerent against India than against Great Britain in Hong Kong or against Portugal in Macao, of wanting to "Sinify" Marxism and of looking forward to the creation of a revolutionary Maquis in France. Thorez condemned any hesitation in these terms:

[30] All quotations from Waldeck Rochet's report are taken from *L'Humanité*, Oct. 8, 1963, pp. 7–8.

Some comrades say that they deplore the Chinese position but do not want to denounce it. This was the argument expressed by Kapo, the representative of the Albanian Party of Labor, at the Bucharest Conference which prepared the 81-party meeting. Kapo contented himself with saying, "One cannot denounce a great party." And why not, if that party fails to follow the commonly accepted line? We have also heard the converse argument: when the Albanians began to affirm their extreme position . . . some said, "But it's a small country! One must understand small countries." If we look at things from this point of view, neither large nor small countries can be judged.[31]

The conclusion is obvious: All heretics, large or small, must be judged, lest "the erroneous theses of the Chinese comrades trouble some spirits."

These speeches, as well as the resolution based on their principal themes, were clearly meant to give notice precisely to those parties (Polish, Italian, Romanian, and Cuban) that hesitated to pronounce an excommunication. By taking responsibility for this warning and by appearing to implore the CPSU the same as all other parties to eliminate any temptation toward conciliation, the PCF rendered a great service to the Soviet leaders.

Peking's reply was prompt. An article published in *Jen-min Jih-pao* and *Hung Ch'i* entitled "Apologists of Neo-Colonialism"[32] contained a very violent passage accusing the PCF of

having given up many years ago the struggle against American imperialism . . . thus definitely handing back to de Gaulle and others the standard of the French national struggle against American imperialism.

The article said that the PCF leaders had "run aground in the mire of chauvinism," defended "the colonial interest of the French imperialists," and "opposed the national liberation movements of the French colonies." This time the Chinese leaders traced the responsibility of the French leaders all the way back to 1946 for having "been divided by the French monopolist bourgeoisie" by accepting the "neo-colonialist ruse of French union." And a passage devoted to the PCF's "chauvinist attitude" on the Algerian question (in connection with which even the Soviet attitude was called shameful) ended with this tirade:

See what frenzy the chauvinism on the part of the leaders of the French Communist Party has reached! Is there a trace of proletarian internation-

[31] *Ibid.*, Oct. 10, 1963.

[32] "Apologists of Neo-Colonialism—Comment on the Open Letter of the Central Committee of the CPSU (4), by the Editorial Departments of *People's Daily* and *Red Flag*, October 21, 1963," *Jen-min Jih-pao* and *Hung Ch'i*, Oct. 21, 1963; *Peking Review*, Vol. VI, No. 43 (Oct. 25, 1963), pp. 6–15; excerpts in Griffith, *The Sino-Soviet Rift, op. cit.*, pp. 475–480.

alism among them? Is there anything proletarian-revolutionary whatever among them? By accepting this chauvinist position, they have betrayed the basic interests of the international proletariat, the French proletariat and the true French national interests.[33]

Three weeks were to elapse before *L'Humanité* carried an embarrassed reply by Léon Feix, accompanied by only brief extracts from the Chinese article.[34]

In the meantime, the PCF reached agreement with its Czech allies at the meeting of a delegation led by Georges Marchais with Antonín Novotný on October 11 where both parties affirmed "their complete support of the Leninist attitude of the CPSU Central Committee in the struggle for peace, peaceful coexistence, and socialism."[35] It then signed with the Dutch Communist Party on October 27 a joint declaration that adopted, word for word, the French proposal for an international conference.[36] These interparty contacts, following in the wake of the exceptionally wide publicity given by *Pravda* to the labors of the PCF Central Committee, aimed at isolating the recalcitrants. Among them was the PCI, whose Central Committee had just reaffirmed, in a long document published by *L'Unità* on October 26, 1963, that

Our party considers it, however, necessary to express its reservations regarding the advisability of calling in the near future a new international conference of the Communist and workers' parties regarding the situation which exists at present in the Communist movement. . . .[37]

33 *Ibid.*
34 *L'Humanité,* Nov. 19, 1963.
35 *Ibid.,* Oct. 12, 1963.
36 *Ibid.,* Oct. 30, 1963.
37 *L'Unità,* Oct. 26, 1963; quoted from Griffith, *The Sino-Soviet Rift, op. cit.,* p. 220. See also François Fejtö, *Chine-URSS, Le Conflit* (Paris, 1966).

CHAPTER THIRTEEN

OPENING TO THE RIGHT

Between October 26 and November 4 an SFIO delegation visited Moscow. Guy Mollet led the delegation, which included presidential aspirant Gaston Defferre, two moderate oppositionists, Albert Gazier and Christian Pineau, and five other SFIO leaders. The communiqué issued at the close of the conversations spoke of a "large measure of agreement" between the SFIO and the CPSU "regarding the need to consolidate the international détente." Going further, the two parties

declared that it is very important to combine the efforts of the working class, the workers, and all democratic and peaceful forces in the struggle for peace, against every war or aggression, and against the danger of a new world war.[1]

Though the communiqué also spoke of continued "important differences in the ideological domain" certain formulas reflected the beginning of a concept of unity of action between Socialists and Communists. To the extent that the definitely intransigent hostility of the SFIO since 1947 to all real unity of action, that is, to any pact resting on a negotiated agreement and not only on circumstantial, limited, and generally oral agreements, had partially disappeared, Khrushchev was right in calculating that a favorable development was taking place with regard to the French Socialists. The PCF leaders, who had launched in their Central Committee meeting of October a campaign for setting up a "common democratic program" in which a presidential candidate could conduct his campaign against de Gaulle, undoubtedly had some hopes in this development. The PCF's demands were, moreover, very moderate: They declared themselves ready in advance to make large concessions to their partners in the desired coalition with regard to the content of the program and to support a non-Communist candidate. In reality, appearances masked the tactical maneuvers tak-

[1] *Le Monde,* Nov. 6, 1963.

ing place inside the SFIO. Guy Mollet would not have been unhappy to bar the road to the presidential candidacy of Gaston Defferre, which had been imposed on the SIFO from the outside by liberal bourgeois groups, expressing themselves mainly in "clubs" and through *L'Express*. As the PCF's support seemed indispensable for any anti-Gaullist candidate, its absence would discourage any competitor from throwing his hat into the ring. However, the combined efforts of Guy Mollet and Maurice Thorez did not suffice to make Defferre withdraw.

Yet it was under the sign of the opening to the right that the PCF Central Committee met at Ivry on January 10, 1964 to undertake preparations for the Seventeenth Congress, postponed until May 14 on account of the local elections in March. All drafts approved by the Central Committee, including the draft of the resolution proposed for discussion at the congress as well as the new and apparently more democratic statutes presented to the activists, were conceived with a view toward making broad alliances easier. The moderation and unusual patience displayed by the PCF leaders vis-à-vis the UEC's persistent lack of discipline can be explained in the same context.

During the same period, the "Week of Marxist Thought," organized by the PCF for the week of January 16, differed from such earlier undertakings in that broader discussions with professors from various disciplines far removed from Marxism were held. These discussions even included Catholic priests, chosen with the consent of the hierarchy. On February 21 at Lyon, Roger Garaudy, a member of the PCF Politburo, in a debate with a Jesuit priest went so far as to disown the theses defended in the Soviet Union by Ilichev with respect to the automatic extinction of religious beliefs in a socialist society. This public display of disagreement with the CPSU, very rare in the history of the PCF, was repeated two months later in connection with a Soviet pamphlet entitled "Judaism without Disguise," the anti-Semitic character of which was condemned by Maurice Thorez and other PCF leaders[2] after similar denunciations by most of the other Western Communist parties. Protests by the Western parties led to a public disavowal of the pamphlet by the CPSU—an unprecedented occurrence in the history of the Communist movement.

But in both cases the affirmation of differences with the CPSU on details in no way jeopardized agreement on fundamentals. On

2 In a letter by Maurice Thorez that appeared in *France Nouvelle*, May 5, 1964, and Victor Michaut, "Contre l'antisémitisme," *ibid.*

the contrary, it might be said that the positions taken by the PCF, designed to show that in certain questions the PCF could maintain its independence with respect to the CPSU, were good tactics with regard to the strategic objective: to remove socialist objections to unity of action and to make the idea of an alliance or a durable coalition with the PCF more generally acceptable to other political currents of opinion.

Besides, the Soviets did not mistake the significance of such gestures of independence on the part of the PCF; far from resenting them, the Soviets called them examples of the results obtained by rapprochement with the socialists. Thus, in an article by A. Chernyayev, "For the Unity of the Labor Class—Communist and Socialist: Perspectives of Cooperation,"[3] the successes obtained by the PCF during previous months with regard to the improvement of its relations with the SFIO were contrasted with the development, "contrary to the true trends of our times," of the situation in the Italian workers' movement, marked by growing tension between the PCI and the Nenni Socialists. To be sure, Chernyayev did not blame this on the Italian Communists. Nevertheless, the PCI's spectacular successes at the polls and in mass movements, particularly the major strikes led by the CGIL under Communist leadership, were played down in comparison with the objectively very minor accomplishments of the PCF.

On balance, the results of the PCF's large-scale policy of unity were very meager. To negotiations on a "common democratic program" as proposed by the Communists, the SFIO had preferred a "public dialogue" on fundamental ideological differences between the two parties. This dialogue, which took the form of a series of articles by Roger Quilliot in *Le Populaire,* the major organ of the SFIO, with unsigned replies in *L'Humanité,* went on from January until March 1964, but succeeded so little in bringing the two viewpoints together that the majority of political observers had good reason to speak of a dialogue between the deaf. As for Gaston Defferre, once he was officially designated by the SFIO Congress as presidential candidate, he not only refused more obstinately than ever to tie himself down with a program but even rejected in principle any negotiations with the Communists. He wanted to gain their vote without having to offer anything in return, simply by making them responsible beforehand—if they did not accept his terms—for the success of de Gaulle or a Gaullist candidate.

[3] *Kommunist,* No. 7, May 1964.

To be sure, the PCF could point to a certain number of successes obtained in the cantonal elections of March 1964, thanks to the mutual agreements on the part of Communists and Socialists to stop running against each other; indeed, the reconstitution of a sort of "popular front reflex" displayed on this occasion by Socialist voters, who voted in a disciplined fashion for the Communist candidate on the second ballot, could be regarded as an encouraging sign. However, the SFIO had never concealed the fact that its electoral alliances were circumstantial and limited and aimed primarily at retaining a certain number of Socialist seats and, where the SFIO candidates had little chance of being elected, at beating the Gaullists. But this did not prevent the Socialist Party from accepting coalitions with the right against the PCF in certain cases.

In these same cantonal elections the PCF pushed its policy of unity against Gaullism so far that it withdrew some of its candidates in favor of politicians of the right, such as Bertrand Motte, who represented in Lille the great traditionalist and anti-Gaullist employers in the north. But there the Communist voters disobeyed the orders of their party en masse to such an extent that Maurice Thorez and Étienne Fajon criticized the desertion, imputing responsibility to the PCF departmental federation. In reality, all such withdawals of candidates had been approved by the Politburo.

Thus, the PCF Central Committee meeting of March 25–26 at Ivry gave Thorez an opportunity to stop or at least limit his overtures to the right. At the same time, as previously with the issue of Algerian self-determination, he profited from this by contrasting (implicitly this time) his own foresight with the errors of other Politburo members. He spoke of the "healthy warning" given by working-class voters to the "horses facing in the wrong direction," "avowed reactionaries," or "groups that always practiced reactionary policies directed against the working class." In short, for Thorez, who had not been able to devote himself personally to the question, the activists in the Nord, Seine-et-Oise, Isère, and Rhône were the ones who had forgotten that the PCF must vote "against personal power and reaction" and who had thought they would be able to support the reaction against de Gaulle's personal power.[4]

While emphasizing that he personally remained indispensable in order to keep the party from committing grave errors, Thorez announced in the same speech an important correction of the systematic anti-Gaullist course pursued by the PCF during the preced-

[4] *L'Humanité*, Mar. 27, 1964.

ing few months. He criticized the tendency to oppose a priori all the measures of the de Gaulle government and noted a whole list of foreign policy *démarches* that Communists should endorse and not oppose: the recognition of Communist China, the proposal for a neutralization of South Vietnam, and the beginnings of an autonomous French policy toward Cuba and Latin America. With regard to Chinese recognition, the only problem was to correct the lack of adroitness with which the Communist press had announced the event—first by minimizing it, then by proclaiming step by step that the government had yielded belatedly to an old Communist demand, and then that the Paris gesture was the result of collusion between de Gaulle and Mao Tse-tung against the Moscow test ban treaty.[5] Thorez said that the PCF should not withhold its support from "positive" measures that might be dictated "by the growth of imperialist contradictions at home and abroad" merely because "de Gaulle allegedly has ulterior motives." In reality, however, behind this "correction" was a whole series of prospects for a Franco-Soviet rapprochement, opened by the journeys of Edgar Faure and Giscard d'Estaing to Moscow and of Podgorny to Paris.

Simultaneously, however, Thorez demonstrated the fragility of the progress made so far regarding unity of action with the Socialists. In fact, the rapprochement with the SFIO, favored by a common hostility to Gaullist domestic policies, was constantly blocked in the area of foreign policy. The SFIO, on the whole, remained faithful to the EEC and NATO, while the government had a much more differentiated attitude with regard to these institutions—a more "positive" attitude from the point of view of Soviet diplomacy, which, as always, basically determined the PCF's position. By stressing the need for appreciating the "positive" aspects of Gaullist foreign policy, Thorez implicitly addressed himself to Moscow as well. Just as he tried to appear vis-à-vis the PCF activists angered by the electoral compromises with the right, as the man indispensable for redressing the errors of other members of the Politburo in domestic politics, he tried to appear in the field

5 See, for example, Léon Feix's interview in *L'Humanité-Dimanche*, Feb. 2, 1964. "Along with France, China is the only great power to refuse to subscribe to the Moscow Treaty." See also a headline in *L'Humanité*, Jan. 18, 1964: "After Five Years of Reflection de Gaulle Becomes Aware that China Exists" and a subhead buried on the third page of *L'Humanité-Dimanche*, Jan. 19, 1964: "The French Government's Recognition of Communist China As Yet Unconfirmed." The PCF Politburo did not publish any communiqué on the occasion, and the following comment is attributed (by a private source of information) to Étienne Fajon: "At last we are to have a daily Chinese information bulletin in Paris!"

of foreign policy in the eyes of the Kremlin as the man who under no circumstances would lose sight of the strategic necessity of subordinating the party line to the general interests of Soviet diplomacy. Looking forward to the PCF Seventeenth Congress, Thorez thus doubly fortified his position.

CHAPTER FOURTEEN

RELAUNCHING THE ANTI-CHINESE CAMPAIGN: THE PCF SEVENTEENTH CONGRESS

In the course of the same Central Committee meeting of March 25–26 Raymond Guyot relaunched the campaign against the Chinese Communist leaders with great violence, accusing them of

wanting to create under their hegemony a factional bloc with its own platform . . . and presenting themselves more and more ambitiously as the sole heirs of the founders of Marxism-Leninism and as the supreme judges of Communist theory and practice.

After denouncing "the creation of fake parties, as in Belgium" and stating that "the few efforts made to organize antiparty groups" in France had "met with failure" (while "calling the Central Committee's attention" to the situation of the Marseille Committee of the "Franco-Chinese Friendship Society")[1] Raymond Guyot insisted on "the convocation, with the least possible delay, of a conference of all Communist and workers' parties of the world."[2] It is interesting to note that this new offensive in favor of an international Communist conference was launched by the PCF less than ten days before the publication in Moscow of the Suslov report, the text of which had remained secret since February 14. A synchronization of these events seems all the more probable because the PCF had carefully avoided echoing the appeal launched on January 21 by Tito and Togliatti

with a view to overcoming the conflicts at present dividing the international labor and Communist movement and . . . to arriving at a new unity preventing the danger of a profound break or even a schism that would lead to an at least temporary weakening of the common struggle of the working class and the progressive forces.[3]

[1] See Chapter Twelve.
[2] L'Humanité, Mar. 27, 1964.
[3] Joint declaration of the PCI and the League of Yugoslav Communists after

In the text of the joint declaration by the two parties most violently attacked by Peking, there was no mention of an international conference. On February 28 *L'Unità* published a communiqué by the PCI Politburo denying a report issued by the news agency Italia concerning a "supposed agreement by the PCI for the convocation of an international conference" as "devoid of all foundation," and reaffirmed that such a conference

would be desirable only if it offered possibilities to obtain positive and unanimous results, while safeguarding the diversity and cohesion of the international Communist movement, which are indispensable necessities, and cannot be renounced.[4]

Put differently, this meant the rejection of the conference in the name of polycentrism.

Still, abandoning the principle of "war on two fronts" for the time being, the PCF Central Committee agreed for the first time, on the occasion of the UEC Seventh Congress, (March 5–8 at Palaiseau) to make important concessions to the "revisionists" in order to defeat the "left." These concessions were all the more surprising because, after working patiently to reconquer student organizations in the provinces, the PCF had succeeded in obtaining the absolute majority of the delegates at the Congress of Palaiseau (approximately 180 out of 325). However, the most important minority consisted of the "left"—Paris, Lyon, Bordeaux, and Nice— and marshaled 90 to 110 votes, depending on the issue, because it was far from homogeneous. The outgoing National Bureau, led by Alain Forner and Pierre Kahn, representing what was called the "Italian" trend, had no more than 45 votes. But to the stupefaction of the orthodox pro-PCF student delegation, the Politburo representative negotiated a compromise with Alain Forner that gave 35 seats in the new UEC National Committee to the "Italians," 35 seats to the orthodox pro-PCF, and only 13 seats to the "left." Thus, the PCF voluntarily sacrificed the absolute majority its strength permitted it to claim, left more than 40 per cent of the leadership posts to a political current representing less than 15 per cent of the votes, and limited to 15 per cent of the leadership posts the representation of the "left," which commanded 30 per cent of the congress. On the one hand, this completely unaccustomed respect for minorities was a gesture in the direction of the Socialists,

---

the January 15–22, 1964 talks, published in *L'Unità*, Jan. 21, 1964. Excerpts were published in *Le Monde*, Jan. 24, 1964; nothing, however, appeared in *L'Humanité*.

4 *L'Unità*, Feb. 28, 1964.

who had declared before the UEC Congress that they would regard the PCF's attitude toward the students as a test of the PCF's protestations of democratization. On the other, it was also a show of the PCF's desire to treat "leftism," allied with the Chinese, as the principal danger by provisionally agreeing to join ranks with "revisionism."[5]

This compromise did not last long, however. In May 1964, on the eve of the PCF Seventeenth Congress, a serious incident caused the UEC's National Bureau, dominated by the "Italians," to oppose the PCF Central Committee. The latter had tried to prevent the publication of an issue of the UEC monthly, *Clarté*, whose editors, despite orders from the party, had refused to withdraw an article by Togliatti. Despite the pressure exercised by the PCF leaders on the printer, the students managed to publish the issue with the objectionable article.

In its tactics vis-à-vis the students the PCF had to act all the more carefully because, first, the "Italian right" was allied with revisionist intellectuals who had just published a new work, entitled *Pour un front de travailleurs*,[6] signed jointly by the circle "Les Voies du Socialisme" (in fact, simply a resurrection of the group of "Voies nouvelles," alias *L'Étincelle*), and, second, because the UEC "left" alone represented the UEC in the leadership of the national student organization, the Union Nationale des Étudiants de France.

However, with the publication of the Suslov report, the PCF was officially joined by the CPSU in its demand for an international conference. In an article entitled "The Proletarian Revolution and Khrushchev's Revisionism," published on March 31 in *Jen-min Jih-pao* and *Hung Ch'i*,[7] the PCF and Maurice Thorez were again personally attacked on several scores. After recalling that, simply as a result of the electoral law, the Communist parliamentary representation in France had declined from 182 seats in 1946 to 10 in 1958, the Chinese article continued:

Certain leaders of the Communist Party of France of whom Thorez is representative have long been pursuing a revisionist line, have publicized

[5] For the Seventh Congress of the UEC, see *La voie communiste*, No. 42 (Mar. 1964), p. 16.

[6] Paris: Julliard, 1964.

[7] "The Proletarian Revolution and Khrushchev's Revisionism: Comment on the Open Letter of the Central Committee of the CPSU (8), by the Editorial Departments of *Jen-min Jin-pao* and *Hung Ch'i* (Mar. 31, 1964); quotations from *Peking Review*, Vol. VII, No. 14 (April 3, 1964), pp. 5–23; in William E. Griffith, *Sino-Soviet Relations, 1964–1965* (Cambridge, Mass.: The M.I.T. Press, 1967), pp. 197–204.

the "parliamentary road" in response to Khrushchev's baton and have actually reduced the Communist Party to the level of a social democratic party. They have ceased to give active support to the revolutionary aspirations of the people and rolled up the national banner of opposition to U.S. imperialism. The result of their pursuit of this revisionist line is that the Communist Party, which once had great influence among the people, has become increasingly isolated from the masses and has deteriorated more and more.[8]

The Chinese were touching here on a very sensitive point: The decline of the PCF and the connection between this decline and its revolutionary vigor was a much discussed and very persistent, although far from clearly defined, subject among the PCF activists. Therefore, on April 25, 1964, Maurice Thorez used an entire page of *Pravda* to reply to the Chinese attack. He accused the Chinese of falsification, vigorously defended the PCF's policies on the "peaceful road" and the "unity front," and concluded with a call for the convocation of the international conference, traditional in PCF publications until the Seventeenth Congress.

But on April 22, when the violence of Sino-Soviet polemics had reached its height, Togliatti, even though he took a position against the Chinese on all the issues between the CCP and the CPSU, renewed before the PCI Central Committee his expression of "doubts on the part of the Italian Communists regarding the usefulness of a new conference."[9] On April 26 the Romanian press published the appeal to all fraternal parties to cease polemics which had just been adopted by the April 15–22 Central Committee session of the Romanian Party of Labor.[10] Under these conditions of profound divisions within the international Communist movement, the PCF Seventeenth Congress, which was scheduled to open on May 14 in the presence of Mikhail Suslov, the "prosecutor" in the hoped-for trial against the Chinese, took on the significance of an international demonstration by the partisans of a conference of excommunication.

The PCF Seventeenth Congress

The Seventeenth Congress of the French Communist Party, held in Paris from May 14 to 17, 1964, was a striking display of solidarity with the Communist Party of the Soviet Union on all principal

8 *Peking Review*, p. 18.

9 *L'Unità*, Apr. 23, 1964.

10 "Statement on the Stand of the Romanian Workers' Party Concerning the Problems of the World Communist and Working-Class Movement," *Scinteia*, Apr. 27, 1964; official translation (Bucharest: Meridiane, 1964), reprinted, with revisions, in Griffith, *op. cit.* For this period, see *ibid.*, pp. 25-41,

questions. The political resolution adopted by the congress[11] repeated point by point the essential theses set forth by Khrushchev:

1. PEACEFUL COEXISTENCE

The forces of peace are now sufficiently strong to impose negotiations and peaceful coexistence on the imperialists. . . . The conclusion of the Treaty [of Moscow], and the joint reduction of production of fissionable materials, is an important step on the road to international détente. To all forces of peace it offers new opportunities for work toward general, universal, and controlled disarmament.

. . . Hundreds of millions of people are aware of the fact that there is no other alternative than peaceful coexistence or thermonuclear war. The positive positions taken by the Eighth Congress of the Socialist International and by John XXIII in his Encyclical *Pacem in Terris* are a reflection of these changes.

In short, the whole of Soviet foreign policy, oriented toward détente and rapprochement with the United States, was approved by the PCF in the very same terms and with the same argumentation customarily found in the documents of the CPSU.

2. THE POSSIBILITY OF A PEACEFUL TRANSITION TO SOCIALISM

The new relationship of forces that has been established in the world in favor of socialism creates new conditions for the transition to socialism. While fifty years ago peaceful transition to socialism was considered by Marxists as possible but not very probable, today, with labor and democratic forces massed in the struggle to eliminate personal power and for ever more advanced democratic reforms, one can appraise the possibilities of a peaceful transition to socialism much more highly.

These sentences of the resolution of the PCF Seventeenth Congress paraphrased almost entirely a passage of the resolution of the Twenty-Second Party Congress of the CPSU on the subject of activities of the Central Committee:

In the conditions prevailing at present, in some capitalist countries the working class, headed by its forward detachment, has an opportunity to unite the bulk of the nation, win state power without a civil war and achieve the transfer of the basic means of production to the people upon the basis of a working-class and popular front and other possible forms of agreement and political cooperation between different parties and democratic organizations. The working class . . . can defeat the reactionary, anti-popular forces, win a solid majority in parliament, transform it from a tool serving the class interests of the bourgeoisie into an instrument serv-

11 For the text of this resolution, from which all following quotations are taken, see *L'Humanité*, May 21, 1964, pp. 7–8.

ing the working people, launch a broad mass struggle outside parliament, smash the resistance of the reactionary forces and provide the necessary conditions for a peaceful socialist revolution.[12]

The resolution of the Seventeenth Congress in Paris presented unity with the Socialists as the principal means of arriving at this "peaceful transfer":

It is precisely in order to contribute to the march toward socialism by the peaceful road that the Communist Party had proposed, and proposes, an entente between the Communist Party and the Socialist Party not only for today but also for tomorrow.

The resolution stressed that in the statutes and programs of the Communist and Socialist parties there are several points of agreement. Actually these were essentially doctrinal references, remnants of the common Marxist heritage of the two parties to be found in important places in their fundamental documents.

To meet the strong objection of the Socialist Party to any agreement beyond a defensive and limited alliance, the resolution affirmed that the Communist Party

has rejected the idea that existence of a single party is a necessary condition for the transition to socialism. This idea, held by Stalin, was a false generalization from the specific conditions under which the October Revolution took place.

On this point the French Communist Party was more explicit than the Soviet Communist Party, which prefers not to accentuate anything that might encourage anyone in the Soviet Union to contest the political monopoly of the Communist Party. The resolution referred to an "experience abroad," which

proves that the objectives common to the parties representing the working classes of the cities and the countryside lead to an increasingly profound unity for the transition to socialism and the building of socialist society.

Thus this theoretical innovation was limited to such an extent that it seemed to refer to the examples of the people's democracies such as Czechoslovakia or the German Democratic Republic, which formally admit the existence of several parties. Therefore this "appeasement" risked creating more uncertainty than assurance. The resolution also added: "There is no doubt that ever since the transition of new countries to socialism this unity and alliance can

12 *The New Soviet Society: Final Text of the Program of the Communist Party of the Soviet Union* (New York: New Leader Paperback, 1962), with annotation and introduction by Herbert Ritvo, p. 78.

still take on new and original shapes"—a definition clearly placed in the text for the sake of the Socialists, who were not likely to be tempted by the prospect of suffering the same fate as their comrades in Prague or East Germany.

Nevertheless, without waiting for these rather long-term prospects, the resolution of the Seventeenth Congress showed the immediate interest of the French Communist Party in obtaining unity of action between the two parties:

The declarations of the delegation of the Socialist Party after its return from Moscow recognize the will for peace on the part of the Soviet Union and the necessity to join together the efforts of the workers and of all forces of peace of the world in the struggle for peace, and the necessity to reinforce the bonds of friendship between France and the Soviet Union, in order to safeguard peace and contribute to unity of action.

The Seventeenth Congress thus revealed the particular attention paid by the PCF to anything that might appear to be a relaxation of the attachment on the part of the Socialists to an Atlantic policy. The impression the PCF wanted to create was that the French Socialists were moving toward a policy of loosening the links between France and NATO, since to accept the "peaceful intentions" of the Soviet Union was, in fact, to deny the menace that justified the North Atlantic Treaty.

3. CONDEMNATION OF THE CHINESE HERESY

The Seventeenth Congress condemns the splitting activity of the Chinese leaders, who by dividing the forces of peace and socialism cause grave injury to the entire movement and make the game of the imperialists easier. . . . The Seventeenth Congress considers that the line elaborated by the leaders of the Chinese Communist Party is dangerous and in opposition to the general line of the international Communist movement. . . . The triumph of the fundamental cause of the Communist movement, peace and socialism, necessitates an ideological and political struggle against the anti-Leninist and neo-Trotskyite positions of the Chinese leaders. A conciliatory attitude toward their leftist, adventurist, and nationalist line would be harmful to the international workers' movement, to the Chinese people themselves, to our party, and its broad policy of unity against personal power.

There we have the entire list of capital crimes: leftism, adventurism, nationalism, neo-Trotskyism, the accusation of playing the game of the imperialists, and "personal power," all of which are included in the vocabulary of the Soviet polemics against China.

4. THE POLICY POSITION ON THE QUESTION OF CONVOKING A
   NEW INTERNATIONAL COMMUNIST CONFERENCE.

The Seventeenth Congress considers it indispensable to reaffirm,[13] in full awareness of the changes that have taken place in the recent past, the general line of the international Communist movement as defined in 1957 and 1960 and to make all decisions necessary for the defense of its unity. It therefore declares itself in favor of calling a conference in the near future of all Communist and workers' parties of the world.

The speaker's rostrum of the congress was made available to Mikhail Suslov, the Soviet delegate, and to a certain number of "fraternal parties" whose only object was to renew their attacks against the leaders of the Chinese Communist Party and to proclaim their agreement with the project of an international conference. The declaration by Enrico Berlinguer, the PCI delegate, was an explosive one in this milieu, since it passed over the projected conference in silence and repeated the original position of his party on this subject:

We must combat the Chinese positions with the most effective means by keeping in mind the complexity and range of actions and initiatives that are necessary. . . . We must, in our opinion, face the new problems posed for us as a result of changes in the world and we must do this by new methods. We must work for the unity of our movement, which at the present time must be unity which also includes differences and autonomy.[14]

These words, which sounded a clearly "polycentric" note, were coldly received by the congress, which, contrary to a well-established habit for this kind of greeting by "fraternal parties," never interrupted the speaker with applause.

Domestic Reaction to the Congress

The debates of the Seventeenth Congress had the advantage of exceptional publicity in France, understandable because of the approaching presidential elections, whose outcome depended to some extent on decisions made by the PCF, and because of the crisis in the world Communist movement.

Moreover, on the internal plane, the congress had some important aspects. The first reactions of the SFIO were quite favorable. In *Le Populaire* Claude Fuzier (representing a Socialist tendency

---

[13] The congress "reaffirmed" the position taken for the first time by the PCF Central Committee on October 6, 1963.

[14] *L'Humanité*, May 18, 1964 and *Le Monde*, May 17–18, 1964.

more favorable to unity of action than Guy Mollet) wrote: "A page of the history of the Communist Party is about to be turned. . . . Maurice Thorez has emerged with greater stature from this Congress."[15] He added: "A broader discussion is now possible with the Communist Party."[16] This trend toward rapprochement was confirmed by a local election that took place toward the end of May in the working-class region of Longwy, in the mining and iron basin of Meurthe-et-Moselle. On May 31, 1964 a Communist deputy replaced a UNR deputy, winning 54.74 per cent of the votes, as against 43.5 per cent in the second round in 1962. The Socialist votes cast during the first round had, in disciplined fashion, gone to the PCF's candidate, who obtained a record vote for that region with respect both to total votes and to percentage of votes cast.

Despite the optimism displayed by the new Secretary-General, Waldeck Rochet, in his speech to a luncheon of the Association of Parliamentary Journalists, where he stated that neither NATO nor the Common Market was any longer an obstacle to agreement between Communists and Socialists,[17] the rapprochement with the SFIO was unable to make further progress while Defferre maintained his persistent refusal to establish contact with the PCF. The polemics, begun with an open attack in an article by Emmanuel d'Astier de la Vigerie in the Gaullist weekly *Notre République* on the PCF's policies in 1940–1941, only poisoned further the relationship between the PCF and its allies. A long-time deputy at the head of a Communist list and director of the progressive weekly *Libération* (financially supported by the PCF), D'Astier had loyally supported the party during the roughest periods of the Cold War. At the core of this controversy was an "Appeal to the People of France" signed by Maurice Thorez and Jacques Duclos in July 1940, referred to by all PCF propaganda since the Liberation as an appeal to anti-Nazi resistance. In reality, this interpretation, resting on excerpts taken out of context, did not stand up to an examination of the entire text, reproduced in Volume 19 of Maurice Thorez' *Oeuvres*.[18] However, since d'Astier had called attention to the fact that the PCF's participation in the anti-Hitler Resistance dated, in fact, from the German attack on the Soviet Union, the always delicate "national" sensibilities of the French Communist leaders came

[15] *Le Populaire,* May 19, 1964.
[16] *Ibid.,* May 21, 1964.
[17] *Le Monde,* June 11, 1964.
[18] See *France-Observateur,* June 18, 1964. For the text of the appeal see *ibid.,* June 25, 1964.

into play together with their defensive reflexes against accusations of obedience to the "baton" in Moscow, a gambit which the Chinese were also busy reviving.

This explained the surprising vehemence of the "historical" controversy, touching on events almost twenty-five years old. The epilogue occurred only several months later. Tension grew between Emmanuel d'Astier and the Communist editors of *Libération* until a day at the end of November when the PCF brutally decided to suppress the newspaper on the very next day by withdrawing financial support—with full knowledge that only a small number of the readers lost could possibly be regained by *L'Humanité*.

CHAPTER FIFTEEN

FROM THOREZ' DEATH TO DE-KHRUSHCHEVIZATION

The PCF after Thorez' Death

The establishment of the position of party President, especially created to permit Maurice Thorez to exercise political leadership of the party while freeing him entirely from all routine work, which was placed under the control of the new Secretary-General, Waldeck Rochet, had made it possible to implement the change at the summit in preparation since the Sixteenth Congress. At the same time, the Seventeenth Congress gave partial satisfaction to the very widespread aspirations in the party for a rejuvenation of the cadres and calmed the somewhat impatient young activists in the apparatus, who had found the excessive stability of many old-timers a barrier to their desire for promotion. Yet among the thirty old Central Committee members (of a total of ninety-nine full and candidate members) not re-elected by the Seventeenth Congress, not all were old-timers. In the case of Jean Llante, Lucienne Maselin, and Jean Tricard it would appear that the opportunity was taken to liquidate the aftereffects of the Casanova-Servin affair by eliminating activists who had compromised themselves at one time with the denounced leaders but for tactical reasons had been spared by the Sixteenth Congress. Other men, such as Raoul Calas, Fernand Grenier, and Marcel Paul, had had notorious clashes with the Politburo on various occasions. In the case of Marcel Dufrische, Georges Thevenin, and Léon Feix (the latter was retained in the Central Committee but expelled from the Politburo) the PCF appeared to be making a concession to the Algerian FLN and other African movements by sacrificing as scapegoats those most responsible for its "colonial" policy. The failure to re-elect Louis Baillot seemed due to the lack of skill which this young candidate member had shown in his relations with the intellectuals and the UEC, for which he had been partially responsible. Finally, well-known and popular trade-union activists, such as Eugène Henaff, secretary of the CGT in the Paris region, Jean Breteau, secretary of the Federation of Metal Workers, and the previously mentioned Marcel Paul (also president of the Federation of Gas and Electrical Workers), were removed from the Central Committee, while one of the secretaries of the CGT, Léon Mauvais, was not re-elected to the Politburo.

There is little to be said about the twenty-five men newly elected to the Central Committee by the Seventeenth Congress, except that they were mainly cadres from district federations, between the ages of thirty and forty. On the level of the real leadership organs, the Politburo and Secretariat, the Seventeenth Congress had not brought about any particularly important changes except for the creation of the Thorez-Rochet tandem.

The Politburo was reinforced with four new candidate members: Roland Leroy and Gaston Plissonier, who had been PCF secretaries before the congress; Henri Krasucki, secretary of the CGT, who replaced the dismissed Mauvais; and René Piquet. The promotion of Piquet, a young activist from Loir-et-Cher and a protégé of Waldeck Rochet, was the only spectacular change. The fourteen full members of the new Politburo had all been members of the preceding Politburo; the three outgoing candidate members were simply promoted to full membership. Thus, while about a third of the Central Committee members were replaced, only two of the sixteen Politburo members, that is, one-eighth, had been changed. Of the nine prewar members who continued to belong to the Central Committee, seven were also Politburo members (Thorez, Rochet, Duclos, Billoux, Fajon, Frachon, and Guyot).

The Secretariat underwent more important changes, as a result of the departure of Jacques Duclos, for reasons of health and age, and of Léo Figuères, undoubtedly for political reasons but hardly because of his rumored Chinese sympathies. He was replaced by René Piquet. The three other secretaries, Georges Marchais, Roland Leroy, and Gaston Plissonier, remained where they were.

As long as Maurice Thorez was alive, none of the "new men" seemed to have a personality strong enough to become a possible rival to the President. But less than two months after Thorez' election, his sudden death on July 11 left the presidency vacant. Thus in the long run the whole equilibrium on which the leadership elected at the Seventeenth Congress rested was placed in jeopardy. Measures that had been pure formalities until then, such as the introduction of the secret vote for elections to the leadership organs under the new statutes modified by the Seventeenth Congress, might in the future produce certain practical effects. (In reality, the list of candidates for election to the Central Committee has always been made up by the Politburo and simply ratified by the congress.)

For several days after Thorez' death, the gravity of the event was masked by the intense and widespread emotion it aroused. The enormous crowd assembled in Paris for the funeral, the messages of condolence and the posthumous eulogies that arrived from every corner of the French political horizon and all foreign Communist parties revealed the extent to which the man who had just died had been identified with the French Communist Party. At the same time he had stood for the masses as a symbol of their revolutionary social aspirations and for the French establishment as a symbol of the stability of an institutionalized, sober, immobile opposition, with a familiar and reassuring face.

To be sure, if one were to draw up a balance sheet of the qualities of Thorez the man, one might say, as Trotsky said of Stalin, that Thorez was the "most eminent mediocrity" in the party. If he was placed so highly above all the others, it was because of his administrative talents, his gift for political maneuvering, the experience he had acquired in the international Communist movement (at a time when the Comintern teachers made great educational efforts to forge cadres), and finally—if not above all—it was because of the ease with which this proletarian parvenu had moved in the petit bourgeois political society of contemporary France.

The reverse side of the coin was the void that Thorez had established around himself by mercilessly destroying all those whose intelligence or courage could have turned them into rivals. Marcel Servin and Laurent Casanova worked in Thorez' personal secretariat before they were promoted to the Politburo and finally eliminated. Auguste Lecoeur, from the same region and the same profession as Thorez, had long been considered his favorite and designated successor.

In the remaining group of leaders the older ones should first of all be singled out. Jacques Duclos and Benoît Frachon, who alone have experience equal to Thorez' with regard to internal affairs and the international Communist movement, seem too old and tired now to be scheming for top positions. But they may be counted on to make use of their prestige and their suggestions for their protégés. Duclos, the great parliamentary specialist, and Frachon, the trade-union leader, have both been associated with the PCF leadership since the thirties; both took over the effective leadership of the clandestine PCF between 1940 and 1944 while Thorez was a refugee in Moscow; and both are the only leaders who still have extensive popularity among the activists and the mass of Communist sympathizers. The Secretary-General, Waldeck Rochet, whose rise we have followed, seemed to be nothing more than a rather lusterless bureaucrat who managed to rise above the others mainly because he knew how to maneuver or keep quiet in delicate situations and because his lack of brilliance made him seem harmless. Even less able than Thorez to understand theoretical problems, little gifted in oratory, incapable of expressing himself otherwise than in the heavy jargon whose balanced formulas betray the extreme prudence of the *apparatchik* anxious to arm himself against all possible changes of line, Waldeck Rochet does not seem to be cast in the mold of a real leader. Yet, paradoxically, the undistinguished character of his mediocrity could serve him well, just as in a similar fashion, during the Third Republic, in order to reduce the shock of the clash of brilliant personalities or disturbing ambitions, a faceless, uncomplicated man, "the most stupid of all," was often selected to preside over the government.

Three other men in the Politburo are of Waldeck Rochet's generation. Of the three, François Billoux is the one whose influence seems to be declining the most. Even if no credence is given to rumors that his being sidetracked is due to the Chinese sympathies attributed to him, he no longer directly controls the important Bouches-du-Rhône federation, and he has been relegated to the role of editor of the weekly *France Nouvelle*. Étienne Fajon occupies a much more important strategic position as editor-in-chief of *L'Humanité*. Raymond Guyot, who has been a devoted and unconditionally loyal theoretician since he betrayed his comrades in the Communist youth organization (Barbé, Célor, Billoux, Lozeray, etc.) to which he belonged, is still the man responsible for the PCF's international relations and is thus considered its "Minister of Foreign Affairs."

To this group of old-timers should be added Thorez' widow, Jeannette Vermeersch (although her election to the Central Committee took place only in 1945), who is very unpopular among her colleagues in the Politburo because of her tyrannical and capricious exploitation of the role of favorite. Her political influence can only decline rapidly. At least, it is probable that from here on it will no longer be she who uses others but others who will eventually try to use her in their game, to exploit for their own purposes the prestige her name still carries. (In fact, since her husband's death she is listed as Jeannette Thorez-Vermeersch in PCF declarations.)

Among the other six full Politburo members, the one who seems most powerful is Georges Marchais, secretary for party organization. He is the prototype of the younger generation of bureaucrats formed in Thorez' school after the Liberation. In comparison with the preceding generation, the outstanding trait of these younger activists is never to have been involved in genuine political debates. Their activity has always been limited to administrative functions, and sometimes to an inquisitorial role after the appearance of this or that "deviation." Thus Marchais owes his promotion to the Central Committee in 1956 to the skill he displayed in the Seine-Sud federation (personally watched over by Maurice Thorez, who had resided and had been elected deputy in that district) in beating down the opposition, particularly at the conferences at Ivry, Champigny, Gentilly, Bagneux, and Malakoff—all important places with Communist municipal governments in the Paris suburbs.

Gustave Ansart, representing the Federation Nord, and Paul Laurent of the Communist Youth have received the same training as Marchais, and three of the four candidate members may be put in the same group: Roland Leroy, Gaston Plissonier, and René Piquet, all three party secretaries. Without doubt, the most intelligent of the three is Roland Leroy, but he is, doubtless, not helped by his former profession as a teacher, in a party where to have been a manual worker in one's youth seems to be a sort of claim to nobility. Both Plissonier, charged with administrative work, and Piquet, young and ambitious, come from the Loir-et-Cher federation, a region long watched over by Waldeck Rochet personally.

There remains a group of trade-union leaders, Georges Seguy, Georges Frischman, and the new candidate member Henri Krasucki. The first two are CGT leaders, of the railroad and postal workers respectively, and the third represents the Paris region with the CGT Confederal Bureau. They might all be tempted to use their union positions to increase their influence in the leadership of the party. Among them the strongest personality is Krasucki, who has the advantage of his youth but whose ambitions might be thwarted by his foreign origin; the PCF has for some time practiced a discreet *numerus clausus* in that regard.

We must discuss separately the case of the only representative of the "intelligentsia" in the Politburo, Roger Garaudy, who is one of the foremost figures of ideological revisionism after having been for a long time one of the most sectarian Zhdanovites. On the political plane, the situation in which he had been placed on the eve of the Seventeenth Congress could have been at first interpreted as a near disgrace. Under the pretext of giving Garaudy more freedom to direct the Centre d'Études et de Recherches Marxistes created by the party, he had been relieved of his functions as editor of *Cahiers du Communisme,* theoretical review of the PCF, in October 1964. (His successor is Léo Figuères, expelled from the Secretariat by the Seventeenth Congress.)

In fact, it would be better to call his change of position a new assignment rather than a disgrace, since the stand taken by Garaudy in the field of the "dialogue" with the Christians and on the question of the freedom of artistic and literary creation, as well as the praises that he was urged to lavish during the opening of the important ideological and cultural debates between Communist specialists in the various disciplines, had widespread political implications. The Politburo had decided in that way to disengage Garaudy from political responsibilities by provisionally reassigning him to the ideological and cultural sector.

Until this time the Centre d'Études et de Recherches Marxistes had played primarily the role of an outlet. While attaching a certain importance to the presence of intellectuals in its ranks and to their recruitment as a factor of prestige for party propaganda, its leaders had just about given up the idea of establishing a strict discipline among the Communist intellectuals. In exchange, these intellectuals had to abstain from any interference in actual political life, other than at the request of the party and as "ornamental elements." Under these conditions, the PCF seemed willing to tolerate henceforth rather unorthodox research, as long as the results did not extend beyond the limited circle of specialists.

However, this "liberal-segregationist" solution had proved insufficient. On the one hand, it was compromised by its failure in the student circles where both the "left" and the "right" of the UEC were persistently questioning the political monopoly of the party. On the other hand, in the event of a large coalition with non-Communist elements, the political role of the intellectuals as a sociological group had automatically increased; their "ideological" assistance became more indispensable to attract the sought-after allies as well as to overcome the "sectarian" resistance of the working class to such alliances. Finally, it was certainly in the "cultural department" that it was easiest to move away from the orthodox Soviet line, thus giving the "proof of independence" from it—an independence demanded of the PCF by the political forces being solicited as allies.

Garaudy's new status constituted an adaptation to a new situation, and offered the leading group a certain number of advantages.

1. His membership in the Politburo gave a certain weight to the positions defended by Garaudy—whether it was in the dialogue with the Christians or in the debates with Communist intellectuals, at the Centre d'Études or elsewhere—thereby giving the leading group some control over the details of these debates under the guise of approving freedom of research and the autonomy of the cultural sector.

2. "Garaudysme," characterized by "humanist" professions of faith and by a tendency to conciliate Marxism and religious ideology, could serve as an instrument in the struggle against "leftism," the main enemy since the split with the Chinese Communists.

3. At the same time, a step was taken in the direction of the tendencies advocated by the PCI, indicating the rapprochement with Rome, which was to take shape in 1965. By the end of 1964, the PCF had made only tentative steps in this direction, waiting to see clearly what would be the move of the leading Soviet team.

For the time being, the demise of Maurice Thorez and the weakness of the PCF leadership, deprived of the man who had seemed to be its brain, led the group to close ranks, particularly because events left this decapitated circle hardly the time to breathe. One month after Thorez' death, Togliatti disappeared from the scene in his turn, leaving behind an explosive "testament" all the more treacherous because it constituted simultaneously an acceptance of the PCI's participation in the conference of the twenty-six parties "preparatory to a world conference," for which the CPSU had finally set December 15, 1964 as the date, and a torpedoing of that conference. (This conference, in fact, brought the PCI more embarrassment than advantage from the moment it promised to become, in the absence of the Chinese "defendants" and their allies, a public confrontation of advocates and opponents of China's excommunication.) In his reply of August 6 in the name of the PCF Central Committee, Waldeck Rochet recalled that the PCF had called for this conference ever since October 1963 and added:

In our opinion, to oppose such a conference would be equivalent to renouncing the necessity of a united front against the imperialist forces and confirming a situation that can only become worse, causing incalculable damage to the cause of socialism. . . . As the majority of parties has declared itself in favor of the conference, we declare ourselves in favor of holding it; we consider it absolutely necessary, even if it cannot bring unanimous agreement.[1]

It was symptomatic that *L'Humanité* on September 5, the very day it published extracts from Togliatti's Testament, (in all, less than one sixth of the full text, which had been published the day before in *Le Monde* and interspersed with commentaries reminding the reader of the PCF's position), the entire top of its international page was taken up by an article devoted to the signing of a joint declaration by the Soviet and Czechoslovak parties, and speeches by Khrushchev and Novotný stressing the necessity for the world conference. Not one line of a long passage containing Togliatti's veritable profession of faith in revisionism was quoted, even though the PCF was directly implicated.

Thus arises the question of the possibility of the conquest of positions of power by the working class within a state that has not changed its character as a bourgeois state, and, therefore, whether the struggle for a progressive transformation of this nature from within is possible.

In countries where the Communist movement is becoming strong, such as in our country (and in France), this is the basic question that today arises in the political struggle.[2]

In these words Togliatti expressed the PCI's claim to extend to France the validity of his "reformist" line. Similarly, his sharp criticism of the WFTU was also aimed at the PCF, which carried out the Soviet line in the Communist international trade-union movement through the intermediary of the docile Louis Saillant.

Finally, *L'Humanité* summarized in ten lines the long passage devoted by Togliatti to problems "of the socialist world." Its content, despite its moderate language, was very harsh with respect to the Soviet Union and the people's democracies. The fact that the PCF opposed the publication of Togliatti's Testament in *L'Humanité*, while the Soviet leaders allowed the publication in *Pravda* of this document of almost revolutionary potential within the Soviet context, clearly showed the limitations of de-Stalinization within the PCF. It took until November 1964 for the PCF leadership to resign itself to publishing the Testament, and then only in the the-

---

1 *L'Humanité*, Aug. 14, 1964.

2 "Promemòria sulle questioni del movimento operaio internazionale e della sua unità," *Rinascita*, Vol. XXI, No. 35 (Sept. 5, 1964), pp. 1–4; also *L'Unità* and *The New York Times*, Sept. 5, 1964 (quotations from *ibid.*); in William E. Griffith, *Sino-Soviet Relations, 1964–1965* (Cambridge, Mass.: The M.I.T. Press, 1967).

oretical journal *Cahiers du Communisme,* whose circulation does not exceed 8,000.

At the same time, September–October 1964, the *Histoire du Parti Communiste Français* finally came off the press. Its publication had been decided upon by the Fourteenth Congress in 1956 and had been announced as being imminent, and it was scheduled for the beginning of 1960, by François Billoux in the July–August 1959 issue of *Cahiers du Communisme.*[3] More than a history, this "manual" for activists was intended to sum up what one now needed to think after the many changes in recent years. But the book had hardly been placed on the stands when a new revision became necessary: The announcement of Khrushchev's removal on October 15 put the "Thorezian leadership without Thorez" established by the Seventeenth Congress, to a new test.

The PCF's Reaction to Khrushchev's Fall

The PCF had already announced the composition of its delegation to the preparatory conference of December 15 (Raymond Guyot, Roland Leroy, and Jean Kanapa) before the majority of the parties invited had even given a firm promise to attend, and when the absence of five Asian parties out of six, and of Albania, was already certain.

By a curious coincidence, it was on October 14, the very day the Central Committee convened in Moscow to "accept" Khrushchev's "resignation," that *L'Humanité* published the report presented by Roland Leroy at Ivry before the PCF Central Committee plenum of October 9–10 on the preparation of the international conference.

Leroy's report contained the beginning of at least a tactical shift with respect to the aims of the conference:

We want the international conference not in order to excommunicate or exclude the Chinese Communist Party, which, moreover, the conference has no right to do. Concerned with maintaining the continued independence of each Communist party, the guarantee of its creative activity, we do not propose the creating of a new centralized international organization.[4]

After making this concession to the PCI's reservations, Leroy immediately added that the PCF also rejected "any proposal to estab-

---

[3] *Cahiers du Communisme,* (July–Aug. 1959), p. 378.

[4] *Le Monde,* Oct. 14, 1964, p. 5. This turning point, however, was not initiated by the PCF. It was inspired by current Soviet declarations (especially those of Khrushchev and Ponomarev) aimed at reassuring reluctant party members about the intentions of the promoters of the conference.

lish groups of parties by continents, regions of the world, or social systems" or "any system of polycentrism that might interfere with the true independence of each Communist party." In fact, a large part of Leroy's report seemed to be devoted to refuting the arguments contained in Togliatti's memorandum, which Leroy euphemistically called "the document recently published" by "our Italian comrades," without mentioning the name of its author. Strangely enough, Leroy contrasted the pessimistic analysis of the outlook for the international situation as contained in Togliatti's Testament with, of all things, a speech made three days before in Berlin by "Comrade Brezhnev," who stated that

neither the aggressive efforts on the part of the imperialists, who are ready to play with fire, nor the activities of the splitters, can jeopardize the fundamental direction of world developments. He rightly demonstrated that whatever new efforts may be made to increase international tension, the trend toward maintenance and reinforcement of peace will certainly win.[5]

The reference to Brezhnev made by Leroy on October 10 in a speech in which the name of "Comrade Khrushchev" was cited only once, with respect to the Chinese propaganda campaign against him, makes one wonder whether Leroy did not have knowledge of the plot being concocted in Moscow to remove Khrushchev from power.

Using veiled language, Leroy in effect reproached those parties which were "hesitant" or expressed "reservations" or "doubts" with regard to the convocation of the conference with being practically accomplices of the divisive work carried on by the Chinese splitters," and he proposed to "substitute bilateral and multilateral conversations." Once more, polycentrism was denounced as hiding the intention of "aiming a blow at the independence and autonomy of parties."

Finally, in his conclusion Leroy vigorously took up again the theme, which had been soft-pedaled for some months, of the "struggle on two fronts":

To question the new relationship of forces in the world can lead to the development of an opportunist point of view on a whole series of questions, to the resumption of the old reformist point of view on the progressive integration of socialism with capitalism, and to looking forward to surrendering the ideological struggle along the entire line.[6]

[5] *Ibid.*
[6] *Ibid.*

This was a clear answer to Togliatti's Testament, and a rejection, as opportunist and reformist, of the line proposed by Togliatti for Italy and France. Leroy also compared the PCI theses to those held by the Casanova-Kriegel-Valrimont group. (Servin was not mentioned; he had been partly "rehabilitated" after his self-criticism and made federal secretary of the Moselle district, but he did not return to the Central Committee.) Leroy's report ended with an unequivocal warning:

We will lead this fight [on two fronts: the term was a quotation from a speech by Thorez to the Seventeenth Congress] firmly, without applying labels, for it is sometimes difficult to discern whether such an attack comes from the right or the left; most often the blow is aimed at the very foundations of our principles.[7]

This was really saying that the "Italian" danger was no less than the "Chinese" danger. The resolution adopted by the Central Committee stressed this point: "Only those can be opposed to a convocation of the conference who, for one reason or another, would like to abandon the principles of 1957 and 1960." And further: "These two dangers nourish each other mutually."[8]

On considering the paroxysm of hostility reached by the Ivry Central Committee meeting in October 1964 with regard to Italian polycentrism, we might propose the hypothesis that for Roland Leroy—who had been warned of, or had foreseen, the serious crises brewing at the CPSU headquarters—it meant the adoption by the PCF of a position of orthodoxy *en pointe*: that is, a position of resistance simultaneously to the pressure from the "left" and "right" in such a manner as to demonstrate the permanence of an unshakable base in the international Communist movement—namely, the French Communist Party.

While one cannot exclude the possibility that Leroy knew of Khrushchev's imminent removal in Moscow, it seems that only a small number in the Politburo shared the secret. In fact, immediately after the Central Committee meeting of October 9–10, and before the announcement of the events in Moscow, two PCF delegations departed: one, led by François Billoux and Gustave Ansart, for a "study trip" to Romania;[9] the second for conversations with

---

[7] *Ibid.*

[8] *Ibid.*

[9] Both were expert at "delicate" missions. François Billoux, who had led the first delegation to attempt a rapprochement with Yugoslavia in 1957, had more recently been charged with responsibility for an attempt at mediation with the Vietnam Workers' Party (Apr. 23–May 8, 1964). He was now being sent to

the FLN in Algeria, with Waldeck Rochet, Raymond Guyot, Georges Frischman, and René Piquet as participants. Thus, at the very moment when the world heard about the replacement of the head of the Soviet Union, six of the seventeen members of the PCF Politburo, among them the Secretary-General and the member responsible for international relations, were traveling abroad. Despite the panic felt by the party, whose most disciplined activists were incapable of answering the demands for explanations, none of the absent leaders considered it necessary to interrupt his trip.

The PCF's reaction to Khrushchev's fall, to the extent that it can be gathered from *L'Humanité* during the last two weeks of October, revealed the confusion reigning in the entire party. On Friday, October 16, the PCF daily published the communiqués by Tass and the Presidium of the Supreme Soviet, some brief extracts from the wire services, and two biographical sketches of Leonid Brezhnev and Alexei Kosygin; but, as the single exception of all the Paris morning papers, *L'Humanité* did not carry a single line of comment on the events. The next day, October 17, the front-page headline read: "No Change in Soviet Policy." Underneath was a communiqué issued by the PCF Politburo, which had met the night before. The communiqué limited itself to reproducing, apparently in a tone of "objective information," the meager indications published in Moscow by that time. Its essential passage was as follows:

Considering the eminent role of the Communist Party of the Soviet Union in international affairs, any decision it makes, in complete independence, concerning the leadership of the Soviet party and state, is of extreme importance for Communists and people everywhere in the world.[10]

This brief sentence contained both a justification for the CPSU (which has the right to make decisions "in complete independence") and a very veiled reproach (such decisions, the Politburo said in effect, are too important to be taken lightly or announced without adequate explanations).

As a matter of fact, it seemed rather difficult to induce the party activists to face the brutal facts, that after having been made to worship a bloody tyrant they were now invited to follow a thoughtless braggart.

It had been necessary to wait until October 19 to find in *L'Humanité* the editorial written by Étienne Fajon devoted to "the de-

Romania. As for Gustave Ansart, it may be recalled that he was the PCF's discreet observer at the Congress of the Albanian Workers' Party in February 1961 (see p. 128, *supra*).

10 Quoted from *Le Monde*, Oct. 17, 1964.

cision of the CPSU." Cautiously, Fajon restricted himself to paraphrasing the Politburo communiqué of October 10–16, to quoting the *Pravda* editorial of October 17, and especially to calling upon the French Communist activists not to ask themselves untimely questions about the events taking place in the Soviet Union.

While the French Communists take deep interest in the decisions of their Soviet Comrades, their main preoccupation is in their own party life. . . . Nothing could be more deplorable than to be diverted from what is our first duty by the legitimate attention that we owe to what is going on in the Soviet Union.

On the same day *L'Humanité* featured the condemnation of the Chinese atomic test by the National Council of the Peace Movement (which had never condemned a Soviet nuclear test) and the *Pravda* version of a declaration of Japanese intellectuals against the pro-Chinese policy of the Japanese Communist Party.

These articles and Waldeck Rochet's silence (Rochet, when interviewed by the "Algerie Presse Service" about Khrushchev's resignation gave an evasive and practically meaningless answer) reveal a double anxiety on the part of the PCF leadership: first, the fear of seeing Moscow renounce its anti-Chinese campaign, search for a compromise with Peking, and abandon the project of an international conference (of which the French party considered itself the initiator); and second, the fear of the discontent of its own activists, which was expressed by the numerous demands for an explanation. Fajon's article urging the activists to take more interest in France and less in the Soviet Union had been, it seems, very little appreciated. Far from appeasing the uproar in the cells, it provoked a new wave of protests to the Central Committee.

Also on October 21, after Rochet's return from Algeria, the Politburo announced its decision to "ask the CPSU Central Committee to receive a PCF delegation." The task assigned to this delegation was "to obtain more complete information and the necessary explanations concerning the conditions and methods by which the changes decided on by the CPSU Central Committee were carried out."[11] The Politburo communiqué, by quoting the key sentence of the previously mentioned October 16 declaration, made an effort to establish some continuity between its immediate reaction (of floundering) and the new *démarche*. The point was to efface the regrettable impression of floundering produced in the first days after

[11] *L'Humanité*, Oct. 22, 1964.

the event, and not to acknowledge that the leadership had yielded to pressure from below.[12]

One cannot help seeing a parallel between the dispatch of this delegation to Moscow in October 1964 and the equally hasty mission to the Kremlin in June 1956 after the publication of the "report attributed to Khrushchev." But this time the delegation comprised only young Politburo members: Georges Marchais, Roland Leroy, and Jacques Chambaz, a historian known mainly for his complete conformism under Stalin and thereafter.

It was with a certain satisfaction that *L'Humanité-Dimanche* wrote on October 25 that "the decision of the French Communist Party to send a delegation to Moscow was followed" by several other Communist parties, including the PCI.

Just at that moment the polemics between French and Italian Communists flared up again. In the WFTU, whose General Council had met at Budapest, Benoît Frachon, coming to the support of Louis Saillant's report, repeated the PCF's classic line on the Common Market ("[it] aggravates the situation of the working class").[13] The Italian delegates, the Communist Agostino Novella and the Nenni Socialist Fernando Santi, patiently continuing the offensive launched three years before,[14] demanded a regional organization, that is, the application of polycentrism in the trade-union sector, and also developed the criticism expressed in Togliatti's memorandum of the immobilism of the WFTU and of the trade-union policies in the socialist countries.[15] The Cubans, Venezuelans, Romanians, and Poles supported the position of the CGIL against the pro-Soviet Frachon and Saillant. Agostino Novella asked for the depoliticization of the WFTU.[16]

On the purely political plane, a very sharp contrast could have been observed between the immediate reaction of the PCF and that of the PCI to Khrushchev's overthrow. In a communiqué published

---

[12] Questioned by the press at a reception on October 23, Waldeck Rochet stated: "It would not be correct to say that we have changed our attitude in deciding to send a delegation to visit the CPSU because our Politburo was forced to do so. . . . Our communiqué of October 16 is entirely consistent with that of October 21. The idea of sending a delegation was already implicitly included in our first communiqué, for it was envisaged in case the information we expected was incomplete. . . . But the Politburo has wished to act without haste by taking things into account, thereby acting as any dedicated party should. . . ." (*L'Humanité*, Oct. 24, 1964.)

[13] For the text of Benoît Frachon's speech, see *ibid.*, Nov. 2, 1964.

[14] See pp. 137 and 146, *supra*.

[15] See *L'Unità*, Oct. 21, 1964.

[16] *Ibid.*, Oct. 23, 1964.

on October 16, the leadership of the PCI "reserves its judgment until it shall be in possession of more complete news" (for the PCF there was no question of expressing judgment). Moreover, the PCI insistently proclaimed that "the new line" of the Twentieth Congress and the policy of peaceful coexistence had had "one of their principal defenders in the comrade Khrushchev."

From October 18 and 19 the principal leaders of the Italian Communist Party, Luigi Longo, Mario Alicata, Pietro Ingrao and the President of the Communist group in the Senate, Terracini, though representing various shades of the PCI leadership, had clearly criticized, sometimes in very sharp terms, the conditions under which Khrushchev's replacement had taken place, thereby bringing up the problem of the unsatisfactory functioning of socialist democracy in the Soviet Union.

On October 24, *Rinascita* published a violent article by Enrico Berlinguer "in reply to Comrade Leroy on the Yalta Memorandum."[17] The article vigorously criticized the bad faith of Leroy in his report to the last PCF Central Committee plenum and reaffirmed the PCI's skepticism with regard to the opportuneness of a world conference of Communist parties, while at the same time perfidiously insisting that there were no differences of principle between French and Italian Communists, but only tactical disagreements. The perfidy consisted in Berlinguer's insinuation that the PCF's attitude was devoid of duplicity; in fact, the tactics advocated by Leroy under the pretext of safeguarding unity led directly toward a split.

The PCF delegation was received in Moscow on October 26–27 by Brezhnev, Podgorny, Suslov, and Ponomarev. Back in Paris on the evening of October 29, it published a rather laconic communiqué that spoke of the "atmosphere of fraternal and sincere friendship" in which the conversations had taken place, and of the desire of both parties "to strengthen brotherly relations, bonds of traditional friendship, and the mutual confidence between the PCF and the CPSU."[18] Not a word about Khrushchev was to be found, but the issue of *L'Humanité* in which the communiqué appeared also carried an extract from an editorial in *Mundo Obrero*, the organ of the Spanish Communist Party, saying, on the one hand, that Khrushchev had been "an outstanding spokesman of the policies of peace and coexistence" and, on the other, that "his merits are shared with the entire CPSU, the entire Central Committee, and, naturally,

17 *Rinascita*, Oct. 24, 1964 (English translation, JPRS 27,299, Nov. 10, 1964).
18 *L'Humanité*, Oct. 30, 1964.

also with the men who are now replacing him—Brezhnev and Kosygin." Thus, in an upside-down fashion, the PCF organ said that the changes that had taken place at the summit in the Soviet Union were acceptable on condition that the new team effectively pursued a policy of "Khrushchevism without Khrushchev."

It is also significant that *L'Humanité* did not mention an appeal for re-establishment of unity between the Soviet and Chinese parties, made on October 28 by Gomułka on the occasion of a meeting in honor of a Mongolian delegation visiting Poland.

With the same prudence, moreover, *L'Humanité* remained silent concerning the violent November 1 editorial in the Albanian paper, *Zëri i Popullit,* which announced the continuation of the struggle against the ideology of "Khrushchevism." *L'Humanité* also did not mention similar declarations by the Indonesian Communist Party leader, Aidit, and Berlinguer's observations after the return from Moscow of the PCI delegation, in which he publicly declared himself dissatisfied with the explanations received, and reaffirmed all the differences already expressed in Togliatti's Testament.[19]

Conversely, the November 5 issue of *L'Humanité* minimized the invitation to Moscow of a Chinese delegation led by Chou En-lai for the anniversary of the October Revolution; and while all other newspapers gave headlines to the event, the Communist organ submerged it in the announcement of the other delegations invited. But *L'Humanité* gave a prominent place to the communiqué signed at the end of their stay by a study delegation to Paris of the League of Communists of Yugoslavia. The delegation had only been headed by a Central Committee member, but it had nevertheless been received by Waldeck Rochet, Jacques Duclos, Raymond Guyot, Georges Marchais, Gaston Plissonier, and René Piquet. The communiqué proclaimed "the need and mutual usefulness of developing closer collaboration between the PCF and the LCY." In the context of the Sino-Soviet rapprochement in process, this statement was unquestionably a protest against the possibility of such a rapprochement, which might take place at Yugoslavia's expense, given the ambiguous references to the Twenty-First Congress made in some Soviet documents in the previous weeks.

[19] *Le Monde,* Nov. 5, 1964.

CHAPTER SIXTEEN

CONCLUSION: THE PCF AFTER KHRUSHCHEV

Not until the special session of the PCF Central Committee of November 6, 1964 at Bagnolet was a position other than a purely evasive one finally taken on the events that were, by then, three weeks old. In symbolic fashion, the front page of L'Humanité of November 7 contained only two texts: the resolution of the PCF Central Committee and a message addressed in the warmest terms by the PCF Central Committee to the Central Committee of the CPSU and to Brezhnev personally.

A highly romanticized version of the conversations held by the PCF delegation in Moscow had been published in L'Express of November 9, but most serious political observers considered these revelations "forged from beginning to end."[1]

The PCI leadership also made clear its position on November 6 after the return of its delegation from Moscow. It will be of interest to compare the attitudes of the two great Western Communist parties after Khrushchev's removal.

Concerning the conflict with China, the PCI's position can be summarized as follows: neither to split nor to compromise with the Chinese. But on the level of state relations the PCI resolution was favorable "to everything that can help restore relations of friendship and collaboration among socialist states," and it even welcomed "with satisfaction the improvement of relations between People's China and the other socialist countries."[2] Conversely, on

---

[1] It is probable that this weekly, whose new "depoliticized" formula tried to imitate that of Time and Newsweek, fell into serious discredit as a result. L'Express, incidentally, brought down on its head a biting and rather witty denial from L'Humanité, under the title "Phantom at L'Express." It is better, in our view, to stick to examining the texts published in L'Humanité even though they are incomplete. The delegation's report, presented by Georges Marchais, was not fully published in L'Humanité of November 9, and nothing became known of the speeches of the Central Committee members except, on reliable authority, that there were many and that they elicited some spirited discussion.

[2] Le Monde, Feb. 8–11, 1965.

the ideological plane, the PCI was just as fearful as the PCF (or the Yugoslav Communists) that a compromise might be concluded at its expense. Under these conditions each party would remain independent, for the Italian concept of polycentrism tolerates de facto the hegemony of the CCP over the other Asian parties. The PCI declaration added:

For all these reasons the PCI leadership confirms again that its reservations with regard to the convocation at this time of a new international conference of Communist parties remain valid.[3]

In contrast, the PCF resolution insisted on the "desire of the two parties . . . to continue to prepare a new international conference of Communist and workers' parties" whose role it would be to

defend the unity [of the movement] by fighting on two fronts, against dogmatism, which today represents the principal danger, and against opportunism from the right, which has not stopped manifesting itself.[4]

Only as a form of lip service did Georges Marchais allude to "certain signs of possible new discussions for the purpose of overcoming the differences" and to "the presence of a Chinese delegation at the November 7 celebrations." While assuring his listeners that "our line has always been to preserve unity and friendship with the Communist Party and the people of China" and that "our party will spare no effort to contribute to the unity of the world Communist movement," Marchais could not hide the fact that he hoped for the failure of the Sino-Soviet discussions. The PCF's position was clear: rather a break than ideological confusion, either with Chinese "leftism" or the de facto polycentrism tolerated by the Italians.

A certain anxiety on Marchais's part showed through when he said that the Soviet negotiators rejected "insinuations to the effect that the CPSU was seeking an ideological compromise with the leaders of the CCP" and also when he discreetly indicated to the Soviets the limits beyond which the PCF would cease to be favorable to any re-establishment of unity:

It is understood that any conciliation with the leftist and nationalist line of the Chinese leaders would be a danger for the international Com-

---

3 *Ibid.* At the Belgrade Congress of December 7–13, 1964, Giancarlo Pajetta, representing the PCI, remained silent on the question of an international conference, as did the Yugoslav speakers. But the Italian and Yugoslav delegates gave their listeners to understand that they approved of other forms of exchange of opinions; they were, as Tito had stated, opposed to all collective decisions having to do with the excommunication of anyone at all.

4 *L'Humanité*, Nov. 7, 1964, p. 1.

munist movement, for the Chinese people themselves, and for our party and its general policy of unity, necessary for the struggle against personal power.[5]

This policy statement is corroborated by information obtained from an entirely trustworthy private source, according to whom Waldeck Rochet is said to have declared at the time of the Soviet meeting with Chou En-lai in November 1964 that, even if the Soviets should decide on a truce in their polemics with China, the PCF would not go along; it was determined to answer all Chinese attacks.

One can then say that the fall of Khrushchev forced the PCF leaders to take a step toward independence, if only through fear of "losing face." They have committed themselves to Khrushchevism; they are not ready to abandon it. They have thrown themselves into the anti-Chinese polemics; they are not disposed to go along, as they had habitually done in the past, with a possible, hasty reconciliation. In their attachment to "Khrushchevism without Khrushchev," they now represent an element of continuity that the Soviets must take into account.

To be sure, the "centralist" line with Moscow as the center was continued by the PCF Central Committee meeting of November 6, but with considerable changes in form and procedure. Instead of unconditionally approving all decisions by the CPSU, as it had done before, the PCF let it be understood that some of these decisions, for example, those concerning internal Soviet policies and changes in Soviet leadership, are exclusively the business of the Soviet Communists and need not be approved by the other parties. Thus, according to Waldeck Rochet,

We say to those who sometimes ask us whether we do or do not approve the decision made [Khrushchev's removal] that in fact it is not up to us either to approve or disapprove, because this involves a decision that belongs to the Central Committee of the CPSU.

At the same time, Marchais and Rochet gave their own interpretation of the declarations published in Moscow after Khrushchev's fall, emphasizing almost exclusively everything that indicated unchanged intransigence with regard to the Chinese question and the holding of the conference. On that subject, Marchais's report contained at least one indication that it was to be quickly refuted by the facts: "The propositions made in favor of holding a new international conference, as well as a meeting of a preparatory

5 *Ibid.*, Nov. 9, 1964, p. 3.

commission of the twenty-six parties on December 15, remain valid." But everything indicates that even then the Soviets had dropped the December 15 date.

As we have seen, as long as the question was one of hostility to an ideological compromise with the CCP, there was to some extent a common attitude among the Western Communist parties. But the PCF also did not want any compromise with "polycentrism" *à l'italienne* and its revisionist implications.

Moreover, the PCI was the target of Marchais's attack against

the majority of members of the National Committee of the UEC, who have adopted a resolution we disapprove of. Under cover of "democratization" they try to mix in inadmissible fashion in the internal affairs of the CPSU. They demand information, they say; but without waiting for it, they criticize the measures taken by the CPSU and give themselves up to speculations. Yet in the last analysis do they want anything except the continuation of the struggle against the proper and reasonable policy of our party? This is a sign of irresponsibility.

Yet, if it is true that the UEC National Committee, toward the end of October 1964, voted with a two-thirds majority of those present ("Italians" and "leftists") in favor of a resolution demanding the publication of the full text of the debates held during the October 14 session of the CPSU Central Committee, including Khrushchev's own speech, then the transgression for which Marchais upbraided the students, namely, having criticized "without waiting" for the requested information, was exactly the same transgression as that committed by the leaders of the PCI.

In fact, the PCF, while refraining from any evaluation of whether the motives and circumstances of Khrushchev's resignation were well founded, emphasized the fact that "legal" norms had been respected and that Khrushchev's "faults," which according to the November 6 resolution "consisted primarily in his methods of work and his excessively personal leadership, contrary to the principles of collective leadership and socialist democracy," had had "negative consequences, particularly in certain areas of *internal* policies of the Soviet Union."[6] This permitted Marchais to stress, with some boldness, the following in the preliminary declaration he made to the CPSU representatives:

We can tell you frankly that some of these criticisms did not surprise us. In fact, on several occasions, our Politburo was worried on this score. For example, we could not understand why Comrade Khrushchev himself

6 *Ibid.*, Nov. 7, 1964. (Our italics.)

made the two reports to the Twenty-Second Congress, and why he dealt with all questions, whether in industry, agriculture, or the arts.[7]

One may ridicule these "worries" concerning the Twenty-Second Congress, which the PCF Politburo had taken good care not to express for three long years. But it is possible to see here an indication of the discreet reappearance of the old hostility, long repressed, by the French Communist leaders toward Khrushchev, the man of the Twentieth Congress.

In comparing the PCF and PCI declarations, one also notices that the latter insisted on the process of democratization in Soviet society (considering it too slow, as partially demonstrated by the manner of Khrushchev's eviction), while the PCF talked only of democratization of the party. This is an important difference, if one agrees that the anti-Khrushchev operation was meant to preserve in large measure the hegemony of the party inside the Soviet Union against Khrushchev's tendency to dismantle its *apparat*, or at least to associate other strata of Soviet society with the tasks of leadership.

However, it should be admitted that explanations given by the Central Committee at Bagnolet were, on the whole, able to assuage the very sharp discontent that had been expressed in the PCF lower and middle echelons during the period of waiting after Khrushchev's fall. Habits of discipline and confidence in the leadership remain solid among the PCF activists, particularly as long as that leadership, lacking the prestige of a Thorez, exercises its inherited authority with the appearance of unity and cohesion.

However, after Thorez' death, the disappearance of Khrushchev from the political scene confronted the PCF with new responsibilities. The event had such far-reaching, world-wide repercussions in all Communist parties, including the traditionally most docile East European satellite parties, because, in view of the manifest weakness of the movement's "center" (the disunity and cracks in the Soviet party, and the lack of elegance of the methods used in making the change of leadership), the other Communist parties found themselves thrown back upon their own resources. They now had to depend on their popular bases and the masses needed for their development, that is, the national conditions of their origin and growth.

For the Italian Communists, despite having obviously come as a surprise, the event was only a confirmation—reassuring on the

7 *Ibid.*, Nov. 9, 1964, p. 3.

whole—of Togliatti's Testament. Things went as he had predicted; there was no real surprise. There was, however, a certain shift toward openly "anti-Soviet" positions. Observers noted that certain Communist candidates in the municipal and provincial elections on November 22–23 (which, moreover, were to yield the PCI a new and spectacular success, contrary to the predictions made before the voting, and to reinforce the national and international prestige of the PCI line) had criticized the Soviet Union with such vehemence that in this respect they could hardly be distinguished any longer from the Christian Democrats. It was as though the death of Togliatti—who had continued to maintain a certain solidarity with the Soviet Union—had made these comrades lose the needle of their compass.

What did the PCF do under these circumstances? It hesitated at first, then chose to flee forward to Moscow, to adopt, finally, an attitude of confirmation of its own illusions. As much as the Italian confirmation seemed real, the French confirmation seemed illusory: Everything is well; everything will be well, as before.

The orientation initiated during the last weeks of the year 1964 had actually taken shape—and an almost coherent shape—by 1965.

To all appearances, we have watched a sudden switchover to the long-resisted Italian positions on the part of the PCF. Yet there is sometimes a tendency to ignore the fact that the PCI, in exchange, has equally taken a step back in the direction of the "French" positions. The preparation and convening of the Eleventh Congress of the PCI at the end of January 1966 have indeed been marked by a return to classical methods of suppressing discussion. Without even having to resort to sanctions or expulsions, Luigi Longo has succeeded in silencing Pietro Ingrao's opposition "from the left" and in making it a prisoner within the leadership.[8] It has been enough for him to conclude a pact with Amendola, leader of the revisionist right, whose history-making *Rinascita* article "Hypothesis on Reunification"[9] published on the eve of the provincial elections in November 1964, proposed the liquidation of the Communist Party as one of the conditions of reconciliation with Nenni's socialists and Saragat's socialist-democrats.

Certainly, Longo's report at the Eleventh Congress gave considerable satisfaction to Amendola on the level of programmatic formulations and tactical propositions, but in exchange the leader of the revisionists ungrudgingly gave up his demands for democratiza-

8 *L'Unita*, Feb. 1, 1966.
9 *Rinascita*, Nov. 28, 1964.

tion. In his closing speech, Longo was very definite on this point; he "was utterly amazed . . . at their demands for more discussion, for democracy, for a greater publicity of the debates," for "we do not want . . . a democracy that would become a permanent matter of discussion, a perpetual questioning of things already settled, which would turn the party into an academy, or a discussion club."

We recognize here a language traditionally employed by the PCF. This does not efface the individual character of the two parties (at the height of the Stalinist period, there was comparatively more democracy in Togliatti's PCI than in Thorez' PCF). But the significance of Longo's tone lies in the atmosphere of the recent evolution. It is as if the policy of the "bureaucratic front" represented in the Soviet Union by the "sacred union" of the CPSU leaders around the Brezhnev-Kosygin tandem—a union sealed during the Twenty-Third Congress—had its counterpart, or its equivalent, in each of the great parties of the international Communist movement. It is against this common background that the national characteristics are brought out: The "flexible" method of the Italians consists in discrediting Ingrao by accusing him of having refused to develop his disagreements before the congress, and then in re-electing him to the leadership of the party; the "hard" method of the French is the liquidation, without further ado, of the opposition of the Communist Students' Union. To do this, the PCF seems to have requested and obtained from the "fraternal" Italian party the abandonment of its French protégés.

If we wish to characterize the evolution of the two years after the fall of Khrushchev, in the light of this analysis, we may say that, simultaneously with the adoption of a flexible opportunist political strategy, the Communist parties of Western Europe (with the possible exception of Sweden) have done their best to reinforce the domination of their leading groups against all centrifugal forces. It is simply that the retreat from democratization was less apparent in the case of the PCF, where less democratization had taken place as a result of the French party's persistent immobility.

On the plane of French domestic policy, 1965 was an important year for the PCF. Indeed, as long as the possibility of Gaston Defferre's candidacy, which was supported by a workers' union between the socialists and the MRP and oriented toward the center, strongly influenced the year-end presidential elections, the appeals to unity by the PCF remained ineffective. The re-entry of the Communists in the political life of France was blocked. The worst was to come: Insofar as Defferre was trying to build up a new political formation, relying on militant trade unionists (essentially members of the CFDT [formerly the CFTC] of the *Force Ouvrière,* and of the *Fédération de l'Éducation Nationale*) and on the "clubs," his venture was designed to shatter the traditional parties and deprive their apparatus of all power, and thus reshape on the left a new "political society."

For the PCF, now integrated into the traditional "political society"—although formally ruled out of the political game—this prospect was dangerous. On the one hand, the pro-American foreign policy orientation of the advocates of the "Operation Defferre" made an alliance with the Communists unlikely. On the other hand, and perhaps above all, a new leftist formation was in a position to exert a force of attraction capable of competing with the PCF itself for its supporters. The Communist leaders have no anxiety of this type with respect to the SFIO led by Guy Mollet (or even with regard to the MRP). In short, the PCF was afraid of being deprived of its intended partners. Consequently there was an objective convergence of interests between the apparatus of the traditional parties, including the PCF, to checkmate "Operation Defferre." Using subtle maneuvers to prevent the creation of the projected federation and thus compel Defferre to renounce his candidacy, Guy Mollet and the leaders of the MRP created the conditions for the re-entry of the PCF in the game of electoral alliances.

Until then, the only weapon of the PCF propaganda had been the threat of a Communist candidate in the presidential elections unless a candidate from the left accepted negotiation with the Communists on a "common democratic program."

According to reliable sources, the leaders of the PCF were supposedly divided into two groups: those who demanded the immediate and public designation of a PCF candidate, and those who with Waldeck Rochet attempted to temporize, to delay the decision, and to use Communist candidacy only as a means of pressure on the other leftist parties.

Yet, considering the new character of the election of the President of the Republic by universal suffrage in France, nobody could foresee whether a possible Communist candidate would obtain more or fewer votes than a candidate of the "non-Communist left." Since the law allowed only the two top candidates in the first round to take part in a second balloting, the main purpose was to come in second behind de Gaulle.

The decision of whether or not to present a Communist candidate depended, in principle, on the analysis of his chances to come in behind de Gaulle. In case he should do so, the situation created for the second round, that of compelling the non-Communist left voters to choose between de Gaulle and the Communist candidate, could bring about a rift that would splinter the regrouping of a "centrist" or "Defferriste" type. In the opposite case, if the Communist candidate came in third (something that Defferre had hoped for a long time), the Communist voters would be placed in an embarrassing situation, being practically obliged to vote for the non-Communist left candidate as the only alternative to running the risk of being accused of playing into de Gaulle's hands.

The torpedoing of Defferre's candidacy in June 1965 followed by the announcement of Mitterrand's long and carefully prepared candidacy, offered a solution to this situation. Certainly, the party had to give up its demand for a common democratic program. In exchange, Mitterrand renounced his anti-Communist position and accepted, in the form of an exchange of letters with Waldeck Rochet, the support of the PCF.

The scenario, whipped into shape with Guy Mollet's active contribution, let at the Drancy Central Committee Meeting on September 23, 1965 to the decision to rally the PCF behind Mitterrand's candidacy. There were protests at least from the lowest echelons, but they were pacified in the name of the unity of the left, achieved at last.

The PCF actually participated effectively in the electoral campaign, proving very active and loyal. It played to the end its game of "overtures to the right," avoiding delicate problems that might have caused disagreement in the coalition supporting Mitterand (particularly everything concerning NATO, European integration, and foreign policy in general). It contented itself with systematically developing the "options" and the "proposals"—which preserved a very vague and general character—of the candidate that it had approved.

Under cover of this campaign, the PCF was, however, working out a "grand comeback" on the political stage. The tribunals of radio, television, and the press were widely opened to its representatives; for example, photographs showed Waldeck Rochet and Guy Mollet together on the occasion of Mitterand's press conference. The specter of isolation was exorcized, and the Communists became participants in a dialogue.

The comparative success scored by Mitterand's candidacy, which gained almost 45 per cent of the votes during the second round, on December 19, 1965, further strengthened the PCF's position. Not only had the mass of Communist voters given the only candidate of the opposition the support of its votes, but the majority of the voters from the left had accepted the alliance with the PCF without being frightened by this cooperation or pushed toward de Gaulle.

Within the party leadership, the position of Waldeck Rochet and of his friends who had recommended first the temporization and then the rallying to Mitterand emerged stronger in contrast to the position of those who had expressed their impatience to nominate a Communist candidate.

Subsequently, it is true, fresh difficulties have arisen. In the pre-electoral union created by the approach of the legislative elections, the decision made by de Gaulle to leave NATO threw an apple of discord into the camp of the allies of the presidential campaign. The new proposals for discussing a "common democratic program" made by the PCF to its former partners found no response. The "little federation" formed under Mitterrand, the essential core of which was the SFIO under Guy Mollet's vigilant control, opposed breaking with the Communists, but at the same time it increased its contacts (less and less discreet) and its overtures in the direction of Jean Lecanuet's *Centre démocratique* which unites the "Atlantic" and non-Gaullist right with the strong support of the entrepreneurial circles.

At least the PCF has obtained spectacular success in another field: the trade-unionist front. On the basis of an agreement achieved for the first time on an organizational level, the CGT and the CFDT agreed on a common social program and jointly organized a general strike in the public sector (May 17, 1966). The *Force Ouvrière* had joined the movement without participating in the organizational talks. The success of this movement amazed the organizers themselves by its immensity. Thus, to a certain extent, trade-union unity (on essentially economic topics) has taken over from purely political unity, which is going through a difficult phase.

As a result of the success scored in the field of domestic politics and in its emergence from isolation, the position of the PCF has also been strengthened within the international Communist movement during the last two years (1965–1966).

The liquidation of the dispute with the PCI was marked by spectacular meetings: Waldeck Rochet and Luigi Longo at Geneva on

May 24–25, 1965 and then the meeting of the two delegations at San Remo, including the two secretaries general, May 3–4, 1966. Each time the French-Italian talks have been followed shortly thereafter by conferences of the Communist parties from the capitalist countries of Western Europe (Brussels from June 1 to 3, 1965, Vienna from May 9 to 11, 1966). More than the decision published at the end of these conferences, the important fact is that the "polycentrism" rejected for a long time by the PCF had begun to function under an *institutional form*—that of a *regional organization* of the Western European Communist parties occurring in fact under a Franco-Italian bipartite leadership.

In the compromise thus achieved between the two major parties of Western Europe, the PCF has adopted most of the Italian positions on the Common Market, the coordination of the trade-unionist struggles on a European scale, etc.—positions that it had fought for a long time. In exchange, the PCI appears to have pledged itself to desist from supporting internal opposition to the PCF, and to have kept its promises.

There is every reason to believe that this application of the principles of polycentrism, which is accompanied by an attempt on the part of the PCF to keep its distance from the Soviet Union, received the blessing of the Kremlin after Khrushchev's overthrow. Indeed, on condition that the leaders keep tight control over their apparatus and their activists, the interests of Soviet diplomacy itself and those of the CPSU in its dispute with the Chinese might be more effectively defended by foreign Communist parties possessing a certain freedom of movement than by a systematic and servile alignment.

However, in practice, this new form of relationship with Moscow did not fail to give rise to difficulties and differences; for example, at the height of the PCF electoral campaign for Mitterrand, an official TASS communiqué encouraged the voters of the left to vote for de Gaulle because of his policy of national independence. The resulting emotion was so great that the party lodged (according to declarations made by PCF leaders to the activists in the cells) an official protest with Moscow. *L'Humanité* restricted itself to objecting curtly to the validity of comments devoted to a domestic French problem by a "foreign agency." A new incident of the same type seems to have taken place in the hall of the CPSU Twenty-Third Congress, in April 1966, when the delegates unanimously cheered de Gaulle, whose name Waldeck Rochet had imprudently pronounced when presenting the positive aspects of Gaullist diplomacy.

Finally, on a quite different level, *L'Humanité* prominently featured a text signed by Louis Aragon, member of the PCF Central Committee, protesting against Moscow's condemnation of the writers Sinyavsky and Daniel, which brought upon the author the attacks of Sholokov—who, it is true, took care not to implicate the leadership of the PCF, whose responsibility in this matter he preferred to ignore. The publication of this text was considered by most political commentators on the French left as a decisive manifestation of the PCF's new independence. Although the questioning of the judgment of a Soviet tribunal was completely new, its interpretation as a revolutionary gesture opening a new era in the relations between the PCF and Moscow does not seem convincing. Indeed, within the context previously mentioned of a flexible support of Soviet policy by the foreign parties—substituted for the former unconditional alignment—it seems obvious that the movement has more to win from the PCF's protest against Sinyavsky and Daniel's condemnation than from the approval, public or tacit, of such a judgment.

On the level of the PCF's internal life, at any rate, the leading group has made no concession to those questioning its power. Resumption of control over the UEC was carried through in two stages. First, after careful preparation, which enabled the party to resume control of the majority of the provincial sections, the Eighth Congress of the UEC (March 1965) permitted the expulsion of the former National Bureau, which was said to be influenced by the Italians, deprived it of Italian support, and reduced it to a negligible minority. (The manifestation of solidarity with the National Bureau of the Communist students, attempted by a hundred university members of the party in a letter to Waldeck Rochet in February 1965, was rejected as "inadmissible" because of its "factional" character, but it did not bring about the expulsion of its authors.) In the second stage, taking advantage of the opposition by the department "Sorbonne-Lettres" of the UEC to the candidacy of François Mitterand in September 1965, the party reacted by expelling the "Lettres" sector of the UEC on January 16, 1966. After the "right" it was the turn of the "left" to be expelled, the other leftist sectors and circles having refused to recognize the arbitrary dissolution of the Sorbonne Students' Organization. (The same sequence of events has been repeated in several provincial cities, especially in Lyon.) At the UEC Ninth Congress (April 1966), the victory of the PCF was completed, and the students of the former "left" decided in their turn to create a new movement, the *Jeunesse Communiste Révolutionnaire,* inspired by militant Trotskyites of the Fourth International.

We must take into consideration the fact that the "democratic" allies of the PCF have shown no reaction to the expulsion of the students. During the electoral campaign at a meeting at the Mutualité François Mitterrand himself called to task the "leftists" amalgamated under the label of "pro-Chinese." For the leaders of the PCF, the passivity and the indifference displayed by the currents of the non-Communist left in this circumstance constitute an encouragement to continue the consolidation of discipline and internal cohesion and eventually even to repression without fearing the reactions of their political partners.

The picture would not be complete without mentioning the recent creation of a new and original opposition, which developed especially among the students, in particular within the circles of the UEC of the École Normale Supérieure on the Rue d'Ulm. (Hence, the name of *ulmiste* or *ulmard* is sometimes given to its proponents.)

The chief inspirer of this trend is a brilliant philosopher, Louis Althusser, whose articles published within the last few years in various reviews (*La Pensée, La Nouvelle Critique*) have been collected in a book edited in 1966 by an ardent pro-Chinese ex-Communist, François Maspero: *Lire Marx.* A second work, written in cooperation with other Communist intellectuals, *Lire le Capital,* was published shortly thereafter.

Attempting simultaneously to return to Marxist orthodoxy and to assimilate the contributions of such disciplines as psychoanalysis and anthropology while severly criticizing the PCF's prolonged theoretical sclerosis, Althusser develops—without leaving the theoretical field, but with great intellectual rigidity—theses with political implications close to the Chinese positions.

This is why the party, which had no difficulty in containing the influence of the "Marxist-Leninist" groups officially supported and subsidized by Peking, was concerned by Althusser's influence, especially from the moment when the leadership of the PCF realized, as a result of the oppositional activities of the "UEC Ulmist" circles who claimed loyalty to Althusser, that the philosopher's theory was not purely speculative.

Next there followed the unusual occasion of a PCF Central Committee meeting devoted especially (during three days from March

11 to March 13, 1966) to "ideological and cultural problems." The topics of discussion were apparently on an academic level: Was there a "Marxist humanism" or not? Did Garaudy depart from Marxism or not in his book *De l'anathème au dialogue,* designed to persuade the Christians?

The answer given by the Central Committee was apparently ambiguous, but only apparently; the resolution worked out by Aragon emphasized the freedom of discussion of theoretical and ideological problems and the necessity of allowing debates "between specialists" as well as research. On certain details, Garaudy's phrasing was corrected in terms of stricter orthodoxy. But the real significance of the apparently liberal resolution was misinterpeted by the majority of commentators.

Fundamentally, in matters of politics the resolution continued the basic ideas of the positions defended by Garaudy. As for Althusser, he was informed that he would be allowed to pursue the activities of a specialist restricted to his field—in which case he would be allowed freedom of expression—but he would be strongly opposed if he ventured further on a political level.

Meanwhile, examination of the speeches at this Central Committee meeting (published in *Cahiers du Commuisme,* May–June 1966) reveals that several members of this organization have themselves been influenced by Althusser, even though they deny agreement with his positions as a whole. In this sense, the prudent vigilance that has been shown by the leadership in this matter seems justified.

The obsession with the "Chinese" danger, which in France could take an "Althusserian" turn, looms very large in the PCF leading group. In this respect at least, the PCF has remained with the Czechoslovak Communist Party on the offensive, in relation to other European parties, in its desire to see the international conference of Communist parties meet in order to proclaim Peking's excommunication.

Since the "little consultative conference" in March 1965, the PCF has never missed an occasion to manifest vehement hatred against the Chinese and impatience to see the resumption of polemics (especially concerning the activity of the small pro-Chinese Marxist-Leninist groups during the French presidential campaign, or concerning Vietnam). However, it has never succeeded in inducing the other Western European parties to adopt its positions, the Italians having firmly held to their previous positions on this point even after the launching by Lin Piao of the great "cultural revolution."

We may conclude the following:

1. The PCF, putting aside its ancient rivalry with the PCI and its attachment to international centralism, will henceforth participate in the "polycentrist" movement, the first promoters and theoreticians of which were the Italians.

2. This is a kind of polycentrism that enjoys—especially since Khrushchev's fall—Soviet sympathy and encouragement. The PCF is no longer, as in the beginning of the period analyzed in this study, "the party of unconditional fidelity," but nobody is asking it to be. It has merely had to adjust its positions to a more subtle comprehensive strategy, which is now determined by the general interests of the Soviet Union and the CPSU. The French Communist Party, along with the Czechs, the Hungarians, and the Mongolians, is one of the most zealous champions of "unity of action for aid to Vietnam," inaugurated by the Soviets in October–November 1964; its violent attacks against the Red Guards in 1966 show that it has not altered its attitude of open hostility toward the Maoists.

3. On the internal plane, the PCF is pursuing (simultaneously with Communist parties in power) two primary and apparently contradictory aims: first, the preservation of the decision-making power and of the totalitarian structures of the party apparatus; and second, greater participation in the national political game under the auspices of the *"unité de la gauche."*

4. In the ideological field, certain overtures to revisionism have been made within the party (pluralism of parties in a socialist regime, the idea of "genuine democracy" as an intermediate form between capitalism and socialism)[10]—overtures that seem to be subordinated to tactics without receiving, except perhaps by Garaudy, a solid theoretical foundation.

5. The future is uncertain for the PCF, depending on changes in internal and external circumstances. It could be pushed either into becoming a party of a social democratic type or on the contrary (in the case of radical mass activity) toward the left. The PCF's evolution hinges upon both the evolution of its support, the French working class, and on that of the CPSU.[11]

6. At any rate, in spite of the vicissitudes of a period of unrest,

[10] See Waldeck Rochet's article, "Sur le capitalisme monopoliste d'Etat," *France Nouvelle,* June 8, 1966.
[11] See Georges Lavau, "Toward a PCF Renaissance," *Esprit,* Oct. 1966.

of questioning doctrine and acquired habits, the force and the guarantee of survival of the French Communist Party lies in the fact that it has managed to maintain a quasi-monopoly over representation of the working class, and in that capacity it is allowed to express discontent and protest against neocapitalist social paternalism of Gaullist France and against the era of affluence in the American style.

7. The much publicized entry of such a personality as the writer Gilbert Mury into the *Fédération des Cercles marxistes-léninistes,* a pro-Chinese movement created in 1964, does not change this author's opinion that the pro-Chinese tendency does not constitute a more serious danger for the PCF than Trotskyite and anarchist groups did in the past. In France Maoist extremism attracts *nostalgiques* of Stalinism such as M. Mury, a former professor at the Party's Central School and Roger Garaudy's assistant at the *Centre d'Études et de Recherches marxistes,* Professor Baby, and a few intellectuals in quest of a New Church, who refuse to renounce ideology, resisting to the end the abolition of the old dream of a saving and purifying revolution.

Mao's simplified Chinese Stalinism has no hold on the bulk of the working and middle classes. The furor of the Red Guards reminds them more of the *Provos* of the Netherlands than the *Gavroches* of French Revolutionary tradition. Some sophisticated writers and readers of *Les Temps Modernes* (directed by Jean-Paul Sartre) or of *Nouvel Observateur* are shaken by the novelty and the strange dynamism of the "great cultural revolution" taking place in China since the spring of 1966. But the well-established cadres and activists of the PCF consider it a deformed caricature of their previous creeds.

In the past many jokes were made about "bolchéviques de salon." Now France will know for a time "maotsétoungistes de salon." Admittedly, a leftist drive of the PCF is a possible development. But if it occurred, such a drive would be conducted in French, not Chinese, terms.

8. Although deeply and durably marked by its historical affiliation to the international Communist movement with the Kremlin as its center, the PCF has put down deep and wide-spreading roots in French soil. It is a "national minority" with representative functions, a great organizational and cultural autonomy, and a remarkable capacity for adjustment to changing circumstances. Even in its isolation, without the possibility of having a direct influence

on the government's decisions, it has balanced and will go on balancing—unless, which seems very unlikely, there is a return in the immediate future to its revolutionary aims—between support of Gaullist foreign policy and support of the SFIO and the center-left against Gaullist social and economic policies.

PCF ELECTION RESULTS SINCE 1924 (LEGISLATIVE ELECTIONS)

The total figures are only of relative interest, because the introduction of the women's vote after World War II distorts comparison with preceding periods. We have therefore taken those percentages that seem the most significant, that is, of Communist voters as against the total of *registered* voters (and not of votes cast, since abstentions are obviously of political significance).

Year	Percentage*
1924	7.9
1928—first round	9.3
1932	6.8
1936	12.6
1945 (October)	20.3
1946 (June)	21
1946 (November)	22.2
1951 (June)	20.1
1956 (January)	21.2
1958 (November)	14.6
1962 (November)	15

* Calculated on the basis of official returns.